Practical Techniques of Business Forecasting

Recent Titles from QUORUM BOOKS

Practical Techniques of Business Forecasting

Fundamentals and Applications for Marketing, Production, and Financial Managers

GEORGE KRESS

Foreword by Al Migliaro

Q

Quorum Books
Westport, Connecticut · London, England

216931

Library of Congress Cataloging in Publication Data

Kress, George.
  Practical techniques of business forecasting.

  Bibliography: p.
  Includes index.
  1. Business forecasting.   I. Title.
HD30.27.K73   1985   658.4'0355   85–6361
ISBN 0–89930–107–X (lib. bdg. : alk. paper)

Library of Congress Catalog Card Number: 85-6361
ISBN: 0–89930–107–X
First published in 1985 by Quorum Books
Greenwood Press
A division of Congressional Information Service, Inc.
88 Post Road West, Westport, Connecticut 06881
Printed in the United States of America

The paper used in this book complies with the
Permanent Paper Standard issued by the National
Information Standards Organization (Z39.48–1984).

10 9 8 7 6 5 4 3 2 1

Copyright Acknowledgments
Grateful acknowledgment is given for permission to reprint the
following:

Figure 6-4 is reprinted by permission of the publisher from Lester Sartorius and N. Caroll Mohn,
Sales Forecasting Models: A Diagnostic Approach (Georgia State
University, College of Business Administration, Atlanta, 1976), p. 121.

Figure 8-3 is reprinted by permission of the American Chemical Society from F. J. Kovac,
"Technological Forecasting—Tires," *Chemtech*, January 1971, p. 22. Copyright 1971 American
Chemical Society.

Figures 9-3, 9-4, and 9-5 are reprinted by permission from
A Guide to Cross-Impact Analysis (Cleveland, OH: Eaton Corp., n.d.).

Chapter 11 is adapted from George Kress, *Marketing Research*, Second
Edition, 1982, Adapted by permission of Reston Publishing Company,
a Prentice-Hall Company, 11480 Sunset Hills Road, Reston VA, 22090.

Contents

Contents

Figures

Tables

Foreword

It was inevitable that sooner or later an author would come along with a book on business forecasting that business managers and business school students could understand and use. George Kress is that author and this is that book.

Both business managers and students who aspire to be business managers will find the book an excellent source of the basic information they need to help them interpret and use forecasts as part of the decision-making process. They'll discover that they don't need an advanced degree in quantitative methods to grasp the essentials. Everything you've always wanted to know about business forecasting but didn't know how to ask is explained in easy-to-understand, jargon-free English.

Kress makes an outstanding contribution to closing the credibility gap between business managers and professional forecasters. He clears up many of the mysteries that cause these two groups to eye each other with suspicion and mistrust. What this book does primarily is to build a manager's confidence in the subject of business forecasting to the level needed to understand forecasting and to ask the right questions. The idea that understanding is the keystone of confidence is the underlying motivation of Kress' book.

The author succeeds in his objective because he:

1. Puts each technique in perspective by stating underlying assumptions in clear, understandable language; this helps managers to test their own assumptions against those of the models, and helps them determine suitable applications for each model.

2. Takes the reader on a step-by-step journey through each technique covered, demonstrating how the technique coincides with the underlying assumption.

3. Sticks to the basics, an understanding of which is a prerequisite to the more advanced techniques.

4. Prepares the reader for certain techniques by first explaining processes incorporated in them; an example is the explanation of "autocorrelation" and "differencing" in preparation for the Box-Jenkins process.

5. Takes nothing for granted other than that the reader knows the four arithmetic functions and high-school algebra.

6. Never goes beyond what an executive should know about certain complex processes as, for example, Box-Jenkins and input-output analysis.

As we trust we have made clear, Kress has identified his audience and written a book that helps its members enhance their executive skills. His audience is made up of business managers without advanced training in quantitative methods.

We suggest that the reader take the time to execute the step-by-step procedures using the data given in the examples to check answers; then execute them a second time using your own company's data (this may not be possible in certain cases because a computer with a suitable program may be needed).

We also suggest that you read the book with an eye on an understanding of the concepts and assumptions of each technique and not on the step-by-step details. It is the concepts and assumptions that will help you gain confidence in your own skills and in the business-forecasting process. Retain the concepts and assumptions associated with the techniques because you can always refer to the table of contents to find the step-by-step procedures.

These suggestions apply with equal force to business school students preparing for a career in any aspect of business—operations, finance, marketing, and so on. Few of you aspire to become professional forecasters. All of you, however, will at some point in your business career face a forecaster either in the form of a computer or a human being. In either case, you need to know how a forecast is derived to make critical business decisions.

One final word: this book is about business forecasting at the company level, a subject that is not taught in most schools of business; they emphasize economic (macro) forecasting. This book fills that gap; we recommend it as an excellent text for undergraduate courses.

Al Migliaro
Executive Editor
The Journal of Business Forecasting

Practical Techniques of Business Forecasting

1

Role of Forecasting in the Business Environment

INTRODUCTION

Decision makers frequently make major commitments of dollars, materials, and personnel based on expected future events. They receive praise when they make right decisions and are criticized when they make errors. Because their necks are on the line, decision makers need to have confidence in the forecast data they use. Such confidence disappears when a forecast is derived from a technique they don't understand.

Decision makers also are reluctant to make decisions based on a forecast derived from another person's subjective judgment, especially when they disagree with some of that person's major assumptions: that is, a forecast prepared for a firm is based on an expected rate of national unemployment of 9.8 percent for 1986, whereas the user of the forecast believes the rate will be closer to 8 percent.

A study by Wheelwright and Clarke provides ample evidence that forecasters and users differ significantly in their evaluation of the other's forecasting skills.[1] Forecasters rated their own technical skills much higher than users rated them. Conversely, users rated their own understanding of various forecasting techniques higher than forecasters rated them. Another area of disagreement involved the forecasters' understanding of many of the user's problems: users believed forecasters were deficient in this area, whereas forecasters believed they had a pretty good grasp of users' problems.

Additional findings from the Wheelwright and Clarke study suggest that the credibility problems between forecasters and users are related primarily to the difference in their perspectives. Forecasters tend to have a technical outlook, whereas users have a managerial outlook. Thus, if the value of forecasters is to be maximized, both sides (users and forecasters) must recognize and appreciate each other's role in the forecasting process.

3

Communication Problems

In addition to the credibility problem, another major problem area between users and forecasters is communication. Forecasters claim that users frequently do not accurately describe their forecasting needs—What is to be forecasted and how will the forecast results be used? Users, on the other hand, believe forecasters either won't or can't explain how a forecast model works. They often use technical jargon that does little to enhance users' understanding.

This communication barrier between users and forecasters explains why such relatively simple forecasting techniques as the jury of executive opinion, sales force composite, and trend projections are most frequently used in business.[2] Most decision makers can understand these techniques and thus feel more comfortable with their output.

The problems of credibility and communication are closely entwined. Users would have more faith in forecasters and their output if they had a better understanding of the forecasting techniques being used. Thus, the ideal forecaster is one who not only possesses the necessary technical skills but who can also communicate effectively with users. He or she provides a total forecast package that includes not only the forecast but also the major assumptions made in developing that forecast, reasons for choosing a particular technique, and the potential weaknesses of the technique.

Users, likewise, have some obligations to forecasters. They should identify how they intend using the forecast, the specific types of information they are seeking, and any critical factors they are aware of that will impact on the forecast.

Thus, if a forecast is to be of maximum value to the user (1) the user must understand how the forecast was derived, (2) it must fit his or her needs, and (3) he or she must believe it will improve decision making.

Mixed Feelings Toward Forecasts

Unless these three issues are effectively addressed, forecasting will continue to receive the mixed reactions depicted in the following statements.

"The sales forecast provides the basis for all of my company's planning activities." "I consume forecast information the same way I consume fresh tomatoes—with a large dose of salt." "How beneficial are forecasts? Well I've always been a firm believer in the adage—something beats nothing all to hell!"

At one extreme are those decision makers who feel a sales forecast is their firm's most valuable planning tool. At the other extreme are those who place little or no value in sales forecasts. The majority of managers seem to fall somewhere in the middle; they recognize the need for sales forecasts, but are reluctant to place complete trust in them.

Reasons for Such Feelings

The reasons for such mixed feelings toward sales forecasts are usually related to one of the following circumstances:

Bad experience with forecast—The user may have been the victim of a forecast that missed the target by a wide margin. Such outcomes are not only an embarrassment to the decision maker, but can be very costly in terms of production overruns or shortages as well as storage expenses, personnel adjustments, and so forth.

Confused by models—Many decision makers are reluctant to accept the output of what they feel are "black box" models. They don't understand the procedures used or the reasons for including certain variables. For example, a multiple regression forecasting model may use advertising expenditures lagged two months and also include a dummy variable to allow for the pricing actions of a major competitor. Unless the decision maker accepts the logic of these models, he or she feels uncomfortable with the forecasts they provide.

Prefer intuitive methods—A number of older decision makers lack both a statistical and computer background. During their careers they have had to rely primarily on their own "seat of the pants" estimates and have come to accept such subjective methods as the most effective forecasting techniques.

Firm's operations not conducive to formal forecasting procedures—Circumstances within the firm itself may not be conducive to the regular use of forecasting models by decision makers.

(a) *Forecasting done only on irregular basis*—If the firm's owners or key manangers don't believe in making forecasts on a regular basis, then subordinates within the firm won't feel the need to develop formalized forecasting methods.

(b) *Lack of people or equipment*—A decision maker may be interested in using some type of formal forecasting model but lacks the personal know-how and does not have access to people knowledgeable about the topic. Or the firm may not have access to the computer equipment needed for sophisticated forecasting models. Both of these deficiencies (lack of people or equipment) can be easily overcome if top management really believes in the importance of forecasting.

(c) *Nature of product*—A firm producing major equipment to the specifications of customers and with only three to five sales a year might not feel the need for a major forecasting effort.

Objective of This Book

Most decision makers recognize the value of making good forecasts; they just disagree as to which is the best method(s) for making such forecasts.

The objective of this book is to familiarize the reader with those methods most frequently used for forecasting and analyzing markets. It will also identify the situations for which each method is best suited. This book exposes decision makers to a variety of forecasting techniques; the more techniques a decision maker feels comfortable with the more effective he or she will be both as a forecaster and as an evaluator of forecasts.

Intended Audience

People needing information about forecasting techniques generally fall into three categories:

(a) Those whose primary job is forecasting. They are employed either by business firms or government agencies and usually have the title of forecaster, statistician, econometrician, or market analyst.

(b) Those whose jobs require that they occasionally make forecasts. This generally includes sales managers, financial managers, production managers, and so on.

(c) Those who do little or no forecasting themselves but must make decisions based on the forecasts of others and thus need to understand the basics of forecasting.

This book is intended for the last two categories of people. It provides a pragmatic look at a variety of forecasting techniques. "Pragmatic" is a nice way of saying the book attempts to follow a fairly low level approach in its handling of these subjects. People in category (a) have extensive math and stat backgrounds and would already be familiar with much of the material in this book.

Another major audience could be colleges of business offering forecasting courses. It would be appropriate as a textbook for either undergraduate or graduate classes dealing with this topic.

This book describes those techniques most commonly used to make forecasts at a micro level, explaining how these techniques work and when they should be used. Little or no coverage is provided of the theoretical backgrounds of each model.

Micro versus Macro Forecasting Models

Virtually any firm, regardless of its size or the nature of its operation (business, government, non-profit), will have to develop some type of forecast. The general nature of these forecasts, however, varies widely among firms and can be separated into two broad categories: micro and macro forecasts.

Micro forecasts are those forecasts related to a firm's own unique needs. They involve forecasts of sales, equipment needs, personnel needs, materials, supplies, and so on.

The firm will also have to make forecasts about what will take place in the economy in general since those conditions will have an impact on their own firm. This broader view is called economic or macro forecasting. It involves estimating how major economic units—households, industries, government—will behave and interact.

Thus, micro forecasting covers situations over which the individual firm has control, whereas macro forecasting involves conditions that affect a firm but over which it has no direct control (interest rates, rate of unemployment in the state, rate of inflation.)

Larger firms such as Ford, Exxon, and Proctor and Gamble, because of the scope of their operations, are very concerned with the general economy. They will even have full-time economists on their staffs to make macro forecasts and incorporate such forecasts into specific forecasts for individual products.

On the other hand, a small firm such as Styro, Inc., a manufacturer of styrofoam materials, may also be concerned about the general economy, but will center its forecasting efforts on its own products and operations.

Although this book concentrates on micro forecasts, this does not mean that macro forecasts and macro data will be ignored, since in many instances macro information is used in a firm's forecasting model (for example, a firm using a multiple regression forecasting model might use the level of national unemployment as one variable in that model). But the primary models used by most firms are micro models and these are the models we will cover.

It should also be emphasized that although many of the examples presented in this book involved forecasting sales of products, the models themselves are also applicable for forecasting in the areas of personnel, production, and finance.

FORECASTING PROCESS

Which Comes First, The Forecast or the Strategy?

Where does the forecast fit into a firm's overall planning activities? Does it guide these plans or is it contingent upon them? Which leads and which follows? To illustrate this controversy, an example involving a marketing plan will be used. Firm A must make some decisions about its target markets and the marketing mix (price, product, promotion, and distribution) that will enable it to reach those markets effectively. Thus, the marketing strategy could be viewed as a firm's "game plan" for a specific time period.

It would seem logical to develop a forecast after the actual marketing plan has been chosen. This acknowledges that any estimates of sales depend on the planned marketing activities. However, how can a final marketing strategy be developed unless it is known what sales under "normal" conditions would be like? Satisfaction or dissatisfaction with initial sales estimates determine Firm A's marketing strategy.

Thus, the development of a sales forecast is really a multi-stage process since both a preliminary and final (formal) forecast are needed. Figure 1-1 illustrates the relationship between a forecast and the firm's selection of a marketing strategy.

In describing the steps of the forecasting process, it will be assumed Firm A's forecasting activities pertain to just one product. For multi-product firms, the same general steps would be duplicated for each product.

Assess Influencing Forces

The initial step of the forecasting process is identifying those external and internal forces expected to affect the product's sales.

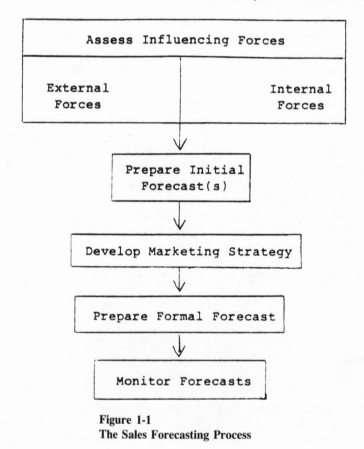

Figure 1-1
The Sales Forecasting Process

External Forces (Factors Outside of Firm's Control)

- Expected general economic conditions (the rate of inflation, the level of interest rates, the level of unemployment)
- Expected actions by the government (tax cuts, new regulations)
- Expected actions by key competitors (changes in their production facilities, increased product offerings)
- Expected social or cultural influences (increased decline in birth rate, increase in number of working wives)

Internal Forces (Factors Inherent to the Firm)

- Changes in the firm's production facilities
- Planned acquisitions
- Introduction of additional products

- Expected costs of raw materials, storage, shipping
- Product's past experience (if existing product)
  - Immediate past sales
  - Market share
  - Recent trend in sales

All of these factors must be integrated so that an overall impression of future sales begins to emerge.

Initial Forecast

After the external and internal conditions that can affect product sales have been evaluated, an initial forecast for the product is made.

The technique(s) used for such a forecast can vary from a fairly sophisticated multiple regression model to a relatively simple procedure such as having individual salespeople estimate their sales over the next 12 months.

Although the label *initial forecast* might imply that this is a relatively unimportant step in the entire sales-forecasting process, that is definitely not the case. The initial forecast is probably the most critical step in the entire process since it really directs the marketing strategy. The majority of time series, causal, and judgmental forecasting techniques described in this and other forecasting books are really methods of developing these initial forecasts.

Developing the Marketing Strategy

The initial forecast is used to guide the development of the firm's marketing strategy or at least that part of the plan related to one particular product. Assume the initial forecast for 1986 for Firm A's product is 15,000 units. Management wishes to surpass that figure and decides to make two major changes in the product's marketing mix: (1) they will increase the promotional budget by 18 percent, with major emphasis on incentive programs for retailers and (2) they will lower the product's price by 5 percent so that it will match the retail price of its main competitor. In light of these actions, they believe sales of their product should increase to 19,000 units and that figure becomes their formal forecast.

Formal Forecast

The formal forecast is then sent to other key people in the firm, some of whom may have even been involved in establishing the initial forecast. These people are asked to react to the formal forecast figure, in light of the proposed strategies. Based on the feedback received, this forecast figure could still be revised. A final forecast figure eventually emerges and is used to guide the firm's production and distribution activities.

Monitor the Forecast

Once actual sales take place, the formal forecast is continually monitored to see how well it depicts what is actually occurring. If actual sales begin to differ significantly from forecasted sales, the forecast will be revised to come closer to the real response of the market.

Overview of Forecasting Processes

The previous example was not intended to provide an in-depth look at the role of forecasting within firms. Rather, it was meant to show the link that exists between forecasting and a firm's planning activities. It emphasizes that these two are interdependent since decisions involving one are contingent upon information about the other.

Because of their close tie, these activities can be enhanced if performed by persons knowledgeable in both areas. A forecaster who views his or her role as strictly a quantitative specialist won't be able to weave the firm's strategies into the forecast. Conversely, a manager with little understanding of forecasting procedures won't really understand how the forecast figures were derived.

Thus, it makes a great deal of sense to provide all decision makers with some training in forecasting and provide forecasters with training in general planning principles. Although each person will still view him or herself as a specialist, the overall performance should be greatly enhanced with this additional background.

SELECTING THE APPROPRIATE FORECASTING MODEL

The person desiring to make a forecast can choose from a large number of forecasting models but not all of them are equally effective for a given situation. Thus, if the success of a forecast is to be maximized, it is crucial that the forecaster select the most appropriate model(s).

The forecaster should consider certain factors in the selection of the forecasting model. These factors are now briefly discussed, with a more extensive discussion postponed (until Chapter 10) when the reader is more familiar with the various forecasting models.

Purpose of the Forecast

What is the forecast intended to do? Is it only to provide information on the expected direction (increase or decrease) of changes or is it intended to be a fairly precise depiction of such changes?

Length of Time Involved

What period of time is to be covered by the forecast? Is the forecast needed on a weekly basis or does it involve a forecast for a period five to ten years in the future? From a time perspective, forecasts generally will be one of three types:

Short-term forecasts—cover a period less than three months in the future.

Medium-term forecasts—cover a period three months to two years in the future.

Long-term forecasts—cover a period greater than two years.

The shorter the time period covered by the forecast, the more accurate the forecast usually will be. This is so because the total business environment becomes more volatile as the length of the forecast period increases.

Degree of Disaggregation Sought

How specific should the forecast be? Will it only cover one product in the firm's total product offerings or will it involve all the firm's products? Will there be a forecast for each specific territory (state or county) or will it cover all territories? Is it intended to forecast impacts on specific divisions of the firm or the impacts on the entire firm or industry?

Degree of Accuracy Sought

The user of the forecast has to define how accurate he or she expects that forecast to be. In some situations, a forecast that is in error by as much as 15 to 20 percent may be acceptable. In other situations, a 2 percent error in the forecast could be disastrous. (In the next chapter, some methods for comparing the accuracy of various models are described.)

Pattern of Past Data

If the forecast involves a product or situation for which there is extensive past data, the pattern of that data can strongly influence the choice of the forecasting model.

Cost of Making Forecast

There are three kinds of expenses associated with a forecasting model: (a) developing the model, (b) accumulating and storing the data used in the model, and (c) actually running or using the model. A comparison of the estimated costs for various models can be the deciding factor as to which model is ultimately chosen.

Types of Data Available

The amount and nature of internal and external information available will strongly influence the forecasting techniques that can be used. If a time series model is used, there should be at least three years of monthly or quarterly data available, especially if the data is to be deseasonalized. Some statisticians believe that to ensure reliability there should be at least four to five periods of data available for each variable in the forecasting model. Thus, a multiple regression model with seven independent variables would need at least 28 to 35 sets of data.

Ease of Application and Understanding

Firms generally use a forecasting technique they feel comfortable with, even though they realize it may not be the most effective one. Many decision makers have neither the quantitative nor computer backgrounds needed to understand the more complicated models such as adaptive filtering or Box-Jenkins. Thus, they choose techniques that make sense to them or enable a forecast to be derived manually.

Product's Stage in Its Life Cycle

Some forecasters believe that the product's position in its life cycle is the single most important factor affecting the forecasting technique. In fact, some forecasting texts are even organized around the different phases of the life cycle.[3] This author believes that while the product's life cycle is an important factor in the forecasting process, it is only one of many that should be considered. An appendix to this chapter describes the impact a product's life cycle can have on forecasts. That appendix is intended for those readers not familiar with the concept of product life cycles.

The Forecast—An Estimate or an Irrevocable Goal

At a forecasting seminar, some product managers were bragging about the forecasting success of their respective firms. A manager of a major food company stated that his firm's forecasts usually came within 50 cases of actual sales. This inspired an elderly sales manager to remark: "That's nothing. For each of the past 25 years my distillery in Scotland has forecasted right down to the last bottle. You see we're not afraid to drink our mistakes."

That story suggests that some firms make a forecast and then take actions that will ensure that this forecast is achieved. For them, the forecast actually becomes an irrevocable goal that dictates their firm's activities. If it looks like sales will fall short of the forecast figure, they initiate major changes that get things back on track.

A forecast should provide an accurate estimate of the results expected from a given plan and under given environmental conditions. The forecast should be continually monitored to see how well it depicts what is actually occurring. However, the forecast should not become a goal that must be met regardless of unforeseen competitive changes or changes in general economic and business conditions. Blindly trying to meet the forecast often results in inefficient use of resources and will usually be detrimental to the firm's overall operations. It is important to understand why a forecast missed its mark, but achieving the actual forecast should never become the firm's all-encompassing goal.

CATEGORIES OF FORECASTING MODELS

It is generally believed that any forecasting method fits into one of three broad categories: (1) time series, (2) causal or (3) judgmental. The material in this book centers on these three categories since they provide a logical basis for comparing and contrasting models.

Time Series Models

These models use past data as the basis for estimating future results. Past patterns are analyzed and attempts are made to compensate for these patterns in the forecasting process. Although there are a wide variety of time series techniques, many are just modifications of some basic time series models. This book describes seven of the better known techniques.

- Classical time series—Decomposition
- Moving averages
- Exponential smoothing
- Adaptive filtering
- Winter's method
- Box-Jenkins
- Census II

Causal Models

The basic premise of causal models is that a particular outcome is directly influenced by some other predictable factor(s). Thus, projections of the "predictors" are first made and then used to make the forecast.

Types of Models Covered

- Regression and correlation
- Leading indicators
- Input-output

Judgmental Models

These forecasting models are often called *subjective* because they rely on intuitive judgments, opinions, and probabilities in deriving forecasts. This does not mean judgmental models only should be used in situations where time series or causal methods are not applicable. Rather, these models are valuable forecasting techniques in their own right and are well suited to long-range forecasting and developing forecasts for new or unique products.

Types of Models Covered

- Expert opinions
- Delphi method
- Surveys of salesmen, potential customers
- Probability

- Simulation
- Technological forecasting

SUMMARY

This chapter provides readers with key background data about forecasting. The remainder of the book describes those models the reader will most likely be involved with in the future. In some cases, he or she may personally use the models to make forecasts. In many cases though, the reader will be using forecasts developed by others. Regardless of who generates the data, however, decision makers must have a reasonable understanding of the strengths and limitations of forecasting techniques if they are to effectively use these methods. The purpose of this book is to provide that kind of information.

APPENDIX: IMPACT OF PRODUCT'S LIFE CYCLE ON FORECASTS

The "product life cycle" is an important marketing concept. The crux of this concept is that products go through a cycle in which sales grow, level off, and then eventually decline. The length of this cycle will vary since some products become instant successes, others go through a lengthy period of continuous but slow growth, and others never reach a satisfactory sales level and are pulled off the market.

There can be anywhere from four to seven separate phases in a product's life cycle depending on a particular author's choice of terms. Some authors include a "maturity" stage, the period in which the growth rate of sales slows down. Others may separate this period into two stages—"slow growth" and "saturation." The differences between various life cycle models are really only semantic ones. A brief description is now presented of the forecasting problems associated with each phase of the product life cycle.

Pre-introduction Phase

The term *new product* covers a number of different situations. A new product includes technological breakthroughs that result in a product category totally new to the market: Polaroid cameras, microwave ovens, silicon chips for computers. A new product also can be a product that is merely an addition to the existing product category: for example, Coors adds a premium beer to its existing product line. A new product can also emerge when an existing product is revamped: an industrial detergent that has been on the market for ten years has another chemical added to cut down on its harshness to the skin.

In each of the above examples, before major production of the product was undertaken, there had to be some evidence (that is, a forecast) that there was a reasonable demand for it. However, each product poses unique problems for forecasters. If the product is a technological breakthrough (microwave ovens), there would be little or no historical data to rely on. Even survey methods are of limited use in this case since potential customers may have trouble visualizing the product and verbalizing their interest in it. If the product is only an addition to existing products (another premium beer), data on comparable products can be used to build a forecast. If the product is a revised version of an existing product, forecasts are much easier to make since the product's past sales data can be used.

Introduction Stage

In this phase, the product is being introduced to potential customers. Little forecasting is done during this period. Instead, close tabs are kept on actual sales to see how well they match the forecasts made during the pre-introduction phase.

Close monitoring of sales is desired but may be difficult to achieve if a long trade channel is used. The producer may have problems tracking the product to the retailer and the ultimate consumer. Heavy original sales to distributors may have overloaded the product pipeline (inventories of middlemen) and a sales decline may follow until these middlemen can lower their inventories.

The introduction phase lasts anywhere from several weeks to several months depending on the nature of the product. For products that are rapidly consumed (food, detergents), the introduction phase usually lasts until repurchase patterns emerge. For products that involve lengthy periods of consumption (microwave ovens, industrial equipment), the introduction stage continues until some pattern of customer acceptance or rejection takes place.

Growth Stage

If the product is accepted by customers, it enters a growth phase where repeat purchases are made or new groups of customers begin to make purchases. This sales data can then be used to update original forecasts or make new ones. This information is crucial to production people since it determines their future levels of operation. It is also the first indication to management of long-term personnel and equipment needs. It is during this period that strong competition often becomes a major influence on the firm's marketing activities.

Maturity Stage

Eventually the product's rate of growth levels off and its market share stabilizes. Except for products in a highly competitive or volatile market, sales in this phase are easiest to forecast. The stability of the market and increasing amounts of past sales data contribute to the forecast's success.

During this phase, the firm monitors its own sales and sales of the industry as a whole. If a firm's product is in the maturity stage, while the industry as a whole is in the growth stage, this indicates the product's sales have stabilized and it is losing market share.

Some products never enter a maturity stage but instead move directly from the growth stage to a rapid decline stage. Fad items such as hula hoops, pet rocks, and Rubik's cubes follow this pattern.

Decline Stage

During this phase sales decrease, but it may still be profitable to produce and sell the product. Because of this decline, it is important to have accurate sales forecasts so that realistic production schedules can be maintained.

Overview of Life Cycle

Forecasters face different challenges in the various stages of the life cycle. During pre-introduction and growth stages, forecasting techniques requiring historical data will be of limited use since little or no sales data exist. In the maturity stage, forecasting gets easier because greater stability occurs and more historical sales data exist. In the decline stage, successful forecasting means the difference between profitably milking a declining product or losing money on it due to production overruns and increased storage expenses.

NOTES

1. Steven C. Wheelwright and Darral Clarke, "Corporate Forecasting: Promise and Reality," *Harvard Business Review* (November-December 1976), pp. 40ff.
2. Ibid., p. 43.
3. Frank Eby and William O'Neill, *The Management of Sales Forecasting* (Lexington, Mass.: Lexington Books—Heath Company, 1977), p. 1.

QUESTIONS AND EXERCISES

1. Susan Sawyer, owner of the Sweaters and Stuff Boutique, is reluctant to design and use a forecasting model in her business because she really doesn't think it will help her make decisions. What would you say to her to convince her otherwise?

2. John Jamison owns a small plant that manufactures water sprinklers. He claims his firm always develops a marketing plan first and then makes the sales forecast. "We never see a forecast until after our plan is developed." How would you respond to Jamison?

3. Describe the key factors that influence the selection of a forecasting model.

4. Explain how the importance and role of sales forecasts change over a product's life cycle.

5. Do you believe a forecast should be a goal for the firm to reach?

6. Distinguish between macro and micro forecasts.

2

Time Series Forecasting Models—Two Key Factors in Their Selection

INTRODUCTION

In Chapter 1, it was emphasized that the forecaster should consider nine different factors to determine which forecasting model is most appropriate. Two of these factors—patterns of past data (for example, sales) and the degree of accuracy sought—are especially critical to the selection and use of time series models. Therefore, before attempting to learn how the various time series models work, the reader first should be able to recognize the different patterns that past data can take and second know how to compare the relative accuracy of the forecasts produced by each of the models.

PATTERNS OF PAST DATA

Identifying Patterns

When time series models are used for a sales forecast, the initial task is to analyze the pattern in the product's past sales. The following four steps, if followed, will identify and confirm the nature of such patterns:

1. Plot historical data on chart.

2. Make visual examination, looking for turning points, count turning points and choose appropriate curve.

3. Compute estimated values for each period using model appropriate for curve.

4. Superimpose curve over historical data. If estimates of computed curve catch turning points and are close to actual historical values, chances are you've got good match. If not, try another curve.

Table 2-1 contains annual sales of Kandid Inc. (a producer of ski boots) over a ten-year period.* The data are plotted on a graph and a line is drawn through the

---

*Although annual sales are used in this example, any time interval (weeks, months, quarters, and so on) can be used depending upon the forecast horizon.

Table 2-1
Annual Sales of Kandid Inc. (in thousands of units)

	#
1971	12
1972	27
1973	34
1974	47
1975	45
1976	49
1977	64
1978	71
1979	68
1980	74

plotted points. The line in Figure 2-1 indicates that Kandid's boot sales have steadily increased over the past ten years. The forecaster could fit a secular trend line to this data and use it to forecast Kandid's sales for 1981. The line in Figure 2-1 is such a trend line. Extension of that line through 1981 provides Kandid with a forecast of approximately 80,000 units.

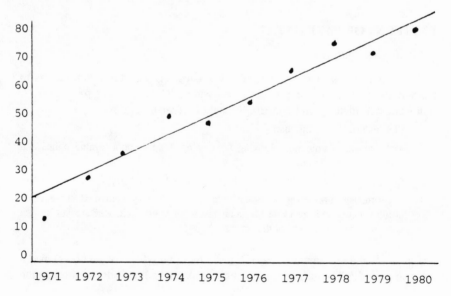

Figure 2-1
Plotted Sales of Kandid Inc. (in thousands of units)

Types of Secular Trends

In Figure 2-1 a straight line is used to depict the general pattern of Kandid Inc.'s past sales. For other sets of data, a curvilinear line might fit better. Trend lines can be described in terms of degrees (see Figure 2-2). A first-degree trend is a straight line (Figure 2-2(a)). A second-degree trend is a curved line, and depicts data growing (or declining) at either a decreasing rate (Figure 2-2(b)) or an increasing rate (Figure 2-2(c)). A third-degree trend (Figure 2-2(d)) is also known as a cubic trend and depicts a wave in the sales pattern.

The number of degrees (first or second or third) really describes the number of changes in the general direction of the trend line. In a first-degree trend, only one general direction is involved. In a second-degree trend, the sales pattern changes once and in a third-degree trend, the pattern changes twice.

Even though there are mathematical procedures available to fit trends to the tenth or eleventh degree, sales forecasters rarely use anything beyond third-degree trend lines. Once you get beyond a third-degree trend, the success of the forecast often depends on the forecaster's "guess" as to the direction of the next sales change.

The discussion in this chapter concentrates on ways to fit first- and second-degree trend lines to the data and on the development of logarithmic trends. These are the most important types of trend lines and knowledge of them enables a forecaster to depict the growth or decline of most time series data.

Fitting a Linear Trend Line

Assume the plotted data indicate that the data are best represented by a straight line (first-degree trend). There are three basic ways to develop such a line: the freehand method, the semiaverage method, and the least squares method.

Freehand Method

The freehand method is the simplest to apply and is used to fit the trend line to the sales data as shown in Figure 2-1. It involves drawing a line through the data points in such a way that the plotted points fall fairly evenly above and below the line. Most forecasters prefer to use a more sophisticated method of fitting a line to the data, such as one of the next two.

Semiaverage Method (Table 2-2, Figure 2-3)

Three steps are involved in the semiaverage method:

(1) The data points in the time series are divided into halves. If there is an uneven number of observations (data points), the central value is included in both halves (Table 2-2).

(2) Arithmetic means are calculated for each half and plotted on the graph adjacent to their respective midpoints (Figure 2-3).

(3) A straight line drawn through these two points is the trend line.

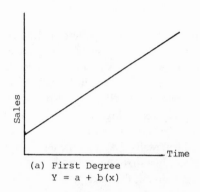

(a) First Degree
    $Y = a + b(x)$

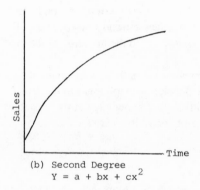

(b) Second Degree
    $Y = a + bx + cx^2$

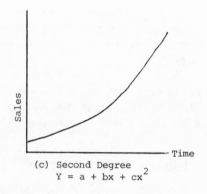

(c) Second Degree
    $Y = a + bx + cx^2$

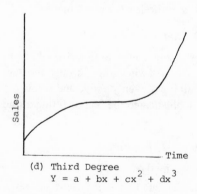

(d) Third Degree
    $Y = a + bx + cx^2 + dx^3$

Figure 2-2
Four Possible Trend Lines

Table 2-2
Using the Semiaverage Method to Develop a Trend Line for Sales of Kandid Inc. (in thousands of units)

Year	Unit Sales (000's)		
	X_1		
1971	12		
1972	27		
1973	34	$\Sigma X_1 = 165$	$\overline{X}_1 = \dfrac{165}{5} = 33$
1974	47		
1975	45		
	X_2		
1976	49		
1977	64		
1978	71	$\Sigma X_2 = 326$	$\overline{X}_2 = \dfrac{326}{5} = 65.2$
1979	68		
1980	74		

Σ = Sum of

$\overline{X}$ = Mean of X

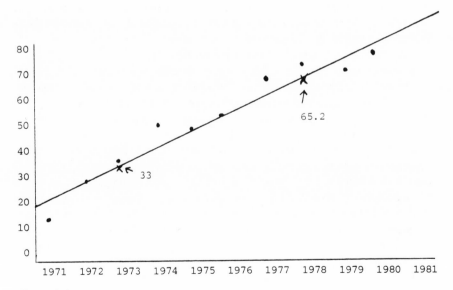

Figure 2-3
Using the Semiaverage Method to Develop a Linear Trend for Kandid Inc. Sales

21

Computations for the semiaverage method are included in Table 2-2 using the ski boot sales data of Kandid Inc. found in Table 2-1. The two semiaverage values are 33,000 and 65,200. These values are plotted at their respective middle years (1973 and 1978) in Figure 2-3.

Least Squares Method

The technique most frequently used to fit a linear trend is least squares because it enables the line to be fitted to the data using a more sophisticated mathematical procedure. This technique fits a trend line to the data in such a way as to ensure that the sum of the squared deviations (the distance between each observation and the line) is at a minimum, thus the least squared differences. This procedure uses the equation for a straight line $[Y = a + b(x)]$ as the basis for its computations. Using least squares analysis requires that values for a and b be identified and incorporated into the formula. Table 2-3 demonstrates the application of the least squares method to the Kandid ski boot sales data.

When the least squares method is used with time series data, the time periods are used as the independent variable (x). To make the computations easier, coded values can be substituted for the actual time periods. The coded values begin with the middle period and move in equal increments backward (using minus values) and forward (using plus values). When an even number of periods is involved, the two center periods are coded -1 and $+1$ and the next periods backward in time become -3, -5, -7, and so on and the ensuing periods forward in time become $+3$, $+5$, $+7$, and so on, maintaining a two-unit interval between periods. If an odd number of periods is involved, the middle period is assigned a value of 0, and the next periods forward in time values of $+1$, $+2$, $+3$, maintaining a one-unit interval between periods.

As stated earlier, the reason for substituting smaller numbers $(1, -1, 3, -3)$ for the actual independent variables (1974, 1975, and so forth) is to make the computations of the a and b values easier. This shortcut is very valuable when the values are computed manually or by hand-held calculator. In this era of personal computers, however, this substitution may not be necessary.

Ideally, when the least squares method is used, 18 to 20 periods of data should be available, although in many instances a smaller number of time periods is used. The reader should be aware that making long-term forecasts (6 or 8 years into the future) is extremely dangerous when only a small number of time periods is used to develop the trend line. Statisticians feel that when long-term forecasts are being made, sales data should be available for twice as many periods as are being forecast (for example, a 10-year forecast should be based on at least 20 years of past data).

As shown in Table 2-3, a value of 49.1 was derived for a, and a value of 3.29 was derived for b. These two values are then placed in the equation: $Y = a + b(x)$. A straight line can now be fit to the data using any two values for x. The years 1973 and 1979 are used in the example below:

$$Y_{73} = 49.1 + 3.29(-5)$$

Table 2-3
Using the Least Squares Method to Develop a Trend Line for Sales of Kandid Inc.

Year	Unit Sales (000's) (Y)	Coded Year (X)	XY	x^2	Trend Value Y_c
1971	12	-9	-108	81	19.5
1972	27	-7	-189	49	26.1
1973	34	-5	-170	25	32.7
1974	47	-3	-141	9	39.2
1975	45	-1	-45	1	45.8
1976	49	1	49	1	52.4
1977	64	3	192	9	59.0
1978	71	5	355	25	65.6
1979	68	7	476	49	72.1
1980	74	9	666	81	78.7
	$\Sigma Y=491$		$\Sigma XY=1085$	$\Sigma x^2=330$	

$$a = \frac{\Sigma Y}{n} = \frac{491}{10} = 49.1 \qquad \text{Value of Y at midpoint between 1975 and 1976}$$

$$b = \frac{\Sigma XY}{\Sigma x^2} = \frac{1085}{330} = 3.29 \qquad \text{Slope, or average increase per year}$$

$$Y_{1981} = a + b(x) \Longrightarrow Y_{81} = 49.1 + 3.29(11) \Longrightarrow Y_{81} = 85.29$$
$$\uparrow$$
$$\text{Code for 1981}$$

$$Y_{73} = 32.65$$

$$Y_{79} = 49.1 + 3.29(7)$$

$$Y_{79} = 72.13$$

These two values are plotted on the graph at their respective years and a line is drawn connecting them. That line, when extended in both directions, becomes the least squares line or the line best depicting the linear trend of the data.

A note of caution: remember that the least squares method can be used to fit a straight line to any set of data, regardless of the type of trend in that data. This does not mean the data actually have a linear trend, since a second-degree or third-degree trend line may be more appropriate. Thus, it is first necessary to plot the past data to determine visually the general nature of the trend.

Situations Affecting Trends

Two situations frequently arise that make it more difficult to fit a trend to time series data: (1) a major turning point occurs (a permanent change) or (2) a major isolated (random) change occurs.

Major Turning Point

When the past data have undergone a major turning point, a single linear trend might not adequately depict the true situation. Such changes usually occur when a firm adds new production facilities, acquires additional stores, or its operation is aided or hurt by a change in government policy.

Two lines are used when the change is permanent. Figure 2-4 illustrates such a situation. In this instance, two linear trend lines represent the past data more effectively than even a single curvilinear line. The linear trend line fitted to the latter years (1976–1980) is used in the example to prepare a forecast for 1981.

Isolated Changes

Some firms may have undergone a major change in sales for just one period that distorts the trend line if included in the computations (see Figure 2-5). If the forecaster can logically explain the discrepancy (for example, morale problems among the firm's employees, fire, poor weather) and believes it will not recur, a figure that is more in line with the norm is substituted for the unusual figure to

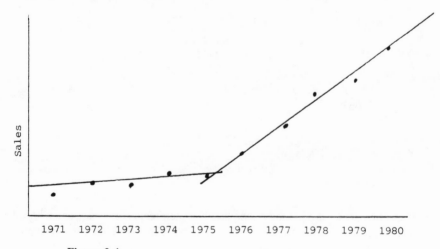

Figure 2-4
Using Two Trend Lines to Depict Turning Point in Past Sales

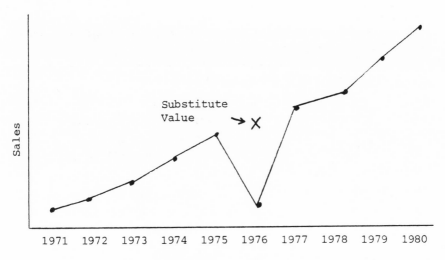

Figure 2-5
Isolated Change in Sales

compute the trend line. Thus, in Figure 2-5, a value close to the other plotted values is substituted for 1976. In Chapter 7 additional coverage is provided on ways to handle temporary disruptions in the variable being forecasted.

Fitting a Second-Degree Trend Line

After the historical data have been plotted, the forecaster may believe that a curvilinear trend best fits the data. This is usually the situation when data values are increasing at a decreasing rate or decreasing at an increasing rate.

The equation for a second-degree trend line is:

$$Y_c = a + bx + cx^2$$

Table 2-4 contains sales data that seem to be best handled by a second-degree trend line because of the turning point at 1975 after a flat period. It also contains the computations needed to derive values for a, b, and c in the above formula.

$$a = \frac{\Sigma Y - c\Sigma X^2}{n}$$

$$b = \frac{\Sigma XY}{\Sigma Y^2}$$

$$c = \frac{n\Sigma X^2 Y - \Sigma X^2 \Sigma Y}{n\Sigma X^4 - (\Sigma X^2)^2}$$

Table 2-4
Using the Least Squares Method to Develop a Second-Degree Trend Line for Annual Sales of Windsor Camera Co. (in thousands of units)

Year	Sales (Y)	Coded Year (X)	x^2	x^4	XY	x^2y	Y_c
1969	20.7	-11	121	14641	-227.7	2504.7	19.14
1970	17.7	-9	81	6561	-159.3	1433.7	19.00
1971	17.6	-7	49	2401	-123.2	862.4	19.16
1972	20.5	-5	25	625	-102.5	512.5	19.63
1973	20.9	-3	9	81	-62.7	188.1	20.41
1974	20.9	-1	1	1	-20.9	20.9	21.49
1975	22.4	1	1	1	22.4	22.4	22.87
1976	25.7	3	9	81	77.1	231.3	24.56
1977	26.6	5	25	625	133.0	665.0	26.56
1978	29.4	7	49	2401	205.8	1440.6	28.86
1979	31.0	9	81	6561	279.0	2511.0	31.46
1980	34.1	11	121	14641	375.1	4126.1	34.37
12	287.5		572	48620	396.1	14518.7	
	ΣY		Σx^2	Σx^4	ΣXY	$\Sigma x^2 y$	

$$c = \frac{n\Sigma x^2 y - \Sigma x^2 \Sigma y}{n\Sigma x^4 - (\Sigma x^2)^2} = \frac{(12)(14518.7) - (572)(287.5)}{(12)(48620) - (572)^2} = .0381$$

$$a = \frac{\Sigma y - c\, \Sigma x^2}{n} = \frac{(287.5) - (.0381)(572)}{12} = 22.14$$

$$b = \frac{\Sigma XY}{\Sigma x^2} = \frac{396.1}{x^2} = \frac{396.1}{572} = .693$$

The final column on Table 2-4 contains the expected, or trend values for each of the time periods. The values derived for a, b, and c used in the formula for the second degree were shown above. For example, the trend value for 1969 was 19.13.

$$Y_{69} = 1 + b(x) + c(x^2)$$

$$Y_{69} = 22.14 + .693(-11) + .0381(121)$$

$$Y_{69} = 19.13$$

The forecast for 1981, based on this second-degree trend line, would be 37,580 units.

$$Y_{81} = 22.14 + .693(13) + .0381(169)$$

$$Y_{81} = 37.58$$

Exponential Trend Lines

The third type of trend line covered in this chapter is the exponential trend line. This is used in situations in which the change in past data occurs at a constant percentage rate, that is, a geometric change or compounded at a fixed rate each year. This type of change follows a curvilinear pattern when plotted on regular graph paper but becomes linear when plotted on semi-log paper.

To understand the difference between regular growth and geometric growth, compare the results of a sales increase of approximately 10,000 units each year versus a sales increase of 10 percent each year (see Table 2-5).

Note the difference in the patterns of change in both sets of data (see Figure 2-6). A constant annual growth in terms of unit sales follows a straight line, whereas a constant percentage growth per year follows a curvilinear path. But if this data were plotted on semi-log paper, the opposite results would occur: the constant percentage growth would be linear and the constant unit growth would be curvilinear.

A formula for fitting an exponential trend to data is:

$$\text{Log } Y_c = \text{Log } a + \text{Log } b(x).$$

This formula will now be used to show how the forecast (Y_c in Column 7) was derived for 1980 (see Table 2-6).

Table 2-5
Regular Growth versus Geometric Growth

	(a) Increase 10,000 units annually	(b) Increase 10% annually (Geometric)
1970	100,000	100,000
1971	110,000	110,000
1972	120,000	121,000
1973	130,000	133,000
1974	140,000	146,300
1975	150,000	160,930
1976	160,000	177,023

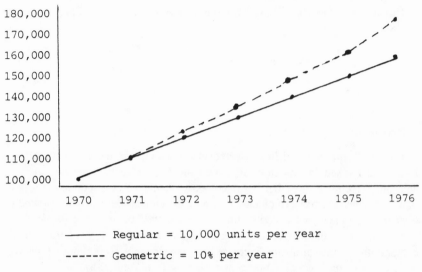

——— Regular = 10,000 units per year

------ Geometric = 10% per year

Figure 2-6
Patterns of Regular and Geometric Growth in Sales

Log Y_{80} = Log a + Log $b(x)$.

The calculated values for Log a and Log b are found at the bottom of Table 2-6. These two values are inserted into the formula along with the appropriate x value for 1980, which is 5.

Therefore, Log Y_{80} = 2.7138 + .0171(5)

$$= 2.7993$$

A table in a statistics book or a calculator with a log key can be used to transform the log values to real numeric values, which in this instance is \$628,000 (Column 7).

The same procedures would be followed in deriving a forecast for 1981.

Log Y_{81} = Log a + Log $b(x)$
       = 2.7138 + .0171(6)
       = 2.8164

The corresponding value found in a common logarithmic table is 653. Therefore, sales for 1981 are estimated to be around \$653,000. Forecasts can also be made for 1982, 1983, and so on by using the appropriate x values (Column 2) for each of those years along with the Log a and Log b values found in Table 2-6.

Table 2-6
Computing the Logarithmic Sales Trend (in thousands of dollars)

Year	$ Sales (Y) (1)	Coded Year (X) (2)	x^2 (3)	Log Y[1] (4)	(Col. 2 x Col. 5) X (Log Y) (5)	Log Y_c* (6)	Y_c^2[2] (7)
1970	446.1	-5	25	2.6494	-13.2345	2.6354	432
1971	452.5	-4	16	2.6556	-10.6224	2.6520	449
1972	447.3	-3	9	2.6506	-7.9518	2.6687	466
1973	475.9	-2	4	2.6775	-5.3550	2.6854	485
1974	487.7	-1	1	2.6882	-2.6882	2.7020	504
1975	497.2	0	0	2.6965	0	2.7187	523
1976	529.8	1	1	2.7241	2.7241	2.7353	544
1977	551.0	2	4	2.7412	5.4824	2.7520	565
1978	581.1	3	9	2.7643	8.2929	2.7687	587
1979	616.7	4	16	2.7900	11.1600	2.7853	610
1980	652.6	5	25	2.8146	14.0730	2.7983	628
	5737.9		110	29.8520	1.8805		
	ΣY		Σx^2	Σ Log Y	ΣX Log Y		

[1] Log values taken from log tables found in most statistics books.
[2] Log values of figures in Column 6.

$$Log\ a = \frac{\Sigma\ \log\ Y}{n} = \frac{29.8520}{11} = 2.7138$$

$$Log\ b = \frac{\Sigma X\ (\log\ Y)}{\Sigma x^2} = \frac{1.8805}{110} = .0171$$

*Log Y_c = Log a + Log b (X)

Overview of Trend Analysis

In the previous sections of this chapter, three general types of trends were presented: linear, curvilinear (second degree), and exponential. These are the types of trends that forecasters most frequently fit to time series data. This chapter employed manual procedures for fitting trends. In Chapter 5, a process using autocorrelations is described in which the computer can be used to identify trends and seasonal factors in data.

MEASURING ACCURACY OF FORECASTS FROM TIME SERIES MODELS

The ultimate test of any forecasting model is how well it forecasts actual data. In the case of time series models, no single technique is considered by forecasters to be the "best" method to measure a model's accuracy. However, some procedures are more widely used than others and three of these are now described.

The basis for comparing the accuracy of models is the difference between actual data for certain time periods and the model's forecast for those periods. One of three approaches can be used to make such comparisons:

(1) Apply the forecast model to all the previous periods to see how well they match the actual data of each of those periods. The drawback of this method is that the model is being tested against the same data from which it was developed.

(2) Build the model from only a limited number of periods of past data (for example, 1967–1976) and test it on more recent historical data that were not used to develop the model (1977–1981). The shortcoming of this method is that it does not include the most recent and possibly the most important data in the model.

(3) The most obvious approach is to evaluate a model solely on the accuracy of its actual forecasts. Compare the forecast for 1982 with the actual outcome of 1982. The major drawback of this approach is that if the model is forecasting annual or quarterly data, a fairly lengthy time period must elapse before the model's accuracy can be measured.

The first two approaches are "ex post" (after the fact), while the third approach is "ex ante" (before the fact). The first approach—applying the model to all the past data from which it is developed—is used most frequently for time series data and some examples of how it is used to measure errors are now presented.

Values Used to Identify Errors

Errors can be measured using actual values (unit or dollars) or percentages. If a forecast for a given period was 1,790 units and actual sales for that period were 1,650 units, then in real terms the forecast was too high by 140 units (1,790 − 1,650 = +140). If percentages were used, the forecast error would be +8.5 percent (140 ÷ 1,650).

In addition to choosing between real values and percentages, the data also should be converted to "absolute values." Absolute values ignore the direction of the error, which means an error of −65 units would be viewed as just an error of 65 units. The reason for using absolute values can be illustrated by developing an arithmetic mean of the error in Table 2-7.

If the individual forecast error for all ten time periods are summed, their overall mean error turns out to be .1 (−7.5 + .9 + 1.3 . . . 4.7 ÷ 10 = .1).

Table 2-7
Actual and Forecasted Sales for Kandid Ski Boots (in thousands of units)

Year (1)	Actual Sales (000's) (1)	Forecast Sales (000's) (2)	Mean Absolute Difference (000's) (1) − (2) (3)	Mean Absolute Percentage Error (3) ÷ (1) (4) %	Mean Squared Error (5) Column (3)^2
1971	12	19.5	-7.5	62.5	56.3
1972	27	26.1	.9	3.3	.8
1973	34	32.7	1.3	3.8	1.7
1974	47	39.2	7.8	16.6	60.8
1975	45	45.8	-.8	1.8	.6
1976	49	52.4	-3.4	6.9	11.6
1977	64	59.0	5.0	7.8	25.0
1978	71	65.6	5.4	7.6	29.2
1979	68	72.1	-4.1	6.0	16.8
1980	74	78.7	-4.7	6.4	22.1
			$\frac{40.9}{10}$ =4.09	$\frac{122.7}{10}$ =12.3	$\frac{224.9}{10}$ =22.5

(MAD) Mean Absolute Difference = $\frac{40.9}{10}$ = 4.09   [(Column 3) 7.5 + .9 + 1.3 ...]

(MAPE) Mean Absolute Percentage Error = $\frac{122.7}{10}$ = 12.3%

(MSE) Mean Squared Error = $\frac{224.9}{10}$ = 22.5

The fallacy of this procedure is that a negative error offsets the positive error, resulting in an unusually low average error per period.

This shortcoming is overcome when absolute values are used. It is also overcome when the error values are squared since this does away with any minus signs (-7.5 units $\times$ -7.5 units = 56.25 units).

Three procedures commonly used to measure and compare errors are now presented: mean absolute difference (MAD), mean absolute percentage error (MAPE), and mean square error (MSE). In all of these examples it is assumed that the forecast values (Column 2, Table 2-7) were developed through the use of a least squares model.

MAD (Mean Absolute Difference)

All the negative values in Column 3 (Table 2-7) are changed to plus values, summed, and the mean of these absolute differences is then derived: 4,090 units.

MAPE (Mean Absolute Percentage Error)

When sales data become quite large (millions or hundreds of thousands of units) it may be difficult to evaluate a forecast's accuracy on the basis of units. Is a forecasting error of 50,000 units bad or good? Therefore, many analysts prefer to measure errors in percentages. Column 4 of Table 2-7 illustrates this procedure. The results show that the mean absolute percentage error (MAPE) produced by the model is about 12.3 percent. This figure may be more useful than knowing that, on the average, the typical annual forecast missed actual sales by 4,090 units (MAD).

MSE (Mean Squared Error)

This procedure penalizes the forecasting techniques that make sizable errors. By squaring the errors (Column 5) the impact of large errors are further magnified. These square values are then summed and their mean determined.

Comparison of Forecast Models

Results from three different models used to forecast Kandid boot sales are included in Table 2-8: least squares model (results from Table 2-7), moving average model, and an exponential smoothing model. At this time the reader should not be concerned with how these specific values were derived (exponential smoothing and moving averages are covered in the next chapter) but instead should be concerned with the size of the forecasting errors of each model.

Table 2-8 indicates that each of the models is superior in one area. Which one should be used? The model eventually chosen usually depends on what aspect of forecasting accuracy is most important to the forecaster. Does the forecaster want a model that provides reasonable accuracy for each period? If so, then MAD or MAPE comparisons will disclose the best model. Or, does the forecaster want a model that minimizes the possibility of a major forecasting error in any one given period? In that case, comparisons of MSE should be used to select the model.

The reader has been introduced to two key time series forecasting activities: identifying the pattern of past sales and comparing the forecasting accuracy of different models. With this background, coverage of the key time series models is provided in the next three chapters.

Table 2-8
Comparison of Three Forecasting Models

Forecasting Model	MAD	MSE	MAPE
Least Squares	4,900	22,500	12.3%
Moving Average	5,700	20,200	12.9%
Exponential Smoothing	5,300	24,000	12.6%

QUESTIONS AND EXERCISES

1. Graph the following sales data. Then develop a trend line using the semiaverage method and the least squares method.

Period	Sales (in thousands of units)
1	10.2
2	9.3
3	12.1
4	15.2
5	12.6
6	12.9
7	13.1
8	17.2
9	16.3
10	14.5
11	16.3

2. What would you do if a first-degree trend line did not seem to fit the data points in your graphed data?

3a. Measure the accuracy of the following forecasts that were based solely on the intuitive judgments of the sales manager. Use MAD, MAPE, and MSE for the analysis.

Period	Sales (in thousands)	Forecasts (Intuitive)
1	10.2	9.5
2	9.3	10.0
3	12.1	10.5
4	15.2	13.0
5	12.6	13.5
6	12.9	14.0
7	13.1	12.5
8	17.2	15.0
9	16.3	15.5
10	14.5	16.0
11	16.3	17.5

 b. How well does the sales manager's intuitive forecast compare with the forecasts (least squares and semiaverages) you made in Question 1? Use MAD, MAPE, and MSE.

4. Distinguish between geometric growth and normal growth.

5. Under what circumstances would a decision maker be most likely to use MSE as the method to evaluate a model? When would MAD be preferable?

3

Time Series Models

INTRODUCTION

Time series forecasting techniques use past data to generate a forecast. The models most frequently used are described in the next three chapters. This chapter covers two rather simple time series models: moving averages and exponential smoothing. Chapter 4 describes the classical decomposition model and Chapter 5 deals with four of the more complicated models: the Winter's method, adaptive filtering, census II, and Box-Jenkins.

Key Element of Time Series

The basic requirement of all time series techniques is that past data exist for the variable being forecasted. In a sales context, for example, they are most appropriate for products that have been on the market for a reasonable period of time, usually products in the "maturity" stage of their life cycles.

An exception would be a new product (Product A) that is very similar to one the firm already has on the market (Product B). The similarity between the two products enables past sales of Product B to be used to estimate sales of the new product. But even this approach is questionable if the overall business environment during Product B's introduction was significantly different from that now facing the new product (A). Therefore, the use of surrogate information is usually best suited to estimating expected rate of growth or general sales patterns, rather than estimating specific sales.

MOVING AVERAGES

Moving average models are one of the most easily understood and applied of all time series models. Their simplicity makes them attractive to firms seeking short-term forecasts for a large number of products, all with a lengthy sales history. The models work best when past sales of the product (or any other variable) follow a reasonably stable pattern, that is, there is little or no slope or trend.

Moving average models are also frequently called "smoothing" techniques, since they level out the distortions caused by occasional random fluctuations. Note the term *occasional* in the previous sentence, since if a product or any other variable has a history of frequent dramatic fluctuations, moving averages are not an effective forecasting tool.

The basic premise of simple moving averages is that the data from a number of consecutive past periods can be averaged to provide a reasonable estimate of sales for the next period ($t + 1$). The greater the number of previous periods included in the forecast model, the greater the smoothing effect. Column 2 of Table 3-1 contains actual sales data for each of 15 periods (in 000s of units) for one of Acme Company's major products: a metal wrench sold in both industrial and consumer markets. Although in this example each data point represents a three-month period, time series models also can be used with weekly, monthly, or yearly data. Column 3 contains forecasts derived from a three-period moving average (MA) model. Figure 3-1 shows the MA model and identifies its symbols.

The sales data from Column 2 are placed in the forecast model from Figure 3-1, resulting in the values in Column 3 of Table 3-1. The first forecast is made for period 4, which is $Y_{t + 1}$ in the formula.

$$Y_{t+1}, \text{ or } Y_4 = \frac{76 + 77 + 70}{3}$$

$$Y_4 = 74.3$$

When the forecast for period 5 is derived, $t + 1 = 5$. Thus:

$$Y_{t+1}, \text{ or } Y_5 = \frac{79 + 76 + 77}{3}$$

$$Y_5 = 77.3$$

This process is continued through period 15 so that a forecast can be developed for period 16.

$$Y_{16} = \frac{S_{15} + S_{14} + S_{13}}{N}$$

$$Y_{16} = \frac{107 + 108 + 103}{3}$$

$$Y_{16} = 106,000 \text{ units}$$

Table 3-1
Using Moving Averages to Develop Forecasts (three- and five-period models)

(1) Time Period	Three Period				Five Period		
	(2) Actual Sales (S)	(3) Forecast Sales (Y)	(4) Absolute Error	(5) Squared Error	(6) Forecast Sales (Y)	(7) Absolute Error	(8) Squared Error
1	70						
2	77						
3	76						
4	79	74.3	4.7	22.1			
5	87	77.3	9.7	94.1			
6	87	80.7	6.3	39.7	77.8	9.2	84.6
7	89	84.3	4.7	22.1	81.2	7.8	60.8
8	92	88.7	3.3	10.9	83.6	8.4	70.6
9	90	89.3	.7	.5	86.8	3.2	10.2
10	94	90.3	3.7	13.7	89.0	5.0	25.0
11	97	92.0	5.0	25.0	90.4	6.6	43.6
12	84	93.7	9.7	94.1	92.4	8.4	70.6
13	103	91.3	11.7	136.9	91.4	11.6	134.6
14	108	94.7	13.3	176.9	93.6	14.4	207.4
15	107	98.3	8.7	75.7	97.2	9.8	96.0
16	–	106.0	–	–	99.8	–	–
Total			81.5	711.7		84.4	803.4
Mean			6.8	59.4		8.4	80.3

etc.

Y_{t+1} = <u>Forecasted</u> sales of <u>next</u> period

S_t = Current period

S_{t-1} = <u>Actual</u> sales of <u>previous</u> period

N = Number of values (time periods) included

$$Y_{t+1} = \frac{S_t + S_{t-1} + S_{t-2}}{N} \qquad (3\text{-}1)$$

Figure 3-1
Symbols Used in Models

Handling Errors

Forecasted sales for period 4 were 74.3 whereas actual sales were 79, resulting in a forecasting error of 4.7 units for that period. Columns 4 and 5 contain information on the absolute differences between forecasted and actual sales for periods 4 through 15. These figures are used to determine the overall error arising from using the three-period moving averages. The mean squared error (MSE) is used to identify the total error in previous periods.

How Many Periods Should Be Used?

A moving average of five periods is also used in Table 3-1 (see Column 6). To determine the amount of error associated with moving averages of different lengths, compare Column 4 with Column 7 and Column 5 with Column 8. The general pattern of the data guides the decision as to the number of periods to include in the moving average model. If the overall pattern of the data is one of regular growth or decline with few random fluctuations, a smaller number of observations would provide more accurate forecasts. On the other hand, if the data have been fairly stable but interrupted by frequent random variations, a larger number of observations should be included.

Including more periods in the model increases its "smoothing" effect, but it also means that the forecasts it produces lag further behind actual data if there is a growth or decline pattern in past data. (It should be emphasized again that the moving average model is not appropriate for sales data that constantly fluctuate or have a strong trend.)

A five-year moving average provides a forecast of 99,800 units for period 16.

There is also a major difference in the mean square errors of both models: 59,400 versus 80,300.

The five-period MA retains data from unusual periods (period 12) in the forecasts longer, resulting in its higher absolute errors and MSE values.

Double Moving Averages

It should now be clear to the reader that a major drawback of using a simple moving average model is that when the value of the variable (such as a product's sales) is steadily increasing or decreasing, the forecast always lags behind the actual values. A double moving average model is intended to overcome this condition.

As its name implies, a double moving average is merely the moving average of a moving average. (The symbol Y' will be used to identify a simple moving average forecast, with Y'' identifying double moving average values.) The values for Columns 3 and 4 of Table 3-2 are derived from the following two formulas, the first of which we have already seen:

$$Y'_t = \frac{S_t + S_{t-1} + S_{t-2}}{N} \tag{3-1}$$

$$Y''_t = \frac{Y' + Y'_{t-1} + Y'_{t-2}}{N} \tag{3-2}$$

The wrench sales data used in Table 3-1 is repeated in Table 3-2 to demonstrate double moving averages.

$$Y'_3 = \frac{76 + 77 + 70}{3}$$

$$Y''_3 = 74.3$$

The computations for the single moving average in Table 3-2 are basically the same as those performed in Table 3-1 with one major difference: in Table 3-1 the single moving average is aligned with period $t+1$ since it is the forecast for that period. However, in Column 3 of Table 3-2, the Y' values are aligned adjacent to the last period used to calculate them (t) as are the double moving average values (Y''). Therefore, the first forecast is for period 5:

$$Y'_5 = \frac{80.7 + 77.3 + 74.3}{3}$$

$$Y''_5 = 77.4$$

Table 3-2
Using Double Moving Average of Three Periods to Forecast Sales for Acme Wrench Co. (in thousands of units)

(1) Time Period	(2) Actual Sales (S)	(3) 3 Period Forecast (Y')	(4) 3 x 3 Forecast (Y")	(5) a	(6) b	(7) Forecast a+b
1	70					
2	77					
3	76	74.3				
4	79	77.3				
5	87	80.7	77.4	84.0	3.3	
6	87	84.3	80.8	87.8	3.5	87.3
7	89	88.7	84.6	92.8	4.1	91.3
8	92	89.3	87.4	91.2	1.9	96.9
9	90	90.3	89.4	91.2	.9	93.1
10	94	92.0	90.5	93.5	1.5	92.1
11	97	93.7	92.0	95.4	1.7	95.0
12	84	91.3	92.3	90.3	-1.0	97.1
13	103	94.7	93.2	96.2	.5	89.3
14	108	98.3	94.8	101.8	3.5	96.7
15	107	106.0	99.7	112.3	6.3	105.3
16						118.6

$$a_t = 2Y_t' - Y_t''$$

$$b_t = \frac{2}{N-1}(Y_t' - Y_t'')$$

Determining a and b Values

Neither the single moving average values (Equation 3-1) nor the double moving average values (Equation 3-2) are intended to be the actual forecast models. Rather, they provide values from which two new variables (a and b) are derived. It is these new variables that are used to make the forecast. Thus, the actual double moving average forecast model is:

$$Y''_{t+1} = a_t + b_t \tag{3-3}$$

Important Relationship

If the values for simple moving average and double moving average for each period were plotted on a chart, the following relationship would emerge. If there is a trend in the data, the simple moving average values lag behind actual data, and the double moving average values lag behind the single moving average values. But, more important, the distance between the simple moving average trend line and the double moving average trend line is about the same as the distance between the simple moving average trend line and the actual trend line. Thus, if the difference between the simple moving average value and the double moving average value is added back to the simple moving average value, a more accurate forecast emerges. The following process is used to find the value of a_t:

$$a_t = 2Y_t' - Y_t'' \text{ (see Column 5 in Table 3-2)}$$

To further improve the forecast, an adjustment (b_t) is made to this a value. This adjustment is based on the difference between the Y' and Y'' values with an allowance made for the number of time periods (N) included in the moving average.

$$b_t = \frac{2}{N-1}(Y_{t'} - Y_{t''}) \qquad \text{(see Column 6 in Table 3-2)}$$

The forecast model for double moving averages that emerges then is:

$$Y''_{t+1} = a_t + b_t \tag{3-3}$$

Applying this model to sales data in Table 3-2 results in the following forecast for period 6.

$$Y_6 = a_5 + b_5$$

$$Y_6 = 84 + 3.3$$

$$Y_6 = 87.3$$

This same procedure is then used for each ensuing period until a forecast for period 16 can be developed.

$$Y_{16} = a_{15} + b_{15}$$

$$Y_{16} = 112.3 + 6.3$$

$$Y_{16} = 118.6$$

A major drawback of using double moving averages is the large amount of historical data needed to make a forecast. In the example (Table 3-2), the moving average model involved three time periods and required six periods of data to make an initial forecast. If 12 time periods had been used in the MA model, 24 data points would be needed for the initial double moving average forecast.

Overview of Moving Average Models

Strengths

- Fairly simple and inexpensive forecasting procedure and thus is appropriate for firms with a large number of products. Best suited to inventory forecasting for low-volume products with fairly stable sales.
- If there are occasional random fluctuations in the data, the impact of these fluctuations on future forecasts will be minimized as more time periods are included in the moving averages.
- The larger the number of time periods included, the greater the smoothing effect. Thus, if it is desirable to react faster to recent changes, fewer time periods should be used.

Drawbacks

- Requires a large amount of historical data.
- Slow adjustment to changes in data patterns.
- Assigns equal weight to each period ignoring the fact that more recent periods usually are more influential in determining the future value of a variable.
- The model's results cannot be statistically tested.

EXPONENTIAL SMOOTHING

Two of the major drawbacks of forecasting with moving averages are: (1) equal weight is given to each time period included in the average and (2) the model may require a great deal of data storage since data for at least the last N time periods must be retained.

Exponential smoothing overcomes both of these drawbacks. The basic premise of exponential smoothing is that the values of the variable in more recent time periods have more impact on the forecast and therefore should be given more weight. Also, because the calculations require only the most recent sales data, the problem of data storage is greatly lessened.

The logic involved in exponential smoothing is expressed in the following model:

$$Y_{t+1} = \alpha S_t + (1 - \alpha) Y_t \tag{3-4}$$

The alpha (α) term is the smoothing constant and must be assigned a value between 0 and 1. The larger its value (closer to 1), the more weight is given to recent sales data. A large α (.8) is comparable to using a small number of time periods (N) in a moving average model, since a small N places more emphasis on recent data. Conversely, a small α (.1) is similar to using a large number of periods in the moving average, since the impact of recent data is lessened. Therefore, exponential smoothing acknowledges past data but assigns less value to more distant periods and progressively greater values to the more recent periods.

Determining α Value

The α value used in the formula can be determined in two ways:

(a) Trial and error methods: A variety of alpha values in increments between 0 and 1 is tested using the exponential smoothing model $[Y_{t+1} = \alpha S_t + (1 - \alpha)Y_t]$ to make a series of forecasts. Each forecast is tested for error and the one with the smallest error (lowest MSE or MAD) is accepted on the assumption that it has the best alpha value. Since manual calculations to find the "best" alpha value are very laborious and time consuming, computer programs should be used.

(b) Substitution: This second way to determine the best alpha value also uses trial and error. However, in this case, the various alpha values are used to find the one that produces a value that is equal to the most recent data point using the model shown below. Assume that the most recent data point equals 34 units and the past data for each period prior to that is as shown in the model. (Only four data points are used for illustration.)

$$S_t = S_{t-1} + S_{t-2}(\alpha) + S_{t-3}(\alpha^2) + S_{t-4}(\alpha^3) \ldots S_{t-n}(\alpha^{n+1})$$
$$34 = 32 + 30(\alpha) + 26(\alpha^2) + 31(\alpha^3) \ldots$$

In the above equations, the value for α was determined to be .063. This alpha value is then used in the exponential smoothing model to prepare a forecast.

Using Exponential Smoothing

The sales data for Acme Company's wrench, previously used to illustrate moving averages, is also used to illustrate exponential smoothing. Equation 3-4, repeated below, is used for the computations.

$$Y_{t+1} = \alpha S_t + (1-\alpha)Y_t$$

Two different α values are used ($\alpha = .2$ and $\alpha = .8$) to illustrate the effect such values can have on the final forecast (see Table 3-3). Because no forecast data exists for period 1, the first forecast that can be made is for period 3. Actual sales for period 1 are used as the forecast for period 2 to initiate the process. There is now enough data to use Equation 3-4 to forecast sales for period 3.

When $\alpha = .2$
Forecast for period 3 $= .2(77) + .8(70)$
$\qquad\qquad\qquad\quad = 71.4$
When $\alpha = .8$
Forecast for period 3 $= .8(77) + .2(70)$
$\qquad\qquad\qquad\quad = 75.6$

Table 3-3
Using Exponential Smoothing to Forecast Sales for Acme Wrench Co. (in thousands of units)

Time Period	Actual Sales		Forecasts Y $\alpha=.2$	Y $\alpha=.8$
1	70		_*	_*
2	77		70.0	70.0
3	76		71.4	75.6
4	79		72.3	75.9
5	87		73.6	78.4
6	87		76.3	85.3
6	87		76.3	85.3
7	89		77.4	86.7
8	92		79.7	88.5
9	90		82.2	91.3
10	94		83.7	90.3
11	97		85.8	93.3
12	84		88.0	96.3
13	103		87.2	86.5
14	108		90.4	99.7
15	107		93.9	106.3
16			96.5	106.8
		MAD	147/14=10.5	72.1/14=5.2
		MSE	121.4	47.8

*Begin the process by assuming that the forecast for period 2 is equal to the actual of period 1 for both alpha values.

When $\alpha = .8$, the MSE was 47.8. When $\alpha = .2$, the MSE has a much higher value: 121.4. Thus the exponential model using the higher alpha value provided a better fit to actual sales. Why? Remember the purpose of a low versus high alpha value. A small alpha is comparable to using a large number of time periods in a moving average model. This means less weight is given to recent data, providing a greater overall smoothing effect. A small alpha is best suited to slow growth or no growth data patterns, interrupted with periods of extreme fluctuations.

A large alpha, on the other hand, places greatest emphasis on the most recent data and will respond more quickly to recent changes. Thus, a large alpha is better suited to data going through some form of consistent growth or decline.

While an alpha of .8 was more accurate than an alpha of .2, there is probably another alpha value even better suited to the sales data. The forecaster should use the computer to identify the most accurate alpha value and use it in the final model. With each new period, figures will be changing so that the best alpha

Table 3-4
Using Double Exponential Smoothing to Forecast Sales for Acme Wrench Co. (in thousands of units; a = .8)

Time Period	Actual Sales	Y'	Y"	a	b	Forecast Value a + b(n) *
1	70	70.0	70.0	-	-	-
2	77	75.6	74.3	76.5	4.4	-
3	76	75.9	75.6	76.2	1.2	80.9
4	79	78.4	77.8	79.0	2.4	77.4
5	87	85.3	83.8	86.8	6.0	81.4
6	87	86.7	86.2	87.2	2.0	92.8
7	89	88.5	88.0	89.0	2.0	89.2
-8	92	91.3	90.6	92.0	2.8	91.0
9	90	90.3	90.3	90.3	0.0	94.8
10	94	93.3	92.7	93.9	2.4	90.3
11	97	96.3	95.5	97.1	3.2	96.3
12	84	86.5	88.3	84.7	-7.2	100.3
-13	103	99.7	97.5	101.9	8.8	91.9
14	108	106.3	104.5	108.1	7.2	110.7
15	107	106.8	106.3	107.3	2.0	115.3
16	-	-	-	-	-	109.3

```
* n = number of periods in the future          MAD = 64.1/13=4.9
      for the forecast.  In this case
      n=1.                                      MSE = 568.5/13=43.7

Y' = Single exponential smoothing
Y" = Double exponential smoothing
```

value will also change. However, the forecaster generally will not alter the alpha value with each new period, but will stay with a particular α until the forecasting errors exceed an acceptable range.

Double Exponential Smoothing

Exponential smoothing, like moving averages, has a major drawback: it always trails a trend in actual data. To overcome this shortcoming, the forecaster can use double exponential smoothing. This model is based on the same premise as that used in the double moving average model.

Adjustments for trend are made by finding the difference between the value derived from single exponential smoothing and that derived from double exponential smoothing (a value). This difference is added back to the single exponential value, with an additional adjustment for its b value (see Table 3-4).

Note the difference between the models. For single exponential smoothing, the formula is:

$$Y_{t+1} = \alpha S_t + (1-\alpha)Y_t \qquad (3\text{-}4)$$

The formula for double exponential smoothing is:

$$Y''_{t+n} = a_t + b_t(n) \qquad (3\text{-}7)$$

The formula for Y'' differs since we are now trying to find Y values for the current period (t), which when incorporated with the values of a and b will produce a forecast for period $t+1$.

Note that the equation for double exponential smoothing (3-7) is similar to the equation for the double moving average (3-3) discussed earlier in this chapter. They both require a and b values, but differ in the way they derive their respective b values. For the double moving average model, b is derived as follows:

$$b_t = \frac{2}{N-1}(Y'_t - Y''_t)$$

In the double exponential smoothing model, since α values are used rather than number of period (N), the b is determined as follows:

$$b = \frac{\alpha}{1-\alpha}(Y'_t - Y''_t)$$

Also note that the Y' and Y'' symbols in each b formula now represent different values in each formula. In the double moving average formula they represent moving average values, whereas in the double exponential smoothing formula they represent exponential smoothing values.

Steps in the Model

Since values for Y' and Y'' are needed to find the a and b values in Equation 3-7, the following steps are needed to derive double exponential smoothing values.

Step 1: $\quad Y'_t = \alpha S_t + (1 - \alpha)Y'_{t-1} \qquad (3\text{-}5)$

Step 2: $\quad Y''_t = \alpha Y_{t'} + (1 - \alpha)Y''_{t-1} \qquad (3\text{-}6)$

Step 3: $\quad a_t = 2Y'_t - Y''_t$

Step 4: $\quad b_t = \frac{\alpha}{1-\alpha}(Y'_t - Y''_t)$

Step 5: $\quad Y''_{t+n} = a_t + b_t(n) \qquad (3\text{-}7)$

(Note: n equals the number of periods into the future for which the forecast is to be made.)

A forecast for period 5 will be used to illustrate how a double exponential smoothing value is derived. In these computations α will be assigned a value of .8 ($\alpha = .8$).

Step 1: $Y'_4 = \alpha S_4 + (1 - \alpha)Y'_3$ (3-5)
               $= .8(79) + (.2)75.9$
               $= 78.4$

Step 2: $Y''_4 = \alpha(Y'_4 + (1 - \alpha)Y''_3$ (3-6)
               $= .8(78.4) + (.2)75.6$
               $= 77.8$

Step 3: $a_4 = 2Y'_4 - Y''_4$
               $= 2(78.4) - 77.8$
               $= 79$

Step 4: $b_4 = \dfrac{\alpha}{1 - \alpha}(Y'_4 - Y''_4)$

               $= \dfrac{.8}{.2}(78.4 - 77.8)$

               $= 2.4$

Step 5: $Y''_5 = a_4 + b_4(n)$ (3-7)
               $= 79 + 2.4(1)$
               $= 81.4$

Forecast for More Than One Period in Advance

If a forecast is to be made three time periods into the future from the current period, the forecast model would be:

$Y''_{t+3} = a + b(3).$

Using the data of period 15 in Table 3-4, the forecast for period 18 ($t+3$) would be:

$Y''_{t+3} = 107.3 + 2(3)$
$Y''_{t+3} = 113.3$

If a forecast for period 20 was desired, it would be derived in the following manner:

$Y''_{t+5} = 107.3 + 2(5)$
$= 117.3$

Table 3-5
Comparison of Accuracy of Four Forecasting Methods for Acme Wrench Co.

	MAD	MSE	(t + 1) Final Forecast
Single Moving Average (3)	6.8	59.2	106.0
Double Moving Average (3)	4.1	32.7	118.6
Single Exponential Smoothing ($\alpha = .8$)	5.2	48.2	106.9
Double Exponential Moving ($\alpha = .8$)	6.1	85.7	109.5

A note of caution: the accuracy of the model diminishes as the forecast period becomes longer. The model is basically intended as a tool for short-term forecasts. Thus, the previous example where $n=5$ is probably too large a time span for this type of model.

Comparison of Models' Accuracy

Table 3-5 discloses that of the four techniques used, the model best suited to the sales data for Acme's wrench is double moving average. Actually, various lengths of time ($N = 3$ versus 4 versus 5, and so on) and various alpha values for the exponential smoothing models should be tested to identify the most accurate model. After those computations, the four resulting models could be compared to see which is best suited to the data. The large number of calculations involved in just these four examples emphasizes the key role computers play in determining the most effective models.

Triple Exponential Smoothing

If the sales data do not show a consistent trend but rather exhibit some curvature, then triple exponential smoothing would be appropriate. The computations involved are merely an expansion of single and double exponential smoothing with some modification in the manner in which a and b values are determined. This method is best exemplified by the Winter's method, which is discussed in Chapter 5.

Overview of Exponential Smoothing

Strengths

- Fairly simple to understand and use.
- Provides more weight to recent data points.
- Does not require much data storage.
- Software packages for these techniques are usually accessible.
- Has fairly good accuracy for short-term forecasts.

Drawbacks

- Can require a great deal of experimentation in the search for the right α value.
- Usually a poor model to use for medium- or long-term forecasts.
- Forecasts can be thrown into great error because of large random fluctuation in recent periods.

QUESTIONS AND EXERCISES

1a. Develop a forecast for period 16 using a four-period moving average on the following set of sales data. Calculate the MAD and MSE.

Period	Sales (000s)
1	14
2	22
3	33
4	50
5	35
6	47
7	52
8	61
9	59
10	48
11	51
12	60
13	65
14	58
15	58
16	

b. What would have been the effect on the forecast if a six-period moving average had been used? What about a three-period moving average?

2. Use the above sales data to develop a forecast using double moving average ($N=4$). Calculate the MAD and MSE.

3. Use the sales data in Question 1 to develop a forecast based on single exponential smoothing and double exponential smoothing. Calculate the MAD and MSE for each.

4. Compare the forecast results of the four models (single and double moving average and single and double exponential smoothing). Which is the most accurate model for this data? What is there about the data that makes this the most accurate model?

5. What is the relationship between the N of moving average models and α of exponential smoothing models?

6. Under what circumstances would a 12-period moving average model be preferable to a 3-period moving average model?

4

Time Series: Decomposition Model

INTRODUCTION

In the previous chapter dealing with moving averages and exponential smoothing, forecasts were derived based solely on the past values of the variable for which a forecast is prepared. Both models were structured on the basic premise of all time series models, that is, the future value of the variable will mimic its own past values.

Thus, it would seem logical that if past annual data of the variable could be used as indicators of its future values, then time periods of less than one year would be even better indicators since they would enable underlying factors to be identified and accounted for, thus improving the accuracy of a forecast. This breakdown of annual data into its component parts is called decomposition, and the entire forecasting procedure is usually referred to as classical decomposition.

Components of Decomposition Model

The decomposition process assumes that sales, for example, are affected by four factors: the general trend of the data, general economic cycles, seasonality, and irregular or random occurrences.

Trend

This is the general movement of the variable both in terms of direction (growth-decline) and rate of change (slope) over the period covered by the historical data.

Seasonal Component

The pattern that recurs within each year. Such patterns are tied closely to holidays, change of seasons, local customs, annual promotions, and so forth.

49

Cyclical Component

This is the up and down fluctuations in general business activity that take place over a fairly long period of time (1 to 12 years). They tend to vary considerably in amplitude and length and are caused by conditions outside an individual firm's control, for example, general economic conditions.

Irregular or Random Component

These are fluctuations in sales that cannot be tied to the seasonal, trend, or cyclical components. Oftentimes they are variations caused by unusual, one-time-only events such as strikes or hurricanes.

Combining all of these components results in the following forecast equation:

$$Y = T(\text{Trend}) \times S(\text{Seasonal}) \times C(\text{Cyclical}) \times I(\text{Irregular})$$
$$Y = T \cdot S \cdot C \cdot I \tag{4-1}$$

This model is called multiplicative because it assumes that while the four components are tied to different factors, they also are related to one another.

An additive model (4-2) can also be used for decomposition, but it assumes each of the components is independent of the other. In other words, no matter how high the trend value becomes, it does not influence the value of the seasonal or cyclical components. This is usually a questionable assumption to make.

$$Y = T + S + C + I \tag{4-2}$$

Of the two, the multiplicative model (4-1) is more widely used and will be the one demonstrated in this chapter.

Major Steps of the Decomposition Model

The following four steps are followed when using the multiplicative decomposition model.

Step One—Identify the length of seasonality and derive the appropriate seasonal indices (S value).

Step Two—Deseasonalize the data and develop a trend line through the deseasonalized data (T value).

Step Three—Divide the moving average value of each period by the trend value of that same period. This provides the cyclical (C) value.

Step Four—Determine the T, S, and C values for the time period to be forecast and derive the actual forecast.

No attempt is made in this text to identify values for irregular movements (I). It is assumed that these values will even out, or be neutralized when moving averages are computed in step one.

DETERMINING THE SEASONAL (S) VALUE

As previously defined, the seasonal component identifies the portion of sales that recur on a regular basis within each year. The sales of children's clothes increase in August because parents are replenishing school wardrobes. Florists' sales increase at such holidays as Valentine's Day and Mother's Day. Automobile sales peak in September-October when new models appear and dealers are trying to get rid of their old models and peak again in spring when car owners are again in a car-buying mood.

The first step in the decomposition process is to eliminate the effect of seasonality from the time series data. The removal of seasonal fluctuation enables the trend in the data to be more easily identified, increasing the overall accuracy of the forecast. The S values (seasonal component) in the decomposition formula (4-1) is derived in two phases. In the first phase, the length of the season for the particular variable is identified. Once this is done, the appropriate seasonal index for the variable is derived.

Determining Length of Season

Ideally, the forecaster wants sales data available in short time periods (weekly, monthly), since the shorter the time period, the greater the insight provided as to why sales are fluctuating. The unit of time that can be used, however, is dictated by the format the firm uses to maintain actual data. Some firms provide only quarterly data (every three months); this means the forecaster can use only a quarterly seasonal format. Or, if industry sales are involved, yearly sales may be the only data available, which means a decomposition model cannot be used. The key point is that each set of moving average figures should contain one entire year of data. Thus, if the data are in a weekly format, 52 periods of data must be included, or 12 periods of monthly data, or 4 periods of quarterly data.

In the example in this chapter, quarterly sales data are used. However, the same basic procedures are followed for monthly or weekly data. The only difference is that a seasonal factor is developed for each month or week, and instead of using a 4-period moving average, a 12-period (monthly) or a 52-period (weekly) moving average is used.

Determining a Seasonal Index

A seasonal index is a number (in a ratio format) that identifies the impact that seasons have on a variable. For example, an index of .92 for July means that for that month the variable's value is typically 8 percent less than normal due to seasonal variation.

There are three reasons for identifying the seasonal indices in a set of time series data.

(1) It provides a better understanding of the seasonal pattern in the data. An airline
     evaluating its passenger loads in the most recent month wants to know how much
     of the traffic is due to normal seasonal variation.

(2) It aids in projecting the future values of a variable. Knowing these seasonal
     variations enables the airline to make allowances for them. (Extra planes needed
     in high traffic months; fewer employees needed in low traffic months.)

(3) It enables the trend and cyclical values to be depicted more accurately. Once the
     seasonal variation is quantified, it can be eliminated from the data, leaving the
     trend and cycle values.

There are a number of ways to determine an index of seasonal variations. The
method most commonly used and the one used in this book is the "ratio to
moving average." The best way to illustrate this method is to show how a
hypothetical firm (Acme Bottlers) determines the seasonality in its sales.

Seasonal Ratios—Acme Bottlers Example

Acme Bottlers is a major soft drink producer in the southern part of the United
States. The classical decomposition model is used to forecast their quarterly sales
for the coming year(s). Sales data of the eight most recent years are used to
develop the model. Case sales per quarter are found in the column identified as
"Unit Sales" (Column 1) in Table 4-1. These data are in 1,000s of cases.

Because quarterly data are involved, the first step is to develop a four-period
moving average (Column 2) for each of the eight years (see Chapter 3). The
following example shows how the four-quarter moving average value for 1973
(Column 2) was derived.

$$MA = \frac{(835.2 + 1,019.5 + 1,104.8 + 1,177.7)}{4} = 1,034.3$$

Centered Moving Average (Column 3, Table 4-1)

Since an even number of periods (four) is used to determine the moving
averages, these values actually fall between the second and third periods. Therefore it is necessary to align the moving average with a specific time period. This
is accomplished by developing a centered moving average (CMA) using each
two succeeding values of the original four-period moving average (see Columns
2 and 3, Table 4-1). Examples:

$$\text{CMA period } 3_{1973} = \frac{1,034.3 + 1,070.9}{2} = 1,052.6$$

$$\text{CMA period } 4_{1973} = \frac{1,070.9 + 1,125.4}{2} = 1,098.2$$

Table 4-1
Seasonal Adjustment of Quarterly Sales of Acme Bottlers (in thousands of units)

Year	Quarter	(1) Unit Sales	(2) 4 Qtr. MA	(3) MA Centered	(4) Ratio to MA (1÷3)	(5) Rounded Seasonal Factor	(6) Sales Seas. Adj. (1÷5)
1973	1	835.2				.88	949.1
	2	1019.5				1.03	989.8
	3	1104.8	1034.3	1052.6	1.050	1.04	1062.3
	4	1177.7	1070.9	1098.2	1.072	1.05	1121.6
			1125.4				
1974	1	981.7	1179.3	1152.4	.852	.88	1115.6
	2	1237.2	1238.6	1208.9	1.023	1.03	1201.2
	3	1320.4	1294.0	1266.3	1.043	1.04	1269.6
	4	1415.2	1349.5	1321.8	1.071	1.05	1347.8
1975	1	1203.1	1384.0	1366.8	.880	.88	1367.2
	2	1459.4	1404.3	1394.2	1.047	1.03	1416.9
	3	1458.2	1439.0	1421.7	1.026	1.04	1402.1
	4	1496.3	1481.8	1460.4	1.025	1.05	1425.0
1976	1	1341.9	1544.2	1513.0	.887	.88	1524.9
	2	1630.9	1590.3	1567.3	1.041	1.03	1583.4
	3	1707.5	1651.3	1620.8	1.054	1.04	1641.8
	4	1681.0	1705.3	1678.3	1.002	1.05	1601.0
1977	1	1585.8	1784.4	1744.9	.909	.88	1802.0
	2	1846.9	1900.4	1842.4	1.002	1.03	1793.1
	3	2023.9	1975.5	1937.9	1.044	1.04	1946.1
	4	2144.9	2104.3	2039.9	1.052	1.05	2042.8
1978	1	1886.2	2216.6	2160.5	.873	.88	2143.4
	2	2362.3	2324.7	2270.7	1.040	1.03	2293.2
	3	2473.0	2411.3	2368.0	1.044	1.04	2377.9
	4	2577.1	2492.8	2452.1	1.051	1.05	2454.4
1979	1	2232.8	2578.5	2535.7	.881	.88	2537.3
	2	2688.2	2691.3	2634.9	1.020	1.03	2609.9
	3	2815.7	2782.9	2737.1	1.029	1.04	2707.4
	4	3028.5	2900.0	2841.5	1.066	1.05	2884.3
1980	1	2599.0	3023.1	2961.6	.878	.88	2953.4
	2	3156.3	3161.6	3092.4	1.021	1.03	3064.4
	3	3308.5				1.04	3181.3
	4	3582.5				1.05	3411.9

Thus, 1,052.6 (Column 3) becomes the moving average value for the third quarter of 1973, with 1,098.2 the MA for the fourth quarter of 1973, and so on. The same procedure is followed when monthly (12) or weekly (52) data are involved since they also have an even number of periods and their moving averages must be centered on a single period.

Seasonal Ratios

The centered moving average value for each period (Column 3) is then compared to actual sales of each matching period (Column 1), and a ratio between
them (Column 4) is developed:

$$\frac{\begin{array}{c}(\text{Column 1})\\ \text{Actual Sales}\end{array}}{\begin{array}{c}\text{Centered Moving Average}\\ (\text{Column 3})\end{array}} = \begin{array}{c}(\text{Column 4})\\ \text{Ratio of Actual Sales}\\ \text{to Centered MA}\end{array}$$

$$\text{Ratio period } 3_{1973} = \frac{(\text{Period } 3_{1973})}{\frac{1{,}104.8}{1{,}052.6}} = 1.05 \text{ (Column 4)}$$
$$(\text{Period } 3_{1973})$$

$$\text{Ratio period } 1_{1974} = \frac{981.7}{1{,}152.4} = .852$$

This means that actual sales in period three of 1973 exceed the average value for
a "typical quarter" of that year by approximately 5 percent, and actual sales of
981,700 units in period one of 1974 were only .852 of what was expected in an
average quarter. (The terms *average quarter* and *typical quarter* in this context
mean the expected volume of sales if they were spread evenly over all four
periods. Hence, the MA is said to smooth the data.)

The same procedure is used to develop a ratio (Column 4) for each time period
in Table 4-1. Note that ratios cannot be developed for the first few and the last
few periods because data are lost in computing moving averages. When monthly
or weekly data are involved, an even larger number of blank periods results.

Developing the Seasonal Index Factors

The next step is to determine how much each quarter deviates from an average
quarter over the entire set of data. The seasonal ratios for the same quarter are
combined, and an average of these ratios is developed (see Table 4-2, Part A).
One of the following three methods is generally used to compute such ratios:

(a) The ratios of the same quarter of each year are added together and divided by the
number of years, resulting in an average ratio for each quarter.

(b) A medial average is determined by dropping the highest and lowest ratios of each
quarter in the data series and computing an average value of the remaining
quarters. This is done to eliminate extreme values that might distort the average
ratio. It also eliminates some of the major irregularities (*I*).

Table 4-2
Computing the Seasonal Ratios for Past Sales of Acme Bottlers

		Quarter				Sums
		1	2	3	4	
A)	Ratios-to-moving averages					
	1973	—	—	1.050	1.072	
	1974	.852	1.023	1.043	1.071	
	1975	.880	1.047	1.026	1.025	
	1976	.887	1.041	1.054	1.002	
	1977	.909	1.002	1.044	1.052	
	1978	.873	1.040	1.044	1.051	
	1979	.881	1.020	1.029	1.066	
	1980	.878	1.021	—	—	

Source: Column 4, Table 4-1.

B) Array of ratios-to moving averages

		1	2	3	4
High Ratios		.909	1.047	1.054	1.072
		.887	1.041	1.050	1.071
		.881	1.040	1.044	1.066
Central Ratios (CR)		.880	1.023	1.044	1.052
		.878	1.021	1.043	1.051
		.873	1.020	1.029	1.025
Low Ratios		.852	1.002	1.026	1.002

C) Calculation of seasonal factors

		1	2	3	4	
1)	Sum of CR	4.399	5.145	5.210	5.265	
2)	$[\dfrac{\text{Sum of CR}}{\text{No. of CR(5)}}]$ = Avg. of CR	.8798	1.029	1.042	1.053=	4.0038
3)	Adjusted average seasonal factors	.8790	1.028	1.041	1.052	
4)	Rounded seasonal factors (Column 5, Table 4-2)	.88	1.03	1.04	1.05=	4.0000

$$\frac{4.0000}{4.0038} = .99905 \text{ Rounding Factor}$$

(c) Use only the middle one-third values. As in (b) above, this method attempts to eliminate extremes and retain the typical values. Because of this, both (b) and (c) require a fairly large number of periods.

In this example, the medial average (b) is used and an average of the remaining values is obtained (Parts B and C, Table 4-2):

(First quarter) $= .887 + .881 + .880 + .878 + .873 = 4.399$
(.852 and .909 were dropped)

$$\frac{4.399}{5} = .8798 \text{ (Part C, lines 1 and 2)}$$

The figure .8798 means that, due to seasonal factors, over the past eight years Acme's first quarter sales were approximately 12 percent $(1 - .8798)$ lower than the amount expected in an average quarter. Fourth quarter sales, on the other hand, were more than 5 percent higher (1.053) than the average quarter.

Adjusting the Seasonal Factor

Because some periods were dropped from the computations, the seasonal ratios for the four quarters do not sum to 4,000. (If months are used, the ratios should sum to 12.00.) Therefore, it is necessary to make an adjustment in the data to ensure that the ratios sum to 4.000, or an average of 1.000 per quarter. A rounding factor must be applied to each ratio to compensate for these variations. The rounding factor in our example (.99905) was determined as follows:

$$\text{Rounding Factor} = \frac{\text{Required Sum of Average Ratios}}{\text{Actual Sum of Average Ratios}}$$
(Line 2, Part C, Table 4-2)

$$\text{Rounding Factor First Quarter} = \frac{4.0000}{4.0038} = .99905$$

This figure (.99905) is then multiplied against the first quarter average of central ratios (.8798), resulting in the adjusted seasonal factor (.8790) for the first quarter. The average seasonal ratios of each of the other three quarters is adjusted in the same manner.

Utilizing the Seasonal Factors

These rounded, or constant, seasonal factors are applied to the actual sales data of each period to eliminate the seasonal impact (see Columns 5 and 6 of Table 4-1). Example:

(Column 1)
$$\frac{\text{Actual Sales}}{\text{(Seasonal Factor)}} = \text{Seasonally Adjusted Sales (Column 6)}$$
(Column 5)

For the first quarter of 1973, for example, the seasonally adjusted sales are 949,100 units.

$$\frac{835,200}{.88} = 949,090 \text{ units}$$

What does this new figure (949,090 units) mean? It means that based on annual sales of the past eight years, sales in the first quarter of 1973 would have been approximately 949,090 units if there had been no seasonal variation. Thus, Column 6, Table 4-1 provides seasonally adjusted or "deseasonalized" data.

Value of Deseasonalized Data

It is much easier to identify the true trend in data if that data is deseasonalized. If Acme's sales data were graphed in two forms—actual sales and seasonally adjusted sales—there would be much greater stability in the line depicting the deseasonalized data.

A second benefit derived from deseasonalizing data is that the analyst can better determine what is actually occurring in a given period. Are sales greater or less than expected?

For example, if actual unit sales in the first quarter of 1981 were 368,700, this could be projected to an annual sales forecast.

$$\frac{\text{Actual Sales for Period}}{\text{Seasonal Index for Period}} \times 4 \text{ (transforming quarterly data into annual data)}$$

$$\frac{368,700}{.88} \times 4 = 1,676,000 \text{ (projected annual sales)}$$

The seasonal impact has been accounted for, and sales are occurring at a level that suggests annual sales of almost 1,676,000 units. Thus, after the first period, the analyst knows whether sales are actually in line with projections.

Checking the Seasonal Patterns

It is important that seasonal ratios not have a consistent pattern (growth or decline). If a consistent pattern emerges, it indicates that an additional factor exists within the data that can distort the forecasts. Plotting the seasonal factors of a quarter will disclose whether such a pattern exists. The data plotted in Figure 4-1 showing the first quarter seasonals for each of seven years are from Column 4 of Table 4-1.

Although the plotted seasonals in Figure 4-1 are not completely random, there does not seem to be any consistent pattern or change occurring. Therefore, seasonals can be used in the forecast model. If some type of consistent pattern is found, some adjustments must be made in the seasonals.[1] Seasonal factors of each of the other three quarters of years 2 through 8 are plotted in the same way and examined for patterns.

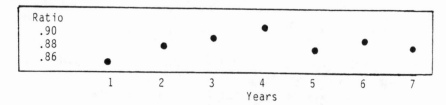

Figure 4-1
Seven-Year Plot of First-Quarter Seasonal Factor for Acme Bottlers

DETERMINING THE TREND

In a multiplicative decomposition model, the trend is the critical value since it is in discrete form (dollars or units), whereas the values of seasonals, cyclicals, and irregulars are ratios (proportions) of the trend. Thus, in developing trend values for each period, it is necessary to derive a real number rather than a ratio.

Using Moving Averages to Determine Trend Values

The centered moving average values developed in Table 4-1 (Column 3) are now used to derive the trend values for the decomposition model. They are used instead of the actual sales data because the moving average values neutralized the seasonal fluctuations of sales and thus give a more accurate picture of the real trend of past sales.

As covered in Chapter 2, a variety of techniques is available to determine a linear trend line for past sales. The moving average value for each period could be plotted on a graph and a trend line visually assigned. Or a semiaverage could be used to affix a trend line to the plotted data. The method most frequently used, however, is the least squares process.

A review of the plotted deseasonalized data in Table 4-1 indicates that a linear trend exists, so the least squares process will be used with "time" as the independent variable and the moving average values as the dependent variable.

Establishing the Trend Value

In Table 4-3, the least squares method provides the two values needed to determine the trend figure for each time period: the a value (intercept) and the b value (slope). The trend value for each period (Column 5, Table 4-3) is found by placing those values in the simple regression formula:

$$Y = a + b(X)$$ (X is the coded period, Column 2, Table 4-3)

Table 4-3
Using the Least Squares Method to Compute Sales Trend of Acme Bottlers

Year	Quarter	(1) X Coded Periods	(2) Y (Central Moving Average) (Table 4-1)	(3) XY	(4) x^2	(5) Trend Value
1973	1					
	2					
	3	-27	1052.6	-28420.2	729	885.8
	4	-25	1098.2	-27455.0	625	959.7
1974	1	-23	1152.4	-26505.2	529	1033.6
	2	-21	1208.9	-25386.9	441	1107.5
	3	-19	1266.3	-24059.7	361	1181.4
	4	-17	1321.8	-22470.6	289	1255.3
1975	1	-15	1366.8	-20502.0	225	1329.2
	2	-13	1394.2	-18124.6	169	1403.1
	3	-11	1421.7	-15638.7	121	1477.0
	4	- 9	1460.4	-13143.6	81	1550.9
1976	1	- 7	1513.0	-10591.0	49	1624.8
	2	- 5	1567.3	- 7836.5	25	1698.7
	3	- 3	1620.8	- 4862.4	9	1772.6
	4	- 1	1618.3	- 1678.3	1	1846.5
1977	1	1	1744.9	1744.9	1	1920.4
	2	3	1842.4	5527.2	9	1994.3
	3	5	1937.9	9689.5	25	2068.2
	4	7	2039.9	14279.3	49	2141.9
1978	1	9	2160.5	19444.5	81	2214.9
	2	11	2270.7	24977.7	121	2288.8
	3	13	2368.0	30784.0	169	2362.7
	4	15	2452.1	36781.5	225	2436.6
1979	1	17	2535.7	43106.9	289	2510.5
	2	19	2634.9	50063.1	361	2584.4
	3	21	2737.1	57479.1	441	2659.8
	4	23	2841.5	65354.5	529	2733.7
1980	1	25	2961.6	74040.0	625	2807.0
	2	27	3092.4	83494.8	729	2881.6
	3					
	4					

$$\Sigma Y = 52742.3 \quad \Sigma XY = 270092.1 \quad \Sigma x^2 = 7308$$

$$a = \frac{\Sigma Y}{n} \qquad b = \frac{\Sigma XY}{\Sigma x^2}$$

$$a = \frac{52742.3}{28} = 1883.7 \qquad b = \frac{270092.1}{7308} = 36.96$$

Trend Value (Column 5) = a + b(x)

Thus, the trend value of the third period of 1974 is:

$Y = 1,883.7 + 36.96(-19)$
$Y = 1,181.5$ units

And the trend value of the second period of 1980 is:

$Y = 1,883.7 + 36.96(27)$
$Y = 2,881.6$ units

For the projected trend value for the first period of 1981, our forecast is:

$Y = 1,883.7 + 36.96(33)$
$Y = 3,103.4$ units

DETERMINING THE CYCLICAL VALUES

The third component of the decomposition model to be determined is the cyclical impact. In the previous section dealing with the trend, it was established that the use of a quarterly moving average will eliminate the seasonal fluctuation and neutralize the irregularities (I). Therefore, what remains is the impact of the cycle and trend.

$$\text{Moving Average} = \text{Trend} \times \text{Cyclical}$$

When the moving average values are divided by the trend values, what remains is the cyclical value.

$$\frac{\text{Moving Average}}{\text{Trend}} = \text{Cyclical Value}$$

Table 4-4 contains the cyclical ratios in Acme soft drink sales for the eight previous years of sales data (Column 3).

Figure 4-2 plots the cyclical ratios of the eight years and indicates the direction of the cyclical activity over that period of time. Since there seems to be a fairly strong cyclical influence in Acme's sales, a cyclical ratio should be included in the decomposition model. In those decomposition models where the cyclical ratios are all very close to 1.00 they can be ignored since they have little or no impact on the actual forecast.

Estimating Future Cyclical Ratios

The future trend values and seasonal factors were both computed mathematically. The future cyclical ratios, however, must be estimated by the fore-

Table 4-4
Computing the Cyclical Ratios for Sales of Acme Bottlers

Year	Quarter	(1) Centered Moving Average (Table 4-1)	(2) Trend* (Table 4-3)	(3) Cyclical (1) ÷ (2)
1973	1	-	-	-
	2	-	-	-
	3	1052.6	885.8	1.19
	4	1098.2	959.7	1.14
1974	1	1152.4	1033.6	1.11
	2	1208.9	1107.5	1.09
	3	1266.3	1181.4	1.07
	4	1321.8	1255.3	1.05
1975	1	1366.8	1329.2	1.03
	2	1394.2	1403.1	.99
	3	1421.7	1477.0	.96
	4	1460.4	1550.9	.94
1976	1	1513.0	1624.8	.93
	2	1567.3	1698.7	.92
	3	1630.8	1772.6	.92
	4	1678.3	1846.5	.91
1977	1	1744.9	1920.4	.91
	2	1842.4	1994.3	.92
	3	1937.9	2068.2	.94
	4	2039.9	2141.9	.95
1978	1	2160.5	2214.9	.98
	2	2270.7	2288.8	.99
	3	2368.0	2362.7	1.00
	4	2452.1	2436.6	1.01
1979	1	2535.7	2510.5	1.01
	2	2634.9	2584.4	1.02
	3	2737.1	2659.8	1.03
	4	2841.5	2733.7	1.04
1980	1	2961.6	2807.6	1.05
	2	3092.4	2881.6	1.07
	3	-	-	-
	4	-	-	-

*Trend values for each period are determined from the regression model
$Y = 1883.7 + 36.96(X)$. The values may differ slightly due to rounding.

caster based on their pattern in the previous time periods. Will the cyclical ratios continue to climb in 1981? Or will they level off and start downward? (See Figure 4-2.)

Although almost eight years of data were used, less than one total cycle has occurred in Acme sales. Thus, a clear picture of a typical cycle in terms of length and magnitude has not yet been established. In our forecast, it is assumed that the cyclical pattern will continue to move toward a peak of 1.17 by the end of 1982.

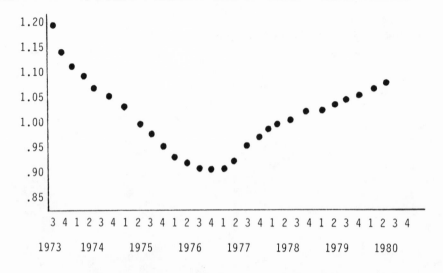

Figure 4-2
Plotting the Cyclical Ratios for Acme Sales

Therefore, the estimated cyclical ratio for the first quarter of 1981 is 1.12. This value falls on a line drawn between the cyclical value for period two, 1980 (1.07) and the estimated cyclical value for period four of 1982 (1.17).

Handling Missing Data

A drawback of using moving averages is that there will always be data missing at both the beginning and ending time periods. For example, in Table 4-4, the centered moving average values end at period 2 in 1980, even though we have actual sales data through period 4. Because of this, the calculated values for the cycle must also end at period two, 1980. This means that if the forecaster wants to improve estimates of the cycle in the forecast period, he or she must first estimate cyclical values (Column 3) for periods three and four of 1980.

One method that would provide the two missing values in Column 1 would be to substitute deseasonalized sales values found in Column 6, Table 4-1. Table 4-5 contains data from just the bottom portion of Table 4-4 and illustrates one method for estimating the two missing cyclical values.

Step One—Obtain deseasonalized values for periods three and four of 1980 from Table 4-1, Column 6 (3,181.3 and 3,411.9).

Step Two—Find a moving average of the three CMA values for periods two, three, and four of 1980.

$$\frac{3,092.4 + 3,181.3 + 3,411.9}{3} = 3,228.5$$

Use that moving average (3,228.5) as the new value for period three, 1980.

Step Three—Find the difference between the CMA values for periods one and two of 1980.

$$3{,}092.4 - 2{,}961.6 = 130.8$$

Then find the difference between the CMA values for period two and the new value for period three.

$$3{,}228.5 - 3{,}092.4 = 136.1$$

Find the average difference between these three periods.

$$130.8 + 136.1 = \frac{226.9}{2} = 133.5$$

Step Four—Add this average difference to the value of period three, 1980 to derive an estimated CMA value for period 4.

$$3{,}228.5 + 133.5 = 3{,}362.0$$

Step Five—Determine the two missing trend values (periods three and four of 1980) by using the least squares model.

$Y = a + b(X)$
Therefore, trend value for period three, $1980 = 1{,}883.7 + 36.96(29)$
$$= 2{,}955.5$$
Therefore, trend value for period four, $1980 = 1{,}883.7 + 36.96(31)$
$$= 3{,}029.5$$

Step Six—Divide the CMA value for each period by the trend value to determine the missing values for the cycle.

Period three, $1980 = 3{,}228.5 \div 2{,}995.5 = 1.08$
Period four, $1980 = 3{,}362.0 \div 3{,}029.5 = 1.11$

These two new cyclical values make the task of estimating C for 1981 much easier. Table 4-5 illustrates just one way missing values can be assigned. There are numerous other methods that might be used to make such assignments.

DETERMINING THE IRREGULAR (I) VALUE

In our example involving the Acme soft drink firm, it is assumed that when the seasonal factors were determined, we had also partially neutralized the impact of irregular events by eliminating the high and low seasonal ratios for each quarter over the eight-year period.

Table 4-5
Assigning Missing Values Caused by Moving Averages

```
Step (1)                 Centered
                         Moving Average

      1980-1             2961.6
        -2               3092.4
        -3                 ?            Use values from Column 6, Table 4-1,
        -4                 ?            Deseasonalized Sales

Step (2)                                        Step (3)
                                     CMA        Difference
      1980-1             2961.6      2961.6 ⎱──── 130.8
        -2               3092.4 ⎫    3092.4 ⎰
        -3               3181.3 ⎬──── 3228.5 ⎰──── 136.1
        -4               3411.9 ⎭
                                              226.9
                                              ───── = 133.5
                                                2

                                     Step (4)

                                     Add this difference to
                                     3228.5 to derive value
                                     for period 4

                                                    3228.5
                                                     133.5
                                                    ──────
                                                    3362.0
Step (4)                             Step (5)       Step (6)
                CMA                  Trend          Cycle
                                                    (1) ÷ (2)

      1980-1    2961.6               2807.6         1.05
        -2      3092.4               2881.6         1.07
        -3      3228.5               2955.5         1.08
        -4      3362.0               3029.5         1.11
```

Not all forecasters agree that such a procedure successfully accounts for the irregular factor. They believe the irregular component remains after seasonals are eliminated and thus must be accounted for separately and given a specific ratio for each time period. Descriptions of procedures for determining the I values are found in texts that provide more extensive coverage of decomposition.[2]

DEVELOPING THE FORECAST

Values for all of the components of the decomposition model have now been developed, and a forecast can be made for some future period. We will make a sales forecast for the first and third periods of 1981.

Forecast for First Period, 1981

$$Y = T \cdot S \cdot C \cdot I$$
$$T = a + b(X)$$
$$= 1,883.7 + 36.96(33)$$

$T = 3,103.38$
$SI = .88$ (first quarter seasonal rates)
$C = 1.12$ (expected cyclical rates in first quarter, 1981)
Therefore, $Y = 3,103,380 \ (.88)(1.12)$
$Y = 3,058,691$ units

Forecast for Third Period, 1981

$T = a + b(X)$
$T = 1,883.7 + 36.96(37)$
$T = 3,251,220$ units
$SI = 1.04$
$C = 1.15$
Therefore $Y = 3,251,220(1.04)(1.15)$
$Y = 3,888,459$ units

OVERVIEW OF DECOMPOSITION MODEL

The decomposition approach has wide acceptance among business firms because it is reasonably simple to understand and, with the availability of computer software packages, it is also fairly simple to administer. Probably its greatest drawback is that it does not lend itself to statistical analysis, that is, confidence limits and tests of significance cannot be applied to the forecasts.

It also suffers from the shortcoming that the only variable used is past data about the variable being forecasted. Thus, other useful explanatory factors are not incorporated into the least squares model.

Finally, if a computer is not available, this procedure requires a large number of calculations, especially if monthly data are involved.

In the next chapter, brief descriptions of some improved (but more complicated) versions of decomposition models are presented.

NOTES

1. Methods for compensating for these patterns are found in: Chow, Y., *Statistical Analysis,* 2d ed. (New York: Holt, Rinehart and Winston, 1975), pp. 722–723.
2. Two texts that deal more extensively with methods of determining irregular values are: Sartorious, Lester, and Mohn, N. Carroll, *Sales Forecasting Models: A Diagnostic Approach* (Atlanta: College of Business, Georgia State University, 1976); and Bowerman, Bruce L., and O'Connell, Richard T., *Forecasting and Time Series* (Belmont, Calif.: Duxburg Press, 1979).

QUESTIONS AND EXERCISES

1. Assume January has a seasonal index of .87. What does that mean in terms of the firm's total sales situation?

2. What values would you expect as the quarterly seasonal indices for a paint company? For a toy company? For a liquor store?

3. Why can we assume the irregular (I) values have been neutralized in the decomposition process?

4. Take the following set of quarterly data and

    (a) Graph the data.

    (b) Develop seasonal indices.

    (c) Develop a trend line.

    (d) Develop a cyclical index (graph it).

    (e) Forecast sales for periods 16, 17, and 18.

Period	Sales
1	14
2	22
3	33
4	50
5	35
6	47
7	52
8	61
9	59
10	48
11	51
12	60
13	65
14	58
15	58

5. Take the following set of monthly data and develop a forecast for June 1982 and August 1982.

Month	1978	1979	1980	1981	1982
January		1,295	1,482	1,948	1,901
February		1,231	1,401	1,785	1,932
March		1,342	1,641	1,839	2,007
April		1,382	1,761	1,976	2,115
May		1,287	1,697	1,890	2,092
June	987	1,402	1,772	2,153	
July	963	1,365	1,752	2,154	
August	1,001	1,441	1,822	1,891	

Month	1978	1979	1980	1981	1982
September	1,056	1,302	1,785	1,820	
October	1,002	1,271	1,582	1,692	
November	1,217	1,440	1,685	1,740	
December	1,156	1,468	1,706	1,830	

5

Additional Time Series Models

INTRODUCTION

The basic premise of any time series model is that the pattern of a product's past sales (or any other variable) is a good indicator of its future pattern and, thus, can be used as the basis of a forecast. However, each time series model differs in the way it uses past data. Moving average models assign equal weight to each period of data used in the equation. Exponential smoothing models, on the other hand, are based on the premise that the values of a variable in more recent periods have a greater impact on that variable's future value and, thus, its values of more recent periods should receive greater weight.

The moving average and exponential smoothing models described in Chapter 3 had two basic advantages: they are easy to understand and they can be computed manually. Their simplicity is obtained at a price, however, and that price is their inability to determine the ideal weights to assign to each period of data.

In this chapter, four higher-level time series models are described: adaptive filtering, Winter's method, Census II, and Box-Jenkins. Although they are merely expanded versions of exponential smoothing, each has a unique way of assigning weights to different periods of data. Because of the large number of computations involved, a computer is needed when using these models.

ADAPTIVE FILTERING

Just as exponential smoothing overcomes the major weakness of moving average models (that is, assigning equal weight to each period of data), adaptive filtering is an improvement over exponential smoothing models. In exponential smoothing, more weight is assigned to the most recent data. However, this weight is chosen in a fairly arbitrary manner and only two weights (α and $1-\alpha$) are involved in each equation.

In adaptive filtering, more weight is also assigned to more recent data, but a formalized process is used to determine the value of each weight. The selection process involves a series of iterations in which the weights are continually revised until the combination of weights that finally emerges provides the most accurate forecast equation (in terms of minimum MSE). The basic formula for adaptive filtering is:

$$Y_{t+1} = W_1 X_t + W_2 X_{t-1} + \ldots W_n X_{t-n+1} \tag{5-1}$$

The above model indicates that the forecast (Y_{t+1}) is derived by assigning weights to certain periods of past data. This means the forecaster must first determine the number of weights to be calculated with the equation. Then values for each of these weights must be derived.

The following formulae are used to derive the individual weights (W values) used in the basic adaptive filtering Equation 5-1.

$$W'_1 = W_1 + 2 Ke X_t \tag{5-2}$$

$$W'_2 = W_2 + 2 Ke X_{t-1} \tag{5-3}$$

$$W'_3 = W_3 + 2 Ke X_{t-2} \tag{5-4}$$

$$W'_i = W_i + 2 Ke X_{t-n+1} \tag{5-5}$$

Components of the Equations

Four statistics are needed to determine the eventual weights $(W_1 \ldots W_n)$ in Equation 5-1.

1. A series of past values of the variable for which a forecast is required $(X_t \ldots X_{t-n})$. In Table 5-1, this would be the unit sales for periods one through eight.
2. The initial weights $(W_1 \ldots W_n)$.
3. The difference between the actual value of the variable being forecasted and the initial forecast value, denoted e.
4. The learning constant, denoted K.

A description is now provided on how to determine the values for these four statistics, and then how to use these values.

Initial Weights

Since adaptive filtering is an iterative process, an initial set of weights must be assigned to start the process. These weights are assigned in one of two ways: (1) arbitrarily by the forecaster based on his or her knowledge and experience or (2) statistically by dividing one by the number of weights used in Equation 5-1. Thus, if four weights are used, each will be assigned an initial value of .25 ($\frac{1}{4}$).

The number of weights used in Equation 5-1 is based on the nature and availability of actual historical data. If the data are affected by seasonality, either 4 or 12 weights are needed depending on whether quarterly or monthly data better depict the seasonality. The minimum number of weights that can be used is two.

The initial weights are assigned to the first 2, 4, or 12 past values of the data series in the following manner: the first weight (W_1) is assigned to the most recent period (t) in the data set being used; the second weight (W_2) to the second most recent period $(t-1)$, the third weight (W_3) to the third most recent period $(t-2)$, and so on. The sum of these initial weights cannot exceed one.

The Forecast Error (e)

The initial weights $(W_1 \ldots W_n)$ and their related past values are used in Equation 5-1 to produce a forecast of the period immediately following the most recent period of the data set being used $(t+1)$. Then this forecast value is subtracted from the actual value of the same period, and this difference is the error term e.

The Learning Constant (K)

The learning constant helps determine the number of iterations needed to find the best weights and also affects the size of the adjustment in the weights between iterations. As its name implies, this value remains constant throughout the entire process.

The K value should be greater than zero and less than one. The smaller the K value, the more iterations needed to identify the weights that will minimize the MSE for this equation. A large K value minimizes the number of iterations used in the search for the best weights but it also means each adjustment in the weights may be too large and the optimal weights might never be found. If the set of data have a great deal of variation, a smaller K value should definitely be used.

The forecaster can either arbitrarily assign a value to K or the following statistical method could be used. The K value is tied to both the actual data in the historical series and the number of weights used in Equation 5-1. The value is obtained by dividing the value 1 by the sum of the squares of the 2, 4, or 12 (value of n in the equation) highest values in the series. To illustrate this procedure, a K value will be assigned to the data series in Table 5-1. Since only two weights will be used $(n=2)$ to keep the example simple, and the two highest values in the data series are 6.2 and 5.8, the resulting K value would be:

$$K = \frac{1}{(6.2)^2 + (5.8)^2} = \frac{1}{72.08} = 0.14$$

Now that the key components of the adaptive filtering equation have been explained, the model will now be used to derive a forecast.

Table 5-1
Sales of Acme Trailers (in thousands of units)

Period	Unit Sales
1	4.2
2	4.4
3	4.8
4	5.1
5	5.0
6	5.5
7	5.8
8	6.2

Procedures for Deriving Final Weights

There are seven steps involved in deriving the weights that will finally be used in Equation 5-1 to make a forecast. Data from Table 5-1 will be used in this example.

Step One—Assign initial weights. Since only two weights will be used in this example, the initial weights are determined by dividing 1 by 2 ($1/n$) producing a weight of .5 for each period.

Step Two—Prepare forecast using initial weights. Transform Equation 5-1 to accommodate the two weights we will be using. Since two weights are involved, the first forecast will be for period 3 ($t+1$). Thus, W_1 refers to the most recent period (period two), and X_t is the actual sales for that period.

$$Y_{t+1} = W_1 X_t + W_2 X_{t-1}$$
$$Y_3 = [.5(4.4)] + [.5(4.2)] = 4.3$$

Step Three—Compute forecast error. Actual sales of period three minus the sales forecasted for that period:

$$4.8 - 4.3 = .5$$

Step Four—Determine K value. A value of .014 is assigned based on the statistical method described earlier.

Step Five—Adjust weights. Since only two weights are used with the Acme Trailer data (Table 5-1), only two equations (5-2 and 5-3) will be needed. Sales for period t (4.4) and period $t-1$ (4.2) will also be used:

$$W'_1 = W_1 + 2 Ke X_t \tag{5-2}$$
$$W'_1 = .5 + (2)(.014)(.5)(4.4) = .562$$

$$W'_2 = W_2 + 2\,Ke\,X_{t-1} \qquad\qquad\qquad\qquad (5\text{-}3)$$
$$W'_2 = .5 + (2)(.014)(.5)(4.2) = .559$$

Step Six—Normalize the weights. The two weights derived in Step five (.562 for period two and .559 for period one) are normalized by summing them and dividing each by that sum. Normalizing these weights reduces the number of iterations eventually needed to determine the final weights. The symbol W'' will be used to represent normalized weights.

.562 + .559 + 1.12

$$W''_1 = \frac{.562}{1.12} = .502$$

$$W''_2 = \frac{.559}{1.12} = .499$$

Step Seven—Use normalized weights to prepare forecast for next period. The two normalized weights are now used as the initial weights for the forecast for the next period (period four) and the procedures are repeated to derive new weights.

$$Y_4 = W''_1 X_3 + W''_2 X_2$$
$$Y_4 = .502(4.8) + .499(4.4)$$
$$Y_4 = 4.6$$

This forecast for period four (4.6) is compared to actual sales for that period (5.1), and their difference becomes the new error term.

$$Y_4 - X_4 = e$$
$$5.1 - 4.6 = .5$$

These results are now incorporated into Equations 5-2 and 5-3 to find two new weights.

$$W'_1 = W_1 + 2\,Ke\,X_t \qquad\qquad\qquad\qquad (5\text{-}2)$$
$$W'_1 = .502 + (2)(.014)(.5)(4.8)$$
$$W'_1 = .569$$

$$W'_2 = W_2 + 2Ke\,X_{t-1} \qquad\qquad\qquad\qquad (5\text{-}3)$$
$$W'_2 = .499 + (2)(.014)(.5)(4.4)$$
$$W'_2 = .561$$

These new unadjusted weights are then normalized.

.569 + .561 + 1.13

$$W''_1 = \frac{.569}{1.13} = .503$$

$$W''_1 = \frac{.561}{1.13} = .497$$

These new normalized weights are then used in Equation 5-1 to forecast sales for period five. This process is repeated until a forecast is developed for period eight. This completes one iteration, or one trip through the set of data. The two normalized weights emerging at the end of the first iteration are then used to begin the second iteration. In other words, they become the new weights for periods one and two in Equation 5-1 to make a forecast for period three.

The total number of iterations depends on how fast the error term is lowered to zero, or a minimum MSE value is reached. The MSE value for each new iteration is compared to the MSE of the previous iteration and, when only insignificant improvements occur, the iterations end. This could require as many as 30 to 40 iterations, which is the reason a computer is needed.

The final weights are then used in Equation 5-1 to make an actual forecast for period nine. Remember all the previous computations were performed to derive the best set of weights for our forecast. In our example, the weights that emerged after the thirtieth iteration were $W_1 = .881$ and $W_2 = .198$. These weights are then used in Equation 5-1 to make a forecast for period nine.

$$Y_9 = W_1 X_8 + W_2 X_7$$
$$Y_9 = .881(6.2) + .198(5.8)$$
$$Y_9 = 6.61$$

Application to Monthly Data

The previous example using the sales data in Table 5-1 was fairly low level since it only involved two weights and eight data points. The typical situation for adaptive filtering involves monthly and quarterly data, which means a much larger number of weights and data points.

Table 5-2 contains five years of monthly sales data (60 periods) for the Big Burp Beer Company. Adaptive filtering was used to derive weights for each month. Thus, Equation 5-1 will include 12 periods of data and 12 weights.

$$Y_{t+1} = W_1 X_{t-1} + W_2 X_{t-2} + \ldots W_{12} X_{t-12} \qquad (5-1)$$

The computer printout showing the MSE for each iteration is contained in Table 5-3, along with the resulting weights to be used in the forecast equation to make a forecast for period 61. As shown in Table 5-3, only minimal reduction in

Table 5-2
Monthly Sales for the Big Burp Beer Co., 1979–1983 (in thousands of barrels)

	1978	1980	1981	1982	1983
January	12.44	11.98	12.87	13.83	14.64
February	11.89	11.48	12.71	13.57	14.72
March	11.89	16.20	15.86	16.89	16.56
April	13.69	16.03	15.62	16.34	16.36
May	15.18	16.79	16.57	16.97	17.97
June	15.76	16.90	16.88	16.77	17.93
July	16.54	15.92	16.74	16.94	18.72
August	16.10	15.31	17.61	16.76	17.02
September	14.31	13.26	14.63	14.70	16.29
October	13.42	12.61	14.01	15.28	14.95
November	11.29	12.02	12.71	13.14	13.02
December	11.19	12.01	12.87	12.18	13.32

Table 5-3
Filtering Weights for the Big Burp Beer Co. (learning performance; learning constant = .075)

Iteration	MSE	MPE	MAPE	% Error Reduction
2	.80	-.31%	4.52%	1.1250
3	.80	-.31%	4.52%	.0020
4	.80	-.31%	4.52%	.0018
5	.80	-.31%	4.52%	.0017
6	.80	-.30%	4.52%	.0016
7	.80	-.30%	4.52%	.0015
8	.79	-.30%	4.51%	.0015
9	.79	-.30%	4.51%	.0014
10	.79	-.30%	4.51%	.0013
11	.79	-.30%	4.51%	.0013
12	.79	-.30%	4.51%	.0013
13	.79	-.30%	4.51%	.0012

Optimal Weights	Weight		Forecasts of 1984	
1	.176		January	13.59
2	.033		February	15.11
3	.096		March	16.55
4	.001		April	17.63
5	-.006		May	18.78
6	.304		June	18.42
7	-.218		July	18.17
8	1.31		August	16.82
9	-.247		September	15.72
10 $(X_{t-2})(W_3)$	-.187		October	14.81
11 $(X_{t-1})(W_2)$	.253		November	13.91
12 $(X_t)(W_1)$	.673		December	14.21

the error (percent error reduction) column occurred after the fourth iteration (.0018 reduced to .0017). The resulting optimal weights were obtained after 13 iterations. These weights are then incorporated into the equation and used to develop forecasts for the 12 months of 1984.

Review of Steps in Adaptive Filtering

(1) Determine the number of weights (n) to be used in Equation 5-1 and their initial values.

(2) Prepare forecast of period $t+1$.

(3) Determine the forecast error (e) (actual value for period $t+1$ and the forecast for that period).

(4) Determine the value of the learning constant (K).

(5) Adjust weights using Equations 5-2, 5-3, and so forth.

(6) Normalize the weights resulting from Step five.

(7) Use normalized weights to prepare forecast for next period.

(8) Repeat this process until forecasts have been made for all periods in the data series. (This completes one iteration.)

(9) Use the weights derived from each iteration in Equation 5-1 to begin a new iteration.

(10) Repeat iteration until only minimal changes occur in the weights (MSE minimized), then use these optimal weights to make actual forecasts for future periods.

Key Points Pertaining to Adaptive Filtering

• The smaller the K value, the more iterations needed to find the best set of weights. A larger K value results in fewer iterations but the adjustments may be too large and the best set of weights might not be discovered.

• The number of weights used in the equation depends on the format of previous data and the seasonality of that data. (Obviously, seasonality will not exist if only annual data is available.)

• The large number of calculations involved in adaptive filtering make it necessary to use a computer program.

• Although the model makes allowances for random variations in past data, adaptive filtering is intended primarily for forecast situations where past data follow a fairly horizontal pattern.

WINTER'S METHOD

The basic exponential smoothing model enables the forecaster to assign greater weight (the alpha value) to more recent data, allowing the model to compensate for recent changes. But even with the use of weights, basic exponential smoothing models cannot effectively account for seasonal variations.

The Winter's method is a sophisticated exponential smoothing model that allows both seasonal and trend influences to be incorporated into the forecast. The unique aspect of the Winter's method is that it enables the forecast equation to be updated continually as new information becomes available.

The Equation

In the chapter dealing with the decomposition model it is stated that the forecaster can do a better job of forecasting if historical data can be separated into its components. Since the Winter's method enables the forecaster to incorporate both trend and seasonality, it is usually a more effective forecasting technique than either exponential smoothing or moving averages for those variables that are affected significantly by seasonality and trend. The adaptive filtering model can also handle seasonality, but it has problems with data that have a strong trend.

Since the Winter's model deals with both trend and seasonality, its equation combines the formula for a straight line $y = a + b(X)$ with a seasonal ratio:

$$Y_{t+n} = a_t + b_t(X) \, (S_{t-L+n}) \tag{5-4}$$

Understanding the Model

The key thing to understand about the Winter's method is that it applies the principles of exponential smoothing to update the intercept (a value), the slope (b value), and the seasonal ratio (S value). Thus, after each new period, all three values may change based on the actual value of the variable in the most recent period.

Since new values of a, b, and S are developed for each ensuing time period, an equation is needed for each value:

$$a_t = \alpha\left(\frac{X_t}{S_{t-L}}\right) + (1 - \alpha)(a_{t-1} + b_{t-1}) \tag{5-5}$$

$$b_t = \beta(a_t - a_{t-1}) + 1 - \beta(b_{t-1}) \tag{5-6}$$

$$S_t = \sigma\left(\frac{X_t}{a_t}\right) + 1 - \sigma(S_{t-L}) \tag{5-7}$$

At first glance, the three equations may seem complicated, but once the basic concepts of the model are understood, the Winter's method becomes fairly easy to use. Each of the above equations has a different symbol to represent a smoothing factor (α, β, σ). These different symbols are used because the forecaster may wish to assign a different weight to each equation, for example, $\alpha = .2$, $\beta = .4$, $\sigma = .3$. The weight assigned to each of the three components can be determined by experimenting to see which combination of weights results in the most accu-

Table 5-4
Application of the Winter's Method to Quarterly Sales of Product M (in thousands of units)

	(1) Period X	(2) Unit Sales S	(3) Trend Line Value	(4) Seasonal (2)÷(3)	(5) S
1978	1	91	99.4	.915	.99
	2	102	103.8	.983	1.05
	3	125	108.3	1.154	1.17
	4	96	112.7	.852	.89
1979	5	118	117.1	1.008	.99
	6	126	121.5	1.037	1.05
	7	146	125.9	1.160	1.17
	8	118	130.4	.905	.89
1980	9	138	134.8	1.024	.99
	10	146	139.2	1.049	1.05
	11	170	143.6	1.184	1.17
	12	139	148.0	.939	.89
1981	13	157	152.5	1.029	.99
	14	177	156.9	1.128	1.05
	15	193	161.4	1.196	1.17
	16	143	165.8	.862	.89
1982	17	157			

rate forecast. The same weight can be assigned to each equation $\alpha = \beta = \sigma = .2$; the only requirement is that each weight have a value greater than 0 and less than 1. The L symbol in equations 5-5 and 5-7 represent the length of seasons (for example, number of months or quarters in a year).

Table 5-4 contains four years of quarterly sales data for product M. A quick perusal of Column 1 indicates an upward trend in the data as well as some seasonal variations. Thus, the Winter's method would be a logical technique to apply to the data.

Steps in Using the Winter's Method

Step One—Identify the trend of previous sales (that is, a and b values).

When the sales data in Table 5-4 is plotted, it indicates that both trend and seasonality exist in the data. A trend line can be developed using either a freehand estimate, the semiaverage method, or least squares analysis. The last mentioned method will provide the best-fitting line but, since this author emphasized the simplicity of the Winter's method, the simplest way of determining the trend is also used in this sample: semiaverage method (Chapter 2).

The two mean values of the sales data in Column 2 are 115.3 and 157.9. When a line is drawn connecting these two points, it intercepts the Y axis at 95, and its value at the last period (period four, 1981) is 166.

The a value, or intercept, for this trend line is 95. The b value, or slope, is determined by subtracting the lowest value on the trend line from the highest value, and dividing this difference by the number of intervening time periods.

$$\frac{166 - 95}{16} = 4.44$$

Thus, the b value, or rate of change in the trend is 4.44. These a and b values are used in the equation ($Y = a + b(X)$) to derive a trend value for each time period (Column 3, Table 5-4).

$$Y_1 = a + b_1(X_1) = 95 + 4.4(1) = 99.4$$

Step Two—Derive seasonal ratios of each time period.

Column 4 of Table 5-4 contains the seasonal values of each time period. Just as in decomposition, the seasonals for each similar time period (that is, all first quarters, all second quarters, and so forth) are summed and a mean value of each quarter is derived (Column 5). Because there are only four years of data in our example, the medial seasonal average is not used.

The three bits of information needed to make a forecast for each period are now available: the intercept, the slope, and the seasonal ratio. Thus, for period 19, the third quarter of 1982, the forecast is:

$$Y_{19} = a + b(X_{19}) (S_{19})$$
$$Y_{19} = 95 + 4.44(19) (1.17)$$
$$Y_{19} \; 209.9$$

A criticism of the above forecast value derived for period Y_{19} is that it is based on what took place over the previous 17 periods, that is, an "averaging" approach is used rather than a scheme that gives more weight to sales of recent periods. The Winter's method allows the user to update the forecast so it gives proper weight to the recent changes in actual sales.

The computations performed thus far are merely preliminary steps of the Winter's method. The Winter's model now takes these three values and updates them by applying the concepts of exponential smoothing. This is the attribute of this model the reader should understand: the Winter's method enables the values used in the forecast equation to be continually updated.

Step Three—Assigning new weights.

There are three components (a, b, and S) in the forecast Equation 5-4. Equations 5-5, 5-6, and 5-7 are used to update these values.

Formula for Updating Intercept

$$a_t = \alpha\left(\frac{X_t}{S_{t-L}}\right) + 1 - \alpha(a_{t-1} + b_{t-1}) \tag{5-5}$$

Formula for Updating Slope

$$b_t = \beta(a_t - a_{t-1}) + 1 - \beta(b_{t-1}) \tag{5-6}$$

Formula for Updating Seasonal Factor

$$S_t = \sigma\left(\frac{X_t}{a_t}\right) + 1 - \sigma(S_{t-L}) \tag{5-7}$$

As previously stated, α, β, and σ are symbols used to represent the weights assigned to each formula. Equal weights can be assigned to each formula ($\alpha = \beta = \sigma$). To avoid confusion, however, each component has a distinct symbol for its weight. A reminder: the weight assigned to each equation must have a value greater than 0 and less than 1 and the sum of the three weights should be 1 or less.

$$Y_{t+n} = a_t + b_t(x)(S_{t-L+n})$$

Step Four—Update the values.

The information in Table 5-4 is now used in the Winter's method to forecast sales for the third quarter of 1982. The starting point is to update the a value since it is needed to derive a new b value. In the initial computations a weight of .3 is used for each of the three equations ($\alpha = \beta = \sigma = .3$).

The most current sales data is for period 17, so that becomes the starting point. Remember, the symbol L represents the length of seasonality. So in this example $t-L$ means the seasonal value four periods prior to the present period ($17-4 =$ seasonal for period 13).

$$a_{17} = \alpha\left(\frac{X_t}{S_{t-L}}\right) + 1 - \alpha(a_{t-1} + b_{t-1})$$

$$a_{17} = .3\left(\frac{157}{.99}\right) + .7(165.8 + 4.4)$$

$$a_{17} = 166.7$$

Note that in the above equation it is assumed that the most up to date value for a was its value on the trend line—165.8. Since this is the first step in the updating, the most recent value for b then would still be 4.4. One way to interpret the new a value is that a new intercept is being derived for each new period and that, in this first computation, the new intercept is the most recent value on the trend line.

Updating b

$$b_{17} = \beta\ (a_t - a_{t-1}) + 1 - \beta(b_{t-1})$$
$$b_{17} = .3(166.7 - 165.8) + .7(4.4)$$
$$b_{17} = 3.35$$

Based on the most recent sales data and the assigned weight of .3, the new slope is 3.35.

Updating S

$$S_{17} = \sigma\left(\frac{X_t}{a_t}\right) + 1 - \sigma(S_{t-L})$$

$$S_{17} = .3\left(\frac{157}{166.7}\right) + .7(.99)$$

$$S_{17} = .973$$

This S value is not immediately useful since it applies to the first period of the year and sales are being forecast for the third period. Thus, this updated value (S_{17}) is stored and used for some future forecast involving a first quarter. The average S for all previous third periods is used as the S_{17} value.

The original a and b are discarded and their new values incorporated into the equation. The a and b values are updated each period and the S value is updated every L period. These updated values are now incorporated into the original equation (5-4) and a forecast for period 19 is developed.

$$Y_{19} = a_t + b(X)\ (S_{t-L+n})$$
$$Y_{19} = 166.7 + 3.37(2)\ (1.17)$$
$$Y_{19} = 202.9$$

Remember, the new present time is period 17, so X in the above computation has a value of 2, since period 19 is 2 periods past 17.

Overview

Although three formulae are involved, the Winter's method is really fairly simple to use. It is best suited to data that have both a trend and a seasonal pattern. It combines the strengths of exponential smoothing—giving more weight to recent data—with the advantage of models that can account for trend and seasonal factors.

AUTOCORRELATIONS AND DIFFERENCING

At this point it is necessary to interrupt the coverage of time series models to introduce two new topics: autocorrelation and differencing. Forecasters must understand these two topics before they can effectively use the Box-Jenkins process or some other forecasting models.

Autocorrelation

Autocorrelation coefficients identify the association that exists between a variable at one time period and that same variable at some other time period. Thus, autocorrelation is really the correlation of a variable with itself. The primary reason for deriving autocorrelation coefficients is to provide insights into the pattern that exists in a set of data.

Table 5-5 shows the initial steps of the autocorrelation process. The data are quarterly production figures of a shower head produced by Griffin Bros. Inc. Their actual output is in Column 1. In Column 2 these figures are all moved ahead one period, creating a new variable Y_1. Another new variable is created by moving the sales data in Column 2 ahead one period, resulting in variable Y_2 in Column 3. Depending on the amount of data available, a large number of such "new" variables could be created.

Table 5-5
Developing Variables for Autocorrelation Analysis for Quarterly Production of Shower Heads (in thousands of units)

Period		Actual Units Y	One Time Change Y_1	Two Time Changes Y_2	Three Time Changes Y_3
1981	1	131	107	192	125
	2	107	192	125	128
	3	192	125	128	115
	4	125	128	115	207
1982	1	128	115	207	131
	2	115	207	131	119
	3	207	131	119	122
	4	131	119	122	215
1983	1	119	122	215	127
	2	122	215	127	
	3	215	127		
	4	127			

It should be noted that as the number of these new variables increases, the total number of data points of the variable decreases. Variable Y_1 has 11 data points, whereas Y_3 has only 9. This influences the degrees of freedom and thus the correlation coefficients between the values of the variable at different time periods.

With the creation of these new values, an analysis can be performed to determine the amount of association that exists between variable Y, actual sales of shower heads, and Y_1, shower head sales changed one period.

The autocorrelation coefficient quantifies this association. This coefficient is similar to a typical correlation coefficient in that its value will vary between -1 and $+1$. The closer this coefficient is to $+1$ or -1, the stronger the relationship between the two values of the variable. For example, a coefficient of $+.73$ or $-.73$ between Y and Y_1 indicates that successive periods of data are closely related. If the value is plus they are moving in the same direction by somewhat comparable amounts. If the value is minus they are moving in opposite directions.

If no relationship exists between successive time periods, the autocorrelation coefficient for one time lag would be close to 0, indicating variations in the data are random and the pattern is stationary (horizontal). Many computer programs now provide autocorrelation coefficients for time series data. In addition to the numerical coefficients, the programs also depict these coefficients on a graph.

Figure 5-1 represents a computer printout for the shower head data. Because of the small number (12) of original data points, only six autocorrelations could be computed. Figure 5-1 indicates that there is little trend in the data, but the high autocorrelation coefficient for time lag 4 (.65) suggests there is seasonality in the data.

The vertical dotted lines in Figure 5-1 are control limits that enclosed an area approximately ± 2 standard deviations from zero (the 95 percent confidence interval). Values falling outside this area, such as the autocorrelation for time lag 4 in Figure 5-1(A) are significantly different from zero. This indicates an actual association exists between data from every fourth period (quarterly data).

If a trend had existed in the data, successive values would be strongly correlated with one another. The autocorrelation of two successive time lags or three time lags might also be high. Figure 5-2(A) shows a set of data that is nonstationary, that is, it has a trend. This trend is depicted in the decreasing value of the autocorrelation coefficients. Figure 5-2(B) shows a set of data that is stationary (trendless), since after one or two time lags the autocorrelation coefficients fluctuate around 0.

Thus, autocorrelation can be used to determine whether there is trend in a set of data and can also determine whether seasonality exists. However, if a strong trend exists in the data, that trend could hide or neutralize the seasonality. Therefore, it is usually necessary to remove the trend so that the seasonality (if it exists) can be identified. The way to remove the trend from a set of data is to perform differencing.

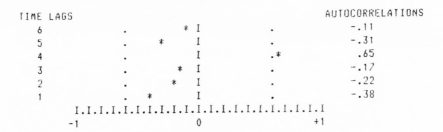

(A) Autocorrelation Coefficients for Shower Head Data.

```
TIME LAGS                                         AUTOCORRELATIONS
   6              .           *  I          .          -.11
   5              .        *     I          .          -.31
   4              .              I        . *           .65
   3              .        *     I          .          -.17
   2              .        *     I          .          -.22
   1              .    *         I          .          -.38
          I.I.I.I.I.I.I.I.I.I.I.I.I.I.I.I.I.I.I.I.I
          -1                     0                  +1
```

(B) Autocorrelation Coefficients - 1st Difference.

```
TIME LAGS                                         AUTOCORRELATIONS
   5              .     *        I          .          -.40
   4              .              I        . *           .66
   3              .        *     I          .          -.30
   2              .              I*         .           .03
   1              .  *           I          .          -.54
          I.I.I.I.I.I.I.I.I.I.I.I.I.I.I.I.I.I.I.I.I
          -1                     0                  +1
```

Figure 5-1
Autocorrelations and First Differences of Shower Head Sales

Differencing

The basic procedure for transforming non-stationary data (data with a trend or pattern) into stationary data is differencing. Rather than use either the sales data or time-lagged data, a new value is created. The differences between the original data at successive time periods are computed and these differences are substituted for the actual values.

Table 5-6 contains the results after differencing has been performed on the shower head data contained in Table 5-5. In this example, there is very little trend in the original data, so the impact of differencing is negligible. However, if the data had contained a major trend, such as in Figure 5-2(A), differencing would have eliminated much of that trend.

If the data are still non-stationary after a first differencing is performed, a second differencing might be needed. Once the trend has been removed through differencing, any seasonality existing in the data is easier to identify. The periods with high autocorrelation identify the length of the seasonality.

Figure 5-2 can also be used to illustrate the effects of differencing on data with a trend. Figure 5-2(A) contains a set of sales data with a very strong trend. Is there also some seasonality in that data? Because the trend is so strong, it is difficult to determine what degree of seasonality (if any) exists. Therefore, first

Table 5-6
First and Second Differences of Shower Head Data

Period		Y Actual Units	Y_t' First Difference $(Y_t - Y_{t-1})$	Y_t'' Second Difference $(Y_t' - Y'_{t-1})$
1981	1	131		
	2	107	-24	
	3	192	85	109
	4	125	-67	-152
1982	1	128	3	70
	2	115	-13	-16
	3	207	92	105
	4	131	-76	-168
1983	1	119	-12	64
	2	122	3	15
	3	215	93	90
	4	127	-88	-181

Example

$$Y_t' = Y_t - Y_{t-1} \qquad\qquad Y_t'' = Y_t' - Y'_{t-1}$$

$$Y_2' = 107 - 131 \qquad\qquad Y_3'' = 85 - (-24)$$

$$Y_2' = -24 \qquad\qquad Y_3'' = 109$$

differences are obtained for each period and autocorrelations are then performed on these new values. Figure 5-2(B) shows the pattern of these first differences. The trend is removed (that is, the data are stationary) and there does not appear to be any seasonality in the data.

Overview of Autocorrelation and Differencing

The reason autocorrelation coefficients are computed is to learn more about the patterns existing in a set of data. Autocorrelation shows whether and to what degree the value of a variable in one period is associated with the value of the same variable in other periods. If the autocorrelation coefficients decrease slowly toward 0, the data are non-stationary. These data can be made stationary through

(A)

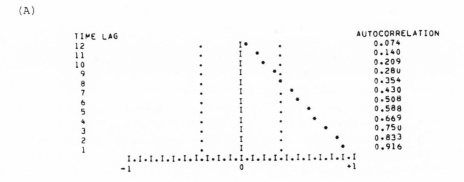

(B)

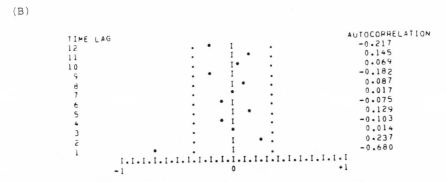

Figure 5-2
Examples of Stationary (A) and Non-Stationary (B) Data

differencing since it neutralizes or removes the trend and allows the seasonality to emerge.

Thus, autocorrelation and differencing, when used together, are effective methods of analyzing patterns in past data. They can be easily performed via most computer forecasting packages. Experienced forecasters use autocorrelation as the first step in the search for the most appropriate forecasting model since it identifies the pattern in the data, an important factor in model selection.

BOX-JENKINS METHOD

To be a successful forecasting tool, a time series model must be able to identify patterns existing in previous data and develop an equation that can integrate these patterns into a forecast. Decomposition models (Chapter 4) accomplish this by first isolating trend, seasonal, and cyclical patterns and then developing values for each to be used in the equation. Adaptive filtering and the Winter's method both use weights to make allowances for patterns in past data.

The technique considered by many to be the most effective way to identify past sales patterns and make allowances for them is the Box-Jenkins method. This is also one of the most costly and complex time series techniques. It requires a great deal of past sales data, which it puts through numerous iterations while searching for the right coefficients. Anyone using this technique must have access to a computer and also possess a fairly solid statistical background.

The Box-Jenkins method is most useful for those situations where forecasts are to be made and an unusual pattern exists in the past data. To analyze these unusual patterns effectively, at least 60 to 70 periods of past data are needed. This means this method is not really appropriate for annual data and works best with weekly or monthly data.

A major strength of the Box-Jenkins method is that it provides a statistical test for determining the adequacy of the fitted model along with confidence intervals for the resulting forecasts.

A Dilemma—How Much to Cover

Because of its complexity, the Box-Jenkins method is usually covered in forecasting texts in either of two ways. One group of authors, while acknowledging its importance, assign only brief coverage to it. At the other extreme are those authors who devote an entire chapter to Box-Jenkins; identifying all of the formulae, presenting the theories behind these formulae and even providing computer printouts for demonstration purposes.

The approach followed in this book falls between these two extremes. Since Box-Jenkins is such an effective forecasting tool, forecasters and decision makers should understand its basic approach. However, an in-depth understanding of all facets of Box-Jenkins is not needed to use the technique effectively. Therefore, its coverage in this text is intended to bring the reader to a level where he or she can use a Box-Jenkins computer package and understand the reports it generates.

Basic Stages of Box-Jenkins

The Box-Jenkins method (named after its two developers) is not a forecasting model per se. Rather, it is an approach or procedure used to select the forecasting model best suited to a variable based on the pattern of that variable's past behavior.

The basic activities of Box-Jenkins fall into three stages: identifying, estimating, and testing or applying. In the first stage, a tentative model format for the forecast is identified by analyzing the pattern of the variable's past behavior. In the second stage, the initial parameters of the model are selected. In the third stage, the forecasting accuracy of the model and its parameters are tested. If the model is judged to be inadequate, a new model format is chosen and all three stages are repeated. The activities involved in each of the three stages are now described.

Stage One—Identifying the Tentative Model

The Box-Jenkins process assumes that any pattern in time series data will fit one of three categories of models. Based on an analysis of a product's past sales, for example, one of these model categories is selected and becomes the basic format of the forecast model.

Categories of Models

The three general types of models are (1) autoregressive (AR), (2) moving average models (MA), and (3) a combination of both, autoregressive–moving average (ARMA). It is important to understand that each of these is a category of models with each category containing a variety of specific models.

Which of the three categories of models is best suited to the sales pattern of a product? The appropriate category is determined by obtaining autocorrelations and partial autocorrelations of the data.[1] The patterns depicted are then compared to the patterns of some theoretical distributions, each of which represents a specific model. Thus, the format best suited to the past sales of a product is the model with the theoretical pattern that most closely matches the past sales pattern of that product.

The above explanation is probably confusing to the reader, since theoretical patterns haven't been discussed as yet. The key thing to understand at this point is that a profile of a product's past sales is developed by means of autocorrelations and this profile of autocorrelation values is then compared to a series of theoretical profiles. Each theoretical profile is associated with a specific format of a forecast model. The theoretical profile that most closely matches a product's profile identifies the initial format of the forecast model.

Formats of Models

As stated earlier, there are three broad categories of models, one of which is best suited to the past sales pattern of a particular product. The term *model format* indicates that within each of the three model categories there is a series of models that differ according to the number of time periods or terms used. Thus, each model has its own format.

Autoregressive Models (AR)

The equation for an autoregressive model is:

$$Y_t = B_1 Y_{t-1} + B_2 Y_{t-2} + \ldots B_p Y_{t-p} + e_t$$

Y_t = Dependent variable
Y_{t-p} = Independent variable (lagged values of the dependent variable)
B_p = Regression coefficient
e_t = Effect of random events on the dependent variable not explained by the equation
p = Number of terms in the model

This model has a format similar to a multiple regression model except it does not have a constant (*a* value). The *B* values and the e_t value are determined by regression analysis. The independent variables are lagged values of the dependent variable. Thus, before this model format can be used, the number of terms (*p*) must be determined along with the specific *B* values.

Moving Average Models (MA)

The equation for a moving average model is:

$$Y_t = e_t - W_1 e_{t-1} - W_2 e_{t-2} - \ldots W_q e_{t-q}$$
Y_t = Dependent variable
$W_1 \ldots q$ = Weight assigned
e_t = Error (residual) of time period t
q = Number of terms

Although this category is called a moving average model, the name is misleading. The model's format (except for the minus signs) and the use of weights make it similar to exponential smoothing models.

Moving average models determine forecasts of Y_t using a linear combination of past errors, whereas autoregressive models base their forecasts on a linear function of a certain number of past values.

Autoregressive–Moving Average Models (ARMA)

As its name implies, this category of models is a combination of the autoregressive and moving average models.

$$Y_t = B_1 Y_{t-1} + B_2 Y_{t-2} + \ldots B_p Y_{t-p} + e_t - W_1 e_{t-1} - W_2 e_{t-2} \ldots W_q e_{t-q}$$

This format implies that the best fit for a product's past sales is achieved when sales of past periods are combined with the errors between actual and forecasted sales.

Choosing the Appropriate Category of Models

Each of the three categories of models (AR, MA, and ARMA) represents a series of models and one specific model in that series is best suited to the past data of a particular variable. Thus, the user must first determine which of the three categories is best suited to his or her set of data and then determine which specific model in that category is most appropriate.

As stated earlier, the primary factor determining the appropriate model format for a product is the pattern of that product's autocorrelations and partial autocorrelations. These patterns, when compared to a set of theoretical patterns, will also determine the number of terms to be included in the selected model format.

The selection of the specific model is accomplished in three stages:

(1)   The data series is made stationary.

(2)   Autocorrelation and partial autocorrelation coefficients are studied to determine the appropriate category.

(3)   The autocorrelation and partial autocorrelation coefficients are reviewed again to determine the number of terms to be included in the model (that is, the p and q terms).

Stationary Data Required

A basic premise of these time series models is that past data follow a horizontal pattern, that is, they are stationary. Thus, if a trend exists in past data, it must be removed before the Box-Jenkins process can be applied.

Table 5-7 contains the weekly sales (in cases) for 1983 of the Studly Dog Food Company. The autocorrelations in Figure 5-3(A) indicate a strong trend in Studly's sales. Thus, if the Box-Jenkins method is to be used to forecast sales for weeks 53, 54, and 55, the data must be transformed into stationary data by removing the trend.

Making Data Stationary

As stated in an earlier section of this chapter, the basic procedure for transforming non-stationary data into stationary data is differencing. Rather than using actual sales data, the values obtained through differencing are substituted for the sales data.

In Figure 5-3(B) the computer printout of the autocorrelations of the first difference indicates the trend in the sales of Studly Dog Food has been removed since the autocorrelation values are all close to zero. Therefore, the first difference values are used in step two.

Analysis of Patterns of Autocorrelations and Partial Autocorrelations

The stationary data are used by the computer program to provide autocorrelation and partial autocorrelation values. Autocorrelations identify the association between values of a time series at different time lags. Partial autocorrelations

Table 5-7
Weekly Sales of Studly Dog Food (in thousands of cases)

Week	Sales	Week	Sales	Week	Sales
1	11.23	19	17.81	37	23.62
2	10.14	20	17.84	38	23.14
3	10.42	21	16.94	39	23.35
4	11.55	22	18.42	40	23.51
5	11.30	23	18.63	41	25.02
6	12.01	24	17.32	42	25.12
7	12.41	25	19.22	43	24.53
8	12.70	26	18.56	44	24.82
9	12.40	27	19.22	45	26.36
10	13.42	28	19.36	46	26.48
11	13.80	29	20.51	47	26.31
12	14.31	30	21.36	48	27.03
13	14.25	31	20.42	49	27.22
14	15.11	32	21.07	50	27.32
15	15.07	33	21.92	51	28.22
16	16.52	34	22.36	52	28.25
17	15.74	35	22.27		
18	16.22	36	22.71		

depict the association between current values of a variable and earlier values of the same variable when the effects of all other time lags are held constant.

Figure 5-4 is a computer printout of two sets of data on Studly Dog Food sales. Figure 5-4(A) contains the pattern of the autocorrelation coefficients of the first differences and Figure 5-4(B) depicts the pattern of partial autocorrelation coefficients. These two patterns determine which of the three categories of models is most appropriate for this set of data.

Evaluating Patterns

The patterns of the data in Figure 5-4 can best be seen if lines were drawn connecting the data points. This profile depicts the pattern of the autocorrelation coefficients. Once a person becomes experienced in using this process, he or she can look at a computer printout of autocorrelations and quickly identify the specific pattern in the data.

There are some basic rules that determine which category of models best fits the pattern shown in a computer printout. For example, if the autocorrelations trail off exponentially to zero, an autoregressive model is indicated. If the partial autocorrelations trail off to 0, a moving average model is indicated. If both values trail off to 0, a mixed ARMA model is probably needed.

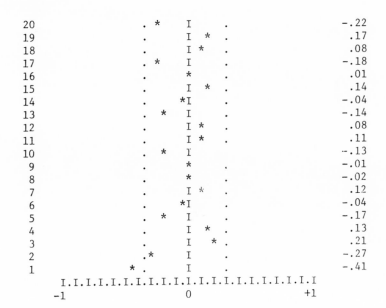

Time Lags		Autocorrelations

(A) Autocorrelations of Basic Data.

```
 20              .      *I      .              -.04
 19              .       *      .               .00
 18              .      I*      .               .04
 17              .      I *     .               .08
 16              .      I  *    .               .13
 15              .      I   * . .               .18
 14              .      I   * . .               .22
 13              .      I    *.                 .27
 12              .      I     *                 .32
 11              .      I    . *                .38
 10              .      I    . *                .43
  9              .      I    . *                .48
  8              .      I    .  *               .53
  7              .      I    .   *              .59
  6              .      I    .    *             .65
  5              .      I    .     *            .70
  4              .      I    .      *           .77
  3              .      I    .       *          .82
  2              .      I    .        *         .88
  1              .      I    .         *        .94
      I.I.I.I.I.I.I.I.I.I.I.I.I.I.I.I.I.I.I.I
      -1                 0                +1
```

(b) First Difference.

```
 20           .  *    I        .              -.22
 19           .       I  *     .               .17
 18           .       I *      .               .08
 17           .  *    I        .              -.18
 16           .       *        .               .01
 15           .       I  *     .               .14
 14           .      *I        .              -.04
 13           .  *    I        .              -.14
 12           .       I *      .               .08
 11           .       I *      .               .11
 10           .  *    I        .              -.13
  9           .       *        .              -.01
  8           .       *        .              -.02
  7           .       I *      .               .12
  6           .      *I        .              -.04
  5           .  *    I        .              -.17
  4           .       I  *     .               .13
  3           .       I   *    .               .21
  2          . *      I        .              -.27
  1        *  .       I        .              -.41
      I.I.I.I.I.I.I.I.I.I.I.I.I.I.I.I.I.I.I.I
      -1                 0                +1
```

Figure 5-3
Autocorrelations and First Differences of Studly Dog Food Sales

(A) Autocorrelations of 1st Difference.

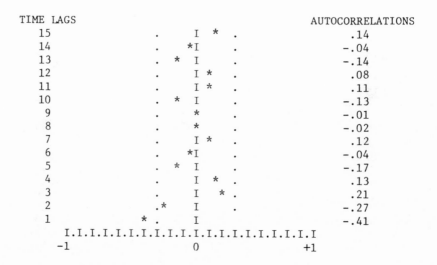

```
TIME LAGS                                          AUTOCORRELATIONS
   15            .         I  *  .                       .14
   14            .        *I     .                      -.04
   13            .     *   I     .                      -.14
   12            .         I *   .                       .08
   11            .         I *   .                       .11
   10            .     *   I     .                      -.13
    9            .         *     .                      -.01
    8            .         *     .                      -.02
    7            .         I *   .                       .12
    6            .        *I     .                      -.04
    5            .     *   I     .                      -.17
    4            .         I  *  .                       .13
    3            .         I   * .                       .21
    2            .*        I     .                      -.27
    1        *   .         I                            -.41
      I.I.I.I.I.I.I.I.I.I.I.I.I.I.I.I.I.I.I.I.I
       -1                  0                  +1
```

(B) Partial Autocorrelations.

```
TIME LAGS                                          AUTOCORRELATIONS
   14            .      *  I      .                     -.09
   13            .        *I      .                     -.04
   12            .         *      .                     -.01
   11            .      *  I      .                     -.12
   10            .      *  I      .                     -.16
    9            .         I*     .                      .07
    8            .        *I      .                     -.03
    7            .         *      .                     -.01
    6            .        *I      .                     -.04
    5            .         *      .                     -.00
    4            .         *      .                     -.01
    3            .   *     I      .                     -.28
    2            *   .     I      .                     -.52
    1            *   .     I      .                     -.41
      I.I.I.I.I.I.I.I.I.I.I.I.I.I.I.I.I.I.I.I.I
       -1                  0                  +1
```

Figure 5-4
**Autocorrelations of First Difference and Partial Autocorrelations of Studly Dog
Food Sales**

This is what is meant in earlier sections where it is stated that the profile of the actual data is matched to some theoretical profiles. Figure 5-5 contains the theoretical profiles for AR(1) and AR(2) models, Figure 5-6 demonstrates the profiles of MA(1) and MA(2) models, and Figure 5-7 contains the theoretical profiles of ARMA(1) and ARMA(2) models.

Ideally, the pattern of the actual data will closely match one of these theoretical patterns. In reality, good fits do not always occur due to randomness in the actual data. This is why the initial selection of the model category is considered just a tentative selection. The tentative model is tested to determine how well it fits past sales. Mean squared errors are used to determine the quality of the fit.

Determining Number of Terms (p, q) in the Model

The number of terms used in the model is determined by counting the number of autocorrelation or partial autocorrelation coefficients that are significantly different from zero. For example, in Figure 5-5(A) the autocorrelations drop exponentially to 0 and there is only one partial autocorrelation coefficient significantly different from 0 (that is, one value fell outside the control limits). This indicates the data should be represented by an AR model with one term: AR(1).

Figure 5-5(B) has two partial autocorrelation coefficients significantly different from 0, thus the appropriate model for this set of data is an AR model with two terms AR(2).

$$Y_t = B_1 Y_{t-1} + B_2 Y_{t-2} + e_t$$

Studly Dog Food Example

Figure 5-4 contains the first difference autocorrelations and partial autocorrelations of the 52 weeks of sales for the Studly Dog Food Company (see Table 5-7). Figure 5-4(A) indicates that the autocorrelation values drop off to 0 and then fluctuate around 0. This suggests an AR model. Two of the partial autocorrelation values in Figure 5-4(B) are significantly different from 0; this implies that an AR(2) model seems to fit this set of data.

Figure 5-8 contains the computer results when an AR(2) model is used on the Studly sales data. It shows the model's success in predicting sales in past periods, and also contains forecasts of three future periods along with a 95 percent confidence interval for those forecasts.

Stage Two—Determining Parameters of Model

The tentative format of the model has been identified. Now, specific values of the model's parameters (the B and Y values) must be selected. The B values eventually chosen should provide the smallest MSE from among possible values of these parameters. Usually, the user has to provide initial estimates for the B

(A)　AR(1)　Model

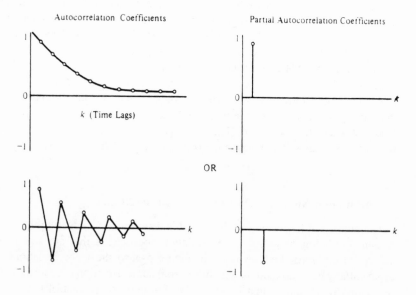

OR

(B)　AR(2)　Model

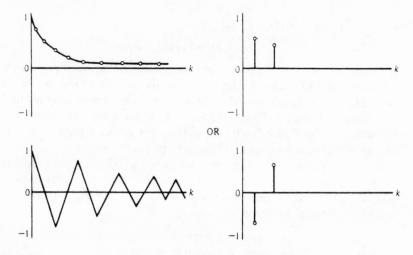

OR

Figure 5-5
Autocorrelation and Partial Autocorrelation Coefficients for an AR(1) and an AR(2) Model

(A)   MA(1) Model

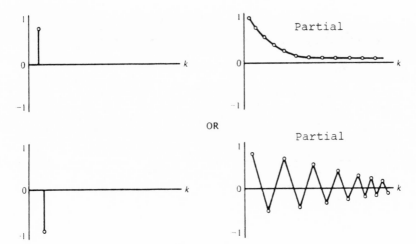

OR

(B)   MA(2) Model

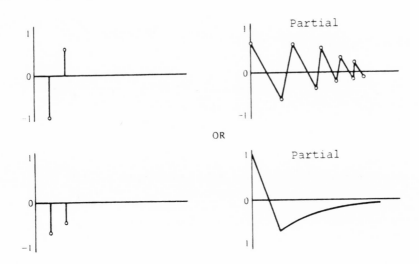

OR

Figure 5-6
Autocorrelations and Partial Autocorrelation Coefficients for an MA(1) and an MA(2) Model

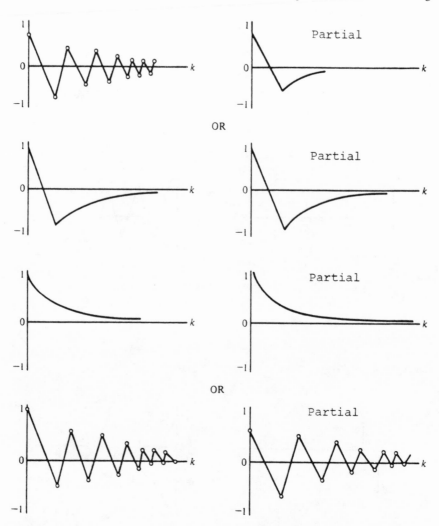

Figure 5-7
Autocorrelation and Partial Autocorrelation Coefficients for an ARMA (1,1) Model

values to start the program. Then the Box-Jenkins computer program performs a search for the optimal values of each parameter. Generally, only a few iterations are needed before the optimal values of the parameters are found. However, if the initial estimates are way off, an extensive searching process will have to take place.

The procedure for finding the most appropriate parameters is similar to that used in regression (AR models) or adaptive filtering (MA models). The optimal parameters are those resulting in the smallest MSE value. Once the optimal

Test of Model's Accuracy

PERIOD	ACTUAL	FORECAST	ERROR	PCT ERROR	95 PCT	BOUNDS
48	27.0	27.4	-.3	1.20	25.7	29.0
49	27.2	27.1	.1	.37	25.5	28.8
50	27.3	27.3	.0	.05	25.7	29.0
51	28.2	27.9	.4	1.29	26.2	29.5
52	28.3	28.4	-.2	.67	26.8	30.1

MEAN PC ERROR (MPE) OR BIAS   =   .13%
MEAN SQUARED ERROR (MSE)   =   .6
MEAN ABSOLUTE PC ERROR   (MAPE) =   3.5%

Actual Forecasts

PERIOD	FORECAST	95 PCT	BOUNDS
53	28.6	26.9	30.2
54	29.2	26.8	31.5
55	29.3	26.4	32.2

Figure 5-8
AR(2) Model Applied to Studly Dog Food Data

parameters are identified, they are incorporated into the model and estimates are made of past periods to determine the general pattern of the errors. The error (residual) values are put through an autocorrelation analysis to determine whether they fall into a random pattern. If an unusual pattern emerges (a number of values significantly different from 0), the model is not appropriate and a new one must be developed. Chi-square tests can also be used to analyze the autocorrelations of the errors.

Stage Three—Application of the Model

If the previous tests indicate that both the model form and its parameters are appropriate, some short-term forecasts are made. As time passes, this model should be reevaluated to make sure it still adequately fits the data. Large errors in later periods suggest that the pattern of one data series is changing and a new model is needed.

Overview of Box-Jenkins Method

The Box-Jenkins process is the most sophisticated of all time series techniques because it is capable of handling almost any pattern of data. It usually provides the most accurate short-range forecasts of any model and even enables statistical tests to be applied to each forecast along with confidence intervals.

However, in spite of its forecasting power it is one of the least used time series methods. Why? It has some major drawbacks that limit its usage.

(1) Because of its complexity, many forecasters and managers shy away from Box-Jenkins.

(2) It is really best suited to short-term forecasts (daily, weekly, or monthly).

(3) It requires a large amount of data; some authorities feel at least six years of data (monthly or weekly) are needed if seasonality exists in the data.

(4) It is difficult to incorporate new information into the model; in fact, it is usually necessary to develop a new model whenever new data appear.

(5) The model is fairly expensive to run on computers and thus does not lend itself to multi-product firms seeking forecasts.

CENSUS II METHOD

Census II is the fourth and final time series model covered in this chapter. It is similar to classical decomposition in that it separates data into its seasonal, cyclical, trend, and random components. However, Census II uses much more sophisticated procedures to accomplish this separation. Census II also provides tests that enable users to verify the accuracy of the decomposition process.

Census II was developed in the mid-1950s for use by the Bureau of the Census. In the ensuing years, the original model has undergone many refinements and the version presently in use is the X-11 model. Census II still finds its widest usage among government agencies. With its increased availability in software packages, however, it is gaining acceptance by business firms.

Coverage in This Book

The Census II techniques involves a large number of steps in which the data is continually refined. Full coverage of the technique would require a great amount of space, so only a few of its various steps are covered in this book.[2] Even with such brief coverage, the reader should be able to grasp the general procedures of Census II and its role as a forecasting tool.

General Procedures of Model

As previously stated, Census II enables the forecaster to decompose past sales into seasonals, trends, cycles, and random factors. However, its decomposition procedures are much more extensive than those used in classical decomposition. In fact, because Census II involves so many refinements of the data, many forecasters feel the technique is guilty of "overkill."

Adjusting for Trading Days

The first refinement that takes place is adjusting the sales data by making allowances for the variations in trading days from month to month. Each month (except February) varies year to year in the number of its Saturdays and Sundays. This affects the number of trading days in a month and, thus, the value of the variable for that month. Therefore, an initial step in Census II is to compensate for differences in trading days so that monthly data more accurately reflect true data from year to year. Table 5-8 shows how such adjustments are made for the month of September from each of the most recent six years. A comparable procedure is used for the other 11 months.

What does this adjustment for trading days accomplish? It provides a more accurate picture of a value's true variation from month to month and thus enables a more accurate seasonal ratio to be developed. For example, actual sales in September of 1978 were 146,000 units. But that September had fewer trading days than a typical September (20 versus 21.5), so sales for September of 1978 are adjusted upward to compensate for this difference.

Table 5-8
Adjusting Data for the Number of Trading Days (September)

Year	(1) \# of Trading Days	(2) Coefficient of Adjustment	(3) Actual Sales (000's)	(4) Sales Adjustment for Trading Days (3÷2)
1978	20	$\frac{20}{21.5} = .930$	146	156.9
1979	21	$\frac{21}{21.5} = .977$	152	155.6
1980	22	$\frac{22}{21.5} = 1.023$	163	159.3
1981	22	$\frac{22}{21.5} = 1.023$	174	170.1
1982	22	$\frac{22}{21.5} = 1.023$	181	176.9
1983	22	$\frac{22}{21.5} = 1.023$	196	191.6

$$\frac{129}{6} = 21.5$$

Additional Steps

Once the data have been adjusted for trading days, seasonal ratios are determined applying 12-month moving averages to the adjusted data.

A procedure is then used to determine whether some extreme values exist in the data. An example of an extreme value is sales that differ from the expected value by two or three standard deviations. Any extreme value is replaced by a value more in line with a "normal" value. Substitutions also can be made for values lost due to the use of moving averages.

Each of the components (seasonal, cycle, trend, random) is decomposed. A variety of tests are then performed to determine whether the decomposition is successful. Some of the most crucial of these tests are the adjacent month test, the January test, and the equality test.

In the adjacent month test, a ratio is developed between the deseasonalized values and average values of the adjacent months. If the data have been effectively deseasonalized, the ratio falls between 95 and 105.

The January test also measures the success of the deseasonalization process. The final seasonally adjusted series of each year is divided by its January value to provide a standardized ratio. If patterns emerge in this ratio, seasonality still exists in the data.

The equality test is used to determine whether the data have been overadjusted due to all of the refinements that have taken place in the previous steps of Census II.

In addition to these three tests, Census II also provides tests that identify the overall impact of each component on sales. These tests calculate the monthly percentage change related to each of the four components.

Overview of Census II

Empirical evidence suggests that Census II is the most effective decomposition technique. And, with the increased availability of software packages, its use is increasing among business firms. Additional methods for refining time series data are constantly being introduced, so the Census II technique, no doubt, will continue to undergo changes.

The Census II method is one of the more expensive forecasting techniques since it has relatively high development costs and fairly high computer costs. In addition, its storage requirements are fairly large. Thus the user must determine whether the additional accuracy of Census II is worth the added expense.

NOTES

1. This identifies the association between a variable with earlier values of that same variable while holding the effects of all other time lags constant.
2. More extensive coverage of Census II can be found in the following book: Spyrus Makridakes and S. Wheelwright, *Forecasting—Methods and Applications* (New York: John Wiley and Sons, 1978).

QUESTIONS AND EXERCISES

1. Four time series models were described in this chapter. Each has unique strengths and weaknesses. Describe the circumstances in which each would be the preferred forecasting technique.

2. How can forecasters use autocorrelations and differencing to enhance the likelihood of their selecting the most appropriate forecasting technique?

3. Why is Box-Jenkins not really considered a specific forecasting model?

4. How does the Winter's method differ from a typical decomposition model?

5. Apply the adaptive filtering and Winter's method to the sales of Studly Dog Food (Table 5-2). How effective is each in forecasting Studly sales? Why aren't they as effective as Box-Jenkins?

6. Make adjustments for differences in trading days for April 1978–1983. Assume original sales for each months as follows:

April 1978	$114,720
1979	$123,614
1980	$132,512
1981	$129,612
1982	$135,114
1983	$136,211

    What would the sales be for each month when adjusted for trading days?

7. Use the following autocorrelation and partial autocorrelation profiles to determine which Box-Jenkins' model should be used.

(A)

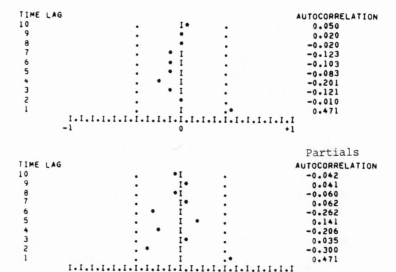

```
TIME LAG                                    AUTOCORRELATION
10                    .          I•      .        0.050
 9                    .          •       .        0.020
 8                    .          •       .       -0.020
 7                    .        • I       .       -0.123
 6                    .        • I       .       -0.103
 5                    .        • I       .       -0.083
 4                    .      •   I       .       -0.201
 3                    .        • I       .       -0.121
 2                    .          •       .       -0.010
 1                    .          I     •.         0.471
         I.I.I.I.I.I.I.I.I.I.I.I.I.I.I.I.I.I.I.I.I
        -1                       0                +1

                                            Partials
TIME LAG                                    AUTOCORRELATION
10                    .        •I         .      -0.042
 9                    .         I•        .       0.041
 8                    .        •I         .      -0.060
 7                    .         I•        .       0.062
 6                    .      •   I        .      -0.262
 5                    .         I  •      .       0.141
 4                    .       •  I        .      -0.206
 3                    .         I•        .       0.035
 2                    .       •  I        .      -0.300
 1                    .         I       •.        0.471
         I.I.I.I.I.I.I.I.I.I.I.I.I.I.I.I.I.I.I.I.I
        -1                      0                 +1
```

(B)

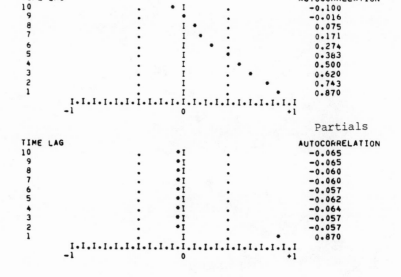

```
TIME LAG                                    AUTOCORRELATION
10                    .        •  I      .       -0.100
 9                    .           •      .       -0.016
 8                    .           I •    .        0.075
 7                    .           I   •  .        0.171
 6                    .           I     •.        0.274
 5                    .           I      •.       0.383
 4                    .           I      .  •     0.500
 3                    .           I      .     •  0.620
 2                    .           I      .       •0.743
 1                    .           I      .        •0.870
         I.I.I.I.I.I.I.I.I.I.I.I.I.I.I.I.I.I.I.I.I
        -1                       0                +1

                                            Partials
TIME LAG                                    AUTOCORRELATION
10                    .         •I        .      -0.065
 9                    .         •I        .      -0.065
 8                    .         •I        .      -0.060
 7                    .         •I        .      -0.060
 6                    .         •I        .      -0.057
 5                    .         •I        .      -0.062
 4                    .         •I        .      -0.064
 3                    .         •I        .      -0.057
 2                    .         •I        .      -0.057
 1                    .          I      • .       0.870
         I.I.I.I.I.I.I.I.I.I.I.I.I.I.I.I.I.I.I.I.I
        -1                      0                 +1
```

6

Causal Models

INTRODUCTION

The basic premise of a causal model is that changes in the value of a particular variable (product A, for example) are closely associated with changes in some other variable(s). Therefore, if fairly accurate information is available on the future value of the other variable(s), it can be used to forecast the future value of the first variable (the sales of product A).

The causal models used most frequently for business forecasting are simple and multiple regression. Simple regression and its accompanying statistical tests are discussed in this chapter and multiple regression is covered in the next chapter.

This chapter also includes a section in which a much simplified version of an input-output model is described. That coverage is not intended to provide readers with the knowledge actually to develop and use input-output analysis. Rather, its purpose is to acquaint them with the general procedures of the technique.

SIMPLE REGRESSION AND INPUT-OUTPUT

Causal versus Association

Although the term *causal* is used to describe regression models, this writer makes a special effort to stay away from stating "variable B causes variable A," even though in some situations that may indeed be the case. For example, a huge snowfall in a community brings about (causes) a sudden increase in the sale of tire chains. But in many other situations, such a direct relationship cannot be established. For example, a close relationship seems to exist between the quarterly sales of Acme tires and the amount of money Acme spends each quarter on advertising. However, such factors as competitors' actions, new car sales, and weather conditions, also affect the sales of Acme tires. Thus, it can't be stated that changes in Acme's advertising expenditures "caused" the changes in their tire sales. Advertising no doubt was a contributing factor, but it was not the sole factor affecting changes in tire sales.

This inability to identify and isolate all possible variables and their impact is the key reason that in business situations regression models should not be used to "prove" cause and effect. These models can be used, however, to demonstrate whether an association exists between two or more variables and the strength of that relationship. That is why regression models are such effective forecasting tools.

Regression versus Correlation

Regression and correlation are statistical techniques for measuring the relationship between a dependent variable (sales) and one or more independent variables but each presents this relationship in a different manner.

Regression analysis identifies the nature of the relationship between variables in the form of an equation ($Y = a + bX$). This equation, derived from past data about both the independent variable (X) and the dependent variable (Y), can be used to estimate future Y values (assuming accurate estimates of future values of the independent variable exist).

Correlation analysis, on the other hand, describes the strength of the relationship between the variables. A coefficient of determination (r^2) is computed and it indicates the portion of changes in the dependent variable (Y) associated with changes in the independent variable (X). For example, an r^2 of .37 means that 37 percent of the variation in the sales of Acme tires is associated with changes in the independent variable (X).

A primary advantage of using regression and correlation is that statistical tests can be applied to their results. Confidence intervals can be developed around the forecast values, the significance of the individual coefficients (a and b values) can be tested and even the significance of the r^2 can be tested. All of these tests are described later in this chapter.

REGRESSION EQUATION

Various terms are used to describe the line derived from the regression equation. It is called the "line of best fit," or "least squares" line. Regardless of its title, its purpose remains the same. An equation is developed that enables a line to be drawn through a set of data points in such a way that the line will minimize the overall distance (sum of squared deviations) between the actual values and corresponding points on this line.

Trend versus Regression Line

In situations where the independent variable is a series of time periods (1971, 1972, and so forth), a "trend line" is developed. When the independent variable is an economic series (advertising expenditures, number of new housing starts, and so forth), a "regression line" is developed. The same general procedures apply in both situations since the purpose of each is to fit a line through the data points.

Application of Model

Joe Page is the new executive director of the Rocky Mountain Council of Bathroom Fixture Wholesalers. As one of his first actions, Mr. Page wants to provide the Council's members with an annual sales forecast for bathroom fixtures in the region. He proposes to use a simple regression model for this forecast and assumes the logical independent variable (X) for the model is new housing starts in the region.

He collects data on housing starts from various state agencies and business associations and then compares these figures with regional sales of bathroom fixtures over the previous 13 years (see Table 6-1).

The first step of the regression process is to plot both sets of data on a graph to determine the general type of association that exists between the two variables. Figure 6-1 indicates a linear relationship between new housing starts and dollar sales of bathroom fixtures. Thus, it is appropriate to apply the equation for fitting a straight line to two variables: $Y = a + bX$.

Once it has been ascertained that a linear relationship exists, it is necessary to find values for a and b in the regression equation. Since it is now assumed that sales of bathroom fixtures are a function of new housing starts, it is desirable to

Table 6-1
Variables for the Simple Regression Model for Bathroom Fixtures

Year	Y Regional Sales of Industry in $ (millions)	X New Housing Starts in Region (000's in units)
1970	101	126
1971	147	196
1972	174	213
1973	136	172
1974	94	115
1975	95	111
1976	138	161
1977	164	216
1978	162	219
1979	161	189
1980	109	123
1981	82	104
1982	74	99

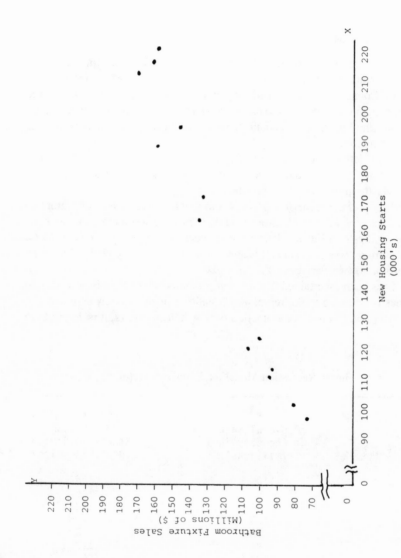

Figure 6-1
Scatter Diagram of New Housing Starts and Sales of Bathroom Fixtures

quantify the nature of this relationship so that estimates of new housing starts can be used to forecast future sales of bathroom fixtures.

Determining the Regression Line

Regression analysis will fit a line through the data points in Figure 6-1 that minimizes the sum of the squared deviations (difference between the actual values and values on the regression line).

The two values to be determined are a, the intercept, and b, the regression coefficient.

a = Intercept is the value of Y when X equals 0. It is the point where the regression line crosses the Y axis.

b = Slope is the amount of change that occurs in Y for each unit of change in X. It is also called the regression coefficient.

Formulae for Determining a and b values

$$b = \frac{\Sigma XY - \dfrac{(\Sigma X)(\Sigma Y)}{n}}{\Sigma X^2 - \dfrac{(\Sigma X)^2}{n}}$$

$$a = \bar{Y} - b(\bar{X})$$

Table 6-2 contains the computations used to derive the a and b values. The computed values are:

a = \$9.7 million
b = .739

This means that the line derived from the formula will intersect the Y axis at 9.7. This can be interpreted as follows: even when there are no new housing starts, bathroom fixture sales will still be \$9.7 million in the Rocky Mountain region.

A b of .739 means that for every one unit change in new housing starts (one unit equals 1,000 starts) bathroom fixtures sales will change \$739,000. (Fixture sales are in units of \$1 million each.)

Forecasting with Regression Equations

Now that the relationship between the two variables has been quantified, the calculated a and b values can be used to make a forecast. Remember, the purpose

Table 6-2
Data and Computations Needed to Derive *a* and *b* Values

(1) Period	(2) Regional Sales Y	(3) New Housing Starts X	(4) Y^2	(5) X^2	(6) XY	(7) $(Y-\bar{Y})^2$	(8) $(X-\bar{X})^2$	(9) $(X-\bar{X})(Y-\bar{Y})$
1970	101	126	10201	15876	12726	621	975	778.2
1971	147	196	21609	38416	28812	444	1503	817.3
1972	174	213	30276	45369	37062	2312	3110	2681.4
1973	136	172	18496	29584	23392	102	218	148.9
1974	94	115	8836	13225	10810	1019	1783	1348.0
1975	95	111	9025	12321	10545	956	2137	1429.4
1976	138	161	19044	25921	22218	146	14	45.5
1977	164	216	26896	46656	35424	1450	3454	2238.0
1978	162	219	26244	47961	35478	1302	3816	2228.7
1979	161	189	25921	35721	30429	1231	1009	1114.5
1980	109	123	11881	15129	13407	286	1172	579.2
1981	82	104	6724	10816	8528	1929	2833	2337.9
1982	74	99	5476	9801	7326	2696	3391	3023.6
n=13	$\Sigma Y=1637$	$\Sigma X=2044$	$\Sigma Y^2=220629$	$\Sigma X^2=346796$	$\Sigma XY=276157$	$\Sigma(Y-\bar{Y})^2=$ 14492	$\Sigma(X-\bar{X})^2=$ 25415	$\Sigma=18770.6$

$$b = \frac{\Sigma XY - \frac{(\Sigma X)(\Sigma Y)}{n}}{\Sigma X^2 - \frac{(\Sigma X)^2}{n}} = \frac{276,157 - \frac{(2044)(1637)}{13}}{346,796 - \frac{(2044)^2}{13}} = \frac{18770}{25416} = \frac{18770}{25416}$$

$b = .739$

$a = \bar{Y} - b(\bar{X}) = 125.92 - .739(157.23)$

$a = 9.7$

$(\Sigma = \text{Sum of})$

$\bar{X} = \text{Mean of X})\ \Sigma X \div n = 2044 \div 13 = 157.23$

$\bar{Y} = \text{Mean of Y})\ \Sigma Y \div n = 1637 \div 13 = 125.92$

Example:

$(Y-\bar{Y})^2_{1970} = (101 - 125.92)^2 = (-24.92)^2 = 621$

of developing a regression equation is to incorporate information about future values of the independent variable into a forecast. In our example, predictions about new housing starts for the coming three years were available from both the federal government and construction trade associations. Predicted new housing starts for 1983 for the Rocky Mountain region were 107,000 units. This estimate is then included in the regression equation and used to forecast sales of bathroom fixtures.

$$Y_c = a + b(X)$$
$$Y_c = 9.7 + .739(107) \text{ (see foot of Table 6-2)}$$
$$Y_c = 88.77$$

Based on this equation, the sales forecast of bathroom fixtures for 1983 is $88.8 million dollars.

Note of caution: Regardless of how strong the relationship is between the two variables, the accuracy of the sales forecast is totally dependent on the accuracy of the prediction of the independent variable. If this prediction is highly questionable, so too will be any forecast derived from it.

Positive Slope versus Negative Slope

The data points on Figure 6-1 slope upward to the right. Such a slope indicates a positive relationship between the two variables—they both move in the same direction. As new housing starts grow, so also do sales of bathroom fixtures. Conversely, when new housing starts decline, bathroom fixture sales decline. If the data points had sloped downward to the right, this would indicate a negative (inverse) relationship between the two variables, that is, an increase in new housing starts results in a decrease in sales of bathroom fixtures.

The nature of the relationship between the variable is identified by the *b* value. If the *b* has a minus sign, a negative relationship exists. It is important to recognize that a negative *b* does not imply a poor relationship exists between the two variables. Instead, it indicates that the relationship is of an inverse nature because the independent and dependent variables move in opposite directions.

Analysis of Regression Equation

A key advantage of using regression models is that statistical techniques can be used to evaluate their accuracy. The first of these determines whether the coefficient *b* is significantly different from 0, that is, is there an actual slope in the regression line? If no slope exists, the regression line is no better a forecasting tool than just using the mean value of Y ($\bar{Y}$).

Since only 13 periods of data were used in the analysis, it is possible that the relationship depicted by *b* might have occurred by chance. If there were no relationship, *b* would have a value of 0 (no slope). Thus, a first test is to see if the calculated b value (.739) is significantly different from zero. Or conversely, if the slope was indeed zero, what is the likelihood of getting a b of .739? Thus, the null hypothesis that will be tested is H_0: $b = 0$.

In determining whether the b value (.739) is significantly different from 0, the unit of measurement will be standard errors. A standard error describes the distribution of sample means around the mean of the population from which they are drawn. How different is .739 from 0 in terms of standard errors? The following formula shows how the standard error value is derived.

$$SE_b = \frac{\text{Col. 5, Table 6-3/(Col. 1)-2}}{\text{(Col. 8, Table 6-2)}}$$

$$SE_b = \sqrt{\frac{\Sigma(Y - Y_c)^2/n - 2}{\Sigma(X - \bar{X})^2}} = \sqrt{\frac{629.44/11}{25,415}}$$

$$SE_b = .0474$$

This computed SE_b value is now used to test the significance of the b value. A t test is used to determine how much difference there is between the computed b value and some hypothetical value, in this case 0.

$$t = \frac{b - \text{hypothetical value}}{SE_b}$$

$$t = \frac{.739 - 0}{.0474}$$

$$t = 15.6$$

Thus, the difference between b and 0 is 15.6 SE_b. A t table is consulted to determine the tabular value of t at the .05 level of significance and n-2 or 11 degrees of freedom.[1]

Tabular $t = 2.2$

Computed $t = 15.6$

Since the computed t greatly exceeds the tabular t, we reject the null hypothesis that b = 0 and accept the alternative hypothesis: H_a: $b \neq 0$. This is statistical evidence that a relationship exists between new housing starts and sales of bathroom fixtures.

Rule of Thumb: A quick assessment of whether a b value is different from zero can be made without having to consult a t table. If the number of observations (n) is between 5 and 20, the tabular t is equal to or greater than 3 at an .05 level of significance. If $n > 20$, the tabular t is around 2.

When Hypothesis Can't Be Rejected

What if the null hypothesis ($b = 0$) can't be rejected? Our personal observations of the data may indicate a slope exists, but in the tests, the calculated t is less than the tabular t. What are the implications of such a result? It is still possible that Y and X are related but in some curvilinear manner. Therefore, we may either have chosen the wrong model to describe the actual situation, or a Type II error (accepting a false hypothesis) may have occurred. In either case, it would be questionable to use this b coefficient as a predictor in a linear model.

Confidence Interval for b Value

A second statistical test that can be used with regression data is the development of a confidence interval (CI) for the coefficient b. In our example, the b value was computed to be .739. Because this figure is derived from only 13 data points, we want to develop an interval that we are confident contains the true value of b.

Again, a rule of thumb can be applied when developing such an interval. When $n < 20$, the 95 percent confidence interval for b is $\pm 3\,SE_b$. When $n > 20$, the 95 percent confidence interval is $\pm 2\,SE_b$.

In our example, the 95 percent confidence interval for b would be .598 to .880. What this means is that we are fairly confident (95 percent) that the true b value falls between .598 and .880.

$$95 \text{ percent CI} = b \pm 3\ (SE_b)$$
$$95 \text{ percent CI} = .739 \pm 3\ (.047)$$
$$= .598 \text{ to } .880$$

Confidence Interval for Y Value

It is important to recognize that although a precise forecast value emerges from the regression equation ($Y_c = a + bX$), this model should really be viewed as providing a range of values in which the true forecast is likely to fall. For example, based on the regression model, the forecast of bathroom fixture sales for 1983 was $88.8 million. It is highly unlikely that actual sales will match that figure. But the regression model enables an error band (interval) to be built around the Y_c value, and the user can be reasonably confident actual sales will fall within that interval. (Again, this assumes the predicted X value is accurate.)

Table 6-3 contains the forecast values of the 13 time periods. Figures in Column 3 (Y_c) are actual forecasts of each period obtained from the regression equation using the X values (Column 3, Table 6-2).

Remember, a basic assumption of regression analysis is that each value on the regression line is really the mean of the Y values associated with a specific X value. It is also assumed that these Y values are normally distributed around an X value. Therefore, it is possible to establish a range in which the true Y value for

Table 6-3
Forecast Values and Residuals

(1)	(2)	(3)	(4)	(5)
				Deviation
			Deviation	Squared
Period	Sales	Forecast	(3-2)	(4^2)
	Y	Y_c	$(Y-Y_c)$	$(Y-Y_c)^2$
1970	101	102.8	-1.8	3.24
1971	147	154.5	-7.5	56.25
1972	174	167.1	6.9	47.61
1973	136	136.8	-.8	.64
1974	94	94.7	-.7	.49
1975	95	91.7	3.3	10.89
1976	138	128.7	9.3	86.49
1977	164	169.3	-5.3	28.09
1978	162	171.5	-9.5	90.25
1979	161	149.4	11.6	34.56
1980	109	100.6	8.4	70.56
1981	82	86.6	-4.6	21.16
1982	74	82.9	-8.9	79.21

$$\Sigma(Y-Y_c)^2 = 629.44$$

each X value is expected to fall. That range is built around the standard error of the forecast (SE_y).

$$SE_y = \sqrt{\frac{\Sigma(Y - Y_c)^2}{n - 2}}\left(\sqrt{1 + \frac{1}{n} + \frac{(X_t - \bar{X})^2}{\Sigma(X - \bar{X})^2}}\right)$$

The above formula contains two components. The first component is the standard deviation of the regression. The second component is really a correction factor to adjust this standard deviation value in light of (a) the number of observations and (b) the distance between the current independent variable (X) and the mean of its previous values ($\bar{X}$). The fewer the observations or the greater the distance between the X value used in the forecast and the $\bar{X}$, the larger the value of SE_y. In our computations we will again assume the 1983 value for X (new housing starts) is projected to be 107,000 units.

$$SE_y = \sqrt{\frac{\Sigma(Y - Y_c)^2}{n - 2}}\left(\sqrt{1 + \frac{1}{n} + \frac{(X_t - \bar{X})^2}{\Sigma(X - \bar{X})^2}}\right)$$

$$SE_y = \sqrt{\frac{629.44}{11}}\left(\sqrt{1 + \frac{1}{13} + \frac{(107 - 157.2)}{25,415}}\right)$$

$$SE_y = (7.56)(1.04)$$

$$SE_y = 7.86$$

This SE_y can be used to develop a 95 percent confidence interval for the 1983 forecast of bathroom fixture sales. Two standard errors of Y are used since they approximate a 95 percent confidence interval (1.96 is more precise):

$Y_c = a + b(X)$
$Y_c = 9.7 + .739(107)$
$Y_c = \$88.77$
95 percent CI $= Y_c \pm 2(SE_y)$
95 percent CI $= \$88.77 \pm 15.72$
95 percent CI $= \$73.05$ to $\$104.49$

Based on these computations it can be stated that if new housing starts are around 107,000 units, we are reasonably confident (95%) that dollar sales of bathroom fixtures will be between $73 million and $104.5 million.

CORRELATION ANALYSIS

Earlier in this chapter it was stated that the regression equation is used to identify the relationship between variables and that this relationship is used to estimate future values of the dependent (Y) variable. Correlation, on the other hand, describes the overall strength of the relationship between these variables.

In correlation analysis, the total variation in the Y values is quantified and separated into those portions that are explained and those that are unexplained. The explained portion is that amount that can be associated with some particular variable(s).

Figure 6-2 illustrates the concept of explained and unexplained variation and the role of the regression equation in identifying these amounts. Figure 6-2 graphs sales for eight different periods. One of these values, point Y_A, is used to illustrate this concept. The regression line explains part of the difference in value between Y_A and the mean of all Y values ($\bar{Y}$). However, some portion of Y_A's deviation from the $\bar{Y}$ line cannot be explained. On the other hand, all of the variation of value Y_B from $\bar{Y}$ is explained by the regression line since the regression line crosses the Y_B value.

The total deviation for any one value equals explained deviation plus unexplained deviation.

$$Y - \bar{Y} = (Y_c - \bar{Y}) + (Y - Y_c)$$

If there were no regression line, the mean ($\bar{Y}$) would have to be used to forecast the Y values for different values of X. Thus, the explained variation is merely the

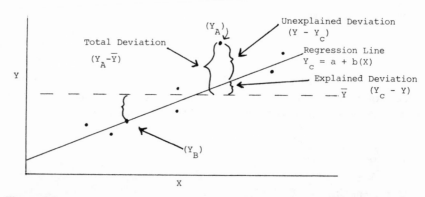

Figure 6-2
Total, Explained, and Unexplained Deviations from Y

improvement the regression line provides over the mean line ($\bar{Y}$) as an estimator of Y values.

Coefficient of Determination r^2

In correlation, the variations (deviations squared) are determined and mathematically apportioned to each independent variable. The term, coefficient of determination (r^2), is used to measure this relationship.

$$r^2 = \frac{\text{Explained variation}}{\text{Total variation}} = \frac{\Sigma(Y_c - \bar{Y})^2}{\Sigma(Y - \bar{Y})^2}$$

The r^2 value will always be between $+1$ and -1. The closer the value is to 1 or -1, the higher the correlation between the variables (that is, the greater the portion of total variation explained by the regression line.) If $r^2 = 0$, this indicates no correlation exists between the variables. The sign of the correlation value is always the same as the sign of the regression coefficient (b). A minus sign merely indicates the correlation is of an inverse nature.

Using data from Columns 7 and 9 of Table 6-2, the following formula is used to derive the r^2 value.

$$r^2 = \frac{\text{Column 9 } (b)}{\text{Column 7}}$$

$$r^2 = \frac{b[\Sigma(X - \bar{X})(Y - \bar{Y})]}{[\Sigma(Y - \bar{Y})]^2}$$

$$r^2 = \frac{.739(18,770.6)}{14,492}$$

$r^2 = .957$

What does the r^2 value mean? It means that 95.7 percent of the variation in previous Y values is associated with variations in the X values. Thus, a very high portion of the variation in Y values is explained by the regression line. In our example, 95.7 percent of the variation in sales of bathroom fixtures is explained by variations in the number of new housing units.

Another method of determining the r^2 value is to determine the ratio between the unexplained variation and the total variation, and subtract this ratio from 1. (There may be a slight difference between answers using the previous formula for r^2 and the following r^2 formula when a small number of observations (n) is involved.)

$$r^2 = 1 - \frac{\text{Unexplained variation}}{\text{Total variation}}$$

$$r^2 = 1 - \frac{\Sigma(Y - Y_c)^2 \text{ (See foot of Column 5, Table 6-3)}}{\Sigma(Y - \bar{Y})^2 \text{ (See foot of Column 7, Table 6-2)}}$$

$$r^2 = 1 - \frac{629.44}{14,492}$$

$$r^2 = 1 - .043$$

$$r^2 = .957$$

The r value is the coefficient of correlation. In the bathroom fixture example, the r value is .978. This value is not nearly as useful for interpreting the association between variables as is the coefficient of determination (r^2). In reality, about the only contribution of r is that it provides a rough measure for identifying the closeness of the association between X and Y and is also the descriptor in the correlation matrix found with multiple correlation.

Testing Significance of r^2

Many users of regression data mistakenly assume that a high r^2 value ($r^2 > .80$) automatically ensures that correlation exists between two variables. Actually, a high r^2 could result from chance, especially when only a small number of data points or observations are involved. (In our example only 13 sets of data are used.) Thus, it is necessary to use a statistical test to determine whether the computed r^2 value is significant. Such a test must consider the number of data points and, in the case of multiple correlation, the total number of variables involved.

The test compares the explained variance with the unexplained variance. Note that the concept of variance, not variation, is now involved. Variance makes allowances for the number of data points (n) and the number of variables (K). The statistical test computes a value of F which is compared to a tabular F value to see if the explained variance is significantly larger than the unexplained variance. The tabular F value is obtained from an F table, at .05 level of significance, with 1 degree of freedom in the numerator and 11 degrees of freedom in the denominator.[2]

The explained variation can be determined by subtracting the unexplained variation (629.4) from the total variation (14,492). This simple subtraction eliminates the need to compute the explained variation. Dividing the explained variation by K-1 then provides the explained variance.

$$14,492 - 629.4 = 13,862.6 \text{ or explained variation}$$

$$F = \frac{\text{Explained variance}}{\text{Unexplained variance}} = \frac{\Sigma(Y_c - Y)^2/K - 1}{\Sigma(Y - Y_c)^2/n - 2}$$

$$F = \frac{13,862.6/1}{629.4/11} = \frac{13,862.6}{57.2} \qquad K = \text{Number of variables}$$

$$F = 242.4 \qquad N = \text{Number of data points}$$

tabular $F = 4.84$

Since the computed F value, in this case (242.4), is significantly larger than the tabular F (4.84), we can safely assume that a linear correlation exists between new housing starts and dollar sales of bathroom fixtures.

Alternate Test for r

An alternate but less accurate method to test the significance of the correlation is to apply a t test to the computed r value.

$$t = r\sqrt{\frac{n - 2}{1 - r^2}}$$

$$t = .978\sqrt{\frac{13 - 2}{1 - .957}}$$

computed $t = 15.6$

tabular $t = 2.2$ (11 degrees of freedom at .05 level of significance)

Again, the computed t is significantly larger than the tabular t, so the hypothesis that there is no correlation between X and Y can be rejected.

Analyzing Residual (Error) Values (Durbin-Watson Test)

Thus far, this description of the regression model has ignored the issue of residuals: the variations in the Y value that are not explained by the regression equation. These residuals are also referred to as error terms (e).

$$Y = a + b(X) + e$$

It would be a rare situation if each actual (Y) value were equal to its forecasted value (Y_c) in the regression equation. There are always some outside factors that affect Y that cannot be included in the regression equation.

Ideally, residual values will fall into a random pattern. Such randomness indicates that although the regression equation does not completely explain the variation in the Y values, it does explain the most critical factor(s). If some pattern does exist in the residuals, however, some factor(s) not included in the equation is strongly affecting sales and may seriously bias the equation's results. This means the levels of significance and ranges set for the forecast are questionable.

The fastest way to determine whether there is a pattern in the residuals is to plot the residual values on a graph around the regression line and visually analyze the pattern. A discernible pattern in the residuals indicates the existence of autocorrelation. Autocorrelation is an association that exists among values of the same variable at different time periods. Figure 6-3 shows four different patterns of residuals. In 6-3(A), 6-3(B), and 6-3(C), some type of pattern exists. This suggests that one or more undetected variable(s) is affecting sales. The pattern in 6(D) is quite random and implies no autocorrelation among the residuals.

The Durbin-Watson test is a statistical method that checks for autocorrelation among the residuals. Most computerized regression models have the Durbin-Watson test built in as one of their statistical tests. The Durbin-Watson test determines the ratio of the first differences of errors to the sum of squared errors. The d value determines whether autocorrelation exists among the residuals.

Table 6-4 contains the data and computations needed to apply the Durbin-Watson test. These values are used to compute the d value. This computed d value is compared to critical values of d determined from a table of Durbin-Watson d values. These tabular values represent both a lower (d_L) and upper (d_U) value for d, based on the number of variables in the regression equation and the number of data points (13). In our example, these tabular values are $d_L = .81$ and $d_U = 1.07$. These are the upper and lower values for d found in a Durbin-Watson table when there is only one independent variable and only 13 data points. A different pair of tabular d values would be used if there were 20 data points or three independent variables. The diagram in Figure 6-4 shows how to use these tabular d values to determine whether the residuals fall into some type of pattern.

Our computed d is 1.95, which means it falls into the region of "no significant

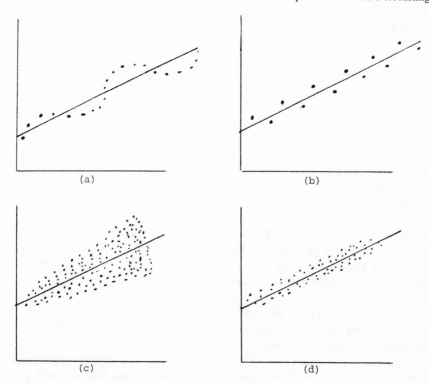

(a)

(b)

(c)

(d)

Figure 6-3
Possible Patterns of Residuals

autocorrelation." Therefore, we can safely assume that no pattern exists in the residuals, which means the independent variable effectively explains the variations in the dependent variables. If no tables are available to derive the appropriate tabular d_L and d_U values, a reasonably safe rule to apply is that a computed "d" between 1.5 and 2.5 indicates a lack of autocorrelation among the residuals.

What if autocorrelation is detected? What can be done to correct or remove it? In the next chapter dealing with multiple correlation models, methods of transformation are identified as ways to handle autocorrelation in residuals.

Non-linear Data

The simple linear regression model is discussed in this chapter along with some key statistical methods that can be used to test the significance of the derived values. Although this chapter concentrated on those relationships that can be depicted with a straight line, many real-world forecasting problems could be handled better by using a non-linear model. Since non-linear relationships

Table 6-4
Comparison of $Y - Y_c$ Residuals

Year	(1) Actual Y	(2) Forecast Y_c	(3) Residual E_i	(4) First Difference E_{i-1}	(5) $E_i - E_{i-1}$ (3-4)	(6) $(E_i - E_{i-1})^2$ (5^2)	(7) $(E_i)^2$ (3^2)
1970	101	102.8	-1.8				3.24
1971	147	154.5	-7.5	-1.8	-5.7	32.49	56.25
1972	174	167.1	6.9	-7.5	14.4	207.36	47.61
1973	136	136.8	-.8	6.9	-7.7	59.29	.64
1974	94	94.7	-.7	-.8	.1	.01	.49
1975	95	91.7	3.3	-.7	4.0	16.00	10.89
1976	138	128.7	9.3	3.3	6.0	36.00	86.49
1977	164	169.3	-5.3	9.3	-14.6	213.16	28.09
1978	162	171.5	-9.5	-5.3	-4.2	17.64	90.25
1979	161	149.4	11.6	-9.5	21.1	445.21	134.56
1980	109	100.6	8.4	11.6	-3.2	10.24	70.56
1981	82	86.6	-4.6	8.4	-13.0	169.00	21.16
1982	74	82.9	-8.9	-4.6	-4.3	18.49	79.21
						Σ1224.89	Σ629.44

Durbin Watson Test

$$d = \frac{\text{sum of squared first differences of errors}}{\text{sum of squared errors}}$$

$$d = \frac{\sum\limits_{i=2}^{n} (E_i - E_{i-1})^2}{\sum\limits_{i=1}^{n} (E_i)^2}$$

$$d = \frac{1224.9}{629.4}$$

Therefore, computed d = 1.95

This computed d is now compared to the appropriate tabular d values to determine if a pattern exists in the residuals.

cannot all be represented by a single model, a number of different curvilinear relationships are needed, which usually make it very difficult to develop and use such a model.

One way of handling such complex relationships is to convert non-linear data to a linear form through transformations, which is discussed in the next chapter.

Overview of Simple Correlation

Strengths

- Usually available in software packages for most computers.
- Fairly inexpensive to run on the computer.
- Technique is usually covered in most statistics courses so increasing numbers of managers are familiar with it.
- Provides statistical tests and confidence intervals for the coefficients and the actual forecasts.
- Provides accurate short-term and medium-term forecasts.

Drawbacks

- Its forecasting accuracy depends upon a consistent relationship with the independent variable.
- An accurate estimate of the independent variable is crucial.
- May still be a "black box" technique for many people.
- Requires the user to understand what all the tests of significance mean. A high r^2 can be misleading.

INPUT-OUTPUT MODELS

As stated at the outset of this chapter, causal models are based on the premise that changes in demand for a product can be directly related to changes in some other variables or products. Thus, knowledge about such relationships can be used to develop better forecasts. Input-output models provide methods of identifying and quantifying interrelationships between products or industries.

Types of Interrelationships

In analyzing demand for a product, we tend to focus attention on the end products. For example, the demand for lawn mowers is the result of the number of those units purchased by households and business firms. But lawn mowers comprise a number of components such as spark plugs, handles, motors, blades. Thus, an increase in demand for lawn mowers also brings about an increase in demand for these components. Moving another step backward, an increase in the

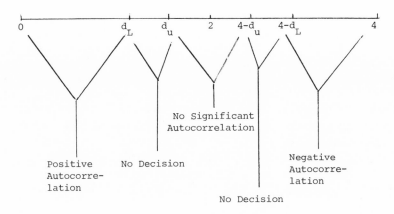

When n = 13, and there is only one independent variable,

Tabular d_L = .81   )
) Values found in Durbin-Watson table.
Tabular d_u = 1.07   )

Therefore,   Range of Values

Positive Correlation =   0 to .81 (0 to d_L)

No Decision =   .81 to 1.07 (d_L to d_u)

No Significant Autocorrelation =   1.07 to 2.93 (d_u to 4-d_u)

No Decision =   2.93 to 3.19 (4-d_u to 4-d_L)

Negative Autocorrelation =   3.19 to 4 (4-d_L to 4)

* Model taken from: Lester Sartorius and N. Caroll Mohn, Sales Forecasting
                      Models: A Diagnostic Approach (Georgia State
                      University, College of Business, 1976), p. 121.

Figure 6-4
Model for Comparing Durbin-Watson Tabular *d* Values to Computed *d*

demand for the components brings about an increase in demand for the materials from which they are made—steel, copper, aluminum, and so forth. Thus, a change in demand for a finished product such as a lawn mower affects the demand for the many intermediate products that go into that finished product.

These interrelationships or linkages among semi-finished products create problems for forecasters. Input-output analysis can be used to identify these linkages and thus can also help develop forecasts. In fact, the further a semi-finished product or commodity is from its final product and the more final products it serves, the more useful input-output analysis becomes.

Basic Premise of the Model

Input-output analysis is based on the simple concept that the sales (outputs) of one industry or industry segment are the purchases (inputs) of another industry or industry segment. It views the economy as an interrelated system in which the actions of one industry segment affect, both directly and indirectly, many other industry segments. Thus, a firm will improve its forecasts if it can (1) identify the other industry segments with which its product(s) are interrelated and (2) quantify these relationships.

The principle tools in the use of input-output analysis are three tables:

(1) Transactions table.

(2) Direct requirements table.

(3) Total requirements table.

The numerical data and ratios in these three tables are derived primarily from the input-output tables periodically issued by the U.S. Department of Commerce. They are found in the "Survey of Current Business," and are identified as national income and product tables.

Coverage in This Text

At present, input-output models are used primarily to analyze the general economy by major firms such as Union Carbide, Phillips Petroleum, National Steel, and General Motors, who can afford the time and expense associated with developing such models. A few universities such as Penn State and Michigan also have developed major econometric models based on input-output methodology.

The reason for including input-output analysis in this book is that a forecaster should at least have a basic understanding of the technique. Also, with increased access to micro-computers and their software packages, middle-sized firms may, in the future, find greater use for input-output models.

The remainder of this section contains a quick look at the input-output approach, showing how data from the three tables can be incorporated into a forecast. Again, the reader should be aware that the example used in this chapter is a very simplified version and not of the same complexity as the ratios and relationships used in actual input-output analysis.

Only three major industries (manufacturing, agriculture, and services) are used to demonstrate the model, whereas in an actual input-output model well over a hundred industry segments might be used. Table 6-5 indicates the purchase and sales activities occurring within each of the three industries. Table 6-6 unites all of the separate accounts into a transactions table.

Table 6-5
Industry Production Accounts

Industry A - Manufacturing

Purchases from Industry A	10	Sales to Industry A	10
Wages	80	Sales to Industry B	20
Depreciation	5	Sales to Industry C	30
Profits	15	Sales to Persons	50
	110		110

Industry B - Agriculture

Purchases from Industry A	20	Sales to Industry C	10
Wages	25	Sales to Persons	25
Depreciation	5	Sales to Government	25
Profits	10		
	60		60

Industry C - Service

Purchases from Industry C	10	Sales to Persons	60
Purchases from Industry A	30	Sales to Industry C	10
Purchases from Industry B	10		
Wages	15		
Profits	5		
	70		70

National Income and Product Account

Wages and Salaries	120	Personal Consumption	
Profits	30	Expenditures	135
Depreciation	10	Government	25
GNP	160		160

Table 6-6
Transactions Table

		(1) A	(2) B	(3) C	(4) Persons	(5) Govern-ment	(6) Total
Intermediate	1. A	10	20	30	50		110
	2. B			10	25	25	60
	3. C			10	60		70
Value Added	4. Wages	80	25	15			120
	5. Other	20	15	5	___	___	40
Total		110	60	70	135	25	

Transactions Table (Table 6-6)

These numbers are dollars moving among sectors of the economy. Each industry is represented by both a row and a column. The rows represent each industry's sales or "output." Industry A sells $20 worth to industry B and $30 to industry C. It also sells $10 to other firms within industry A.

The columns represent each industry's purchases or "input." Industry A paid $80 in wages, bought $10 of materials from other A industries, and purchased an additional $20 from other sources.

Direct Requirements Table (Table 6-7)

The values from the transactions table (Table 6-6) are converted into percentages. The columns (inputs) are summed and each individual value in the column is divided by the column's total to identify the percentage of input from each source. Thus, 9 percent of the total expenses of industry A are purchases from itself ($10 \div 110 = .09$). Forty-two percent of industry B's expenses are wages ($25 \div 60 = .42$).

Total Requirements Table (Table 6-8)

Now things become complicated. This table shows both the direct and indirect effects of final demand on each industry. Assume industry C had an increase in sales of $1,000. C would then require the following: 44 percent of input from industry A; 14 percent from B, and 14 percent from C. It would also need to pay wages and obtain materials from "other" sources.

But the overall impact on all accounts will be much greater than just the percentages found in Table 6-7. For example, C will have a direct increase in wages of $210 ($1,000 × 21 percent) and wages in A and B will also be affected. Because industry A has sales of $440 to C, it will need to pay $321 in wages (440 × 73 percent). Industry B will have additional wage expenses of $58 ($140 × 42

Table 6-7
Direct Requirements Table

	(1) A	(2) B	(3) C	(4) Persons	(5) Govern- ment
1. A	.09	.33	.44	.37	
2. B			.14	.19	1.00
3. C			.14	.44	
4. Wages	.73	.42	.21		
5. Other	.18	.25	.07		
Total	1.00	1.00	1.00	1.00	1.00

Table 6-8
Total Requirements Table

	(1) A	(2) B	(3) C
1. A	1.099	.363	.622
2. B		1.000	.163
3. C			1.163
Total	1.099	1.363	1.948

percent). Since C also buys 14 percent from firms in its own industry, this will add another $29 to labor payments. Thus the total impact on labor from the $1,000 increase in industry C is $618.

Wages in A	$321
Wages in B	58
Wages in Other C	29
Original C Wages	210
Total Impact on Wages:	$618

But there are also indirect effects. To produce $1,000 of product, industry C must produce $140 for its own use. Thus, its total output is really $1,140. To produce $1,140, industry C will require $159 of input from industry B ($1,140 × .14 = $159). To produce $159, B, in turn must obtain $52 of input from A ($159 × .33). This means, in order for industry C to produce $1,000 of new product, industry A must produce $553 of new product ($501 + 52). But since A also uses 9 percent of its own product it will produce a total of $602 of product because of that original $1,000 increase in demand within industry C.

This illustrates the direct and indirect relationships that occur in an economic system. These interrelationships are quantified in the total requirements table (Table 6-8). Thus, in order for industry C to produce $1,000 of output, it must really produce $1,163. When its interactions with the other industries are considered, a $1,000 increase in C's output will bring about a total output of $1,948 in the economy.

Conversely, an increase in output of $1,000 in industry A will only result in a total output of $1,099, since A does not buy from the other industries.

Use of Input-Output Model

This simplified example illustrates why input-output analysis can be used in forecasting sales. If a multi-industry model were developed, each industry could see the impact on its sales from extensive changes in other industries or industry segments.

The impact of a bad year in the auto industry can be traced through the other industries it affects such as steel, glass, aluminum, and coal.

At present, input-output has its widest usage among federal and state government agencies. For example, there is a number of state models showing the demand for water associated with industrial and population growth. Theimpact of tax cuts or increases also can be traced via input-output models.

A key drawback to the use of input-output models is that it is difficult to obtain accurate, up-to-date coefficients. Many of the coefficients used in government tables are from 1967 and may no longer be appropriate.

Again, it is emphasized, this is a quick look at input-output analysis and is intended to provide the reader with just a basic understanding of the process. A great deal more background would be needed before the reader could effectively use this technique as a sales forecasting tool.

NOTES

1. Degrees of freedom identify the number of data points used for different tests (t test, F test, Chi-square test). The formulae associated with these tests usually identify the number of degrees of freedom to use $(n-K)$.
2. Levels of significance indicate the probability of making an error by rejecting a hypothesis that actually is a true hypothesis. The two levels generally used to test sample results are .05 and .01. A .05 level of significance means there is only a 5 percent (or less) chance of making such an error in this situation.

QUESTIONS AND EXERCISES

1. (a) Do causal models prove "cause and effect" between variables?
   (b) What is the difference between these two terms: *associated with* and *caused by*?
2. Distinguish between regression and correlation.
3. What does a negative slope in a regression line indicate? Give an example of such a relationship.
4. Why does the existence of patterns in residuals indicate that there are problems in the regression model?
5. Why is it necessary to test the hypothesis that $b = 0$?
6. The Buzz Company manufactures and sells electric table saws for the home craftsman. In the past, Buzz has had problems developing forecasts for their sales districts. John Heinz, their new sales manager, feels a simple regression model, using number of lumber yards in a district as the independent variable, would be an effective forecasting tool.

   Below is information on the company's unit sales in ten of their sales districts, along with the number of lumber yards in each district. Use this information to answer the following questions.
   (a) Is the b value significant?
   (b) What is the 95 percent confidence interval for the$b$ value?

(c) What unit sales would be expected in a district with 23 lumber yards?

(d) What is the 95 percent confidence interval for the district with 23 lumber yards?

(e) What is the r^2 value? Is it significant?

(f) The Durbin-Watson value for this data is 2.2. What does this imply about the residuals? About the value of the model?

(g) Does the number of lumber yards in a district directly affect (or cause) sales of the electric saw?

District	Saw Sales	Lumber Yards
1	15	9
2	16	13
3	17	14
4	18	15
5	20	16
6	20	16
7	22	17
8	24	19
9	23	20
10	25	21

7. Why are input-output models viewed as causal models?

8. Describe how an input-output table could be used to forecast future water demands in your state.

7

Multiple Regression and Correlations

INTRODUCTION

In the preceding chapter, simple regression is used to determine the association between new housing starts and the sales of bathroom fixtures. The resulting r^2 of .957 indicates that most of the variation in sales of bathroom fixtures is related to changes in new housing starts.

It is unusual for a single independent variable to play such an important role in estimating the value of a dependent variable. Usually the r^2 value between two variables is less than .8, necessitating a search for additional independent variables that can improve the forecasting strength of the regression model.

When more than one independent variable is included in the regression equation, a multiple regression model is needed. Although the basic concepts of simple regression also apply to multiple regression, the computations to derive the regression coefficients are much more cumbersome. Thus, a computer is needed to perform multiple regression.

Selection of Independent Variables

The starting point in the use of a multiple regression model is identifying those variables that management believes are associated with the sales of the product or services to be forecasted (the dependent variable). What other variable(s) might affect the sales of bathroom fixtures? Some likely choices are new office construction, average size of families, average size of new homes, and disposable personal income.

Once the variables that might affect sales (the dependent variable) are identified, each must be evaluated to determine its potential value as a predictor.

Key Questions to Ask

When evaluating possible predictor variables, five key questions should be asked:

Does adequate past data exist on the variable? There must be enough data on the proposed variable to enable the true nature of its association with the dependent variable to emerge. In fact, the amount of data needed in the model is related to the total number of variables in the equation. A suggested ratio is that there should be at least five periods of data for each independent variable. Thus, if the final equation has four independent variables, there should be at least 20 periods of data for each variable.

Does data exist in the appropriate time frame? Not only must sufficient past data be available, it must be available in the desired time frame. You may be developing a regression model using quarterly data, but if the only data that exists on a possible independent variable is annual data, the variable must be rejected. The time frame factor is a stumbling block for many forecasting models using monthly data.

Are future projections available on the independent variable? Since the independent variable is to be used to forecast future sales, accurate estimates of future values of that predictor must exist. If you intend to use new housing starts to predict sales of bathroom fixtures of 1987, accurate estimates of new housing starts must exist for that year.

Is the relationship between the two variables likely to continue? The value of each regression coefficient (b value) is a measure of the amount of change in the dependent variable that occurs with each one unit of change in the independent variable to which it relates. If that b value is to be an effective predictor, the relationship between both variables should be fairly consistent over time. For years, the demand for steel was closely associated with the number of new automobiles produced. In recent years, however, because more plastic and other non-steel products are used in cars, the relationship between these two variables is changing.

Government actions can also alter such relationships. The federal and state tax credits given for solar installations have led to a change in demand for natural gas in Colorado. Thus, the relationship between new housing starts (the predictor) and demand for natural gas has dramatically changed in that state.

Is the proposed predictor linearly related to the dependent variable? There must be a linear association between each independent variable and the dependent variable. Or, if such a relationship does not initially exist, can the data be adjusted (transformed) so that linearity can be created?

Computer Analysis

Positive answers to those five questions are required before bringing any variable into the regression model. If a variable passes these five hurdles, it is subjected to additional hurdles within the computer program before it can be included in the final regression equation.

Computer analysis provides information about the strength of the relationship between different independent variables (multi-collinearity). It can determine whether an unusual pattern exists among the residuals, suggesting that all of the key independent variables have not been included in the equation, that is, the model has been mis-specified. It can also identify which of the independent variables are most closely related to the dependent variable. These and other tests are covered later in this chapter.

Developing the Regression Model

In simple linear regression, the model used is:

$$Y = a + b(X)$$

The basic model for multiple regression is an expanded version of the above model, since it incorporates additional independent variables.

The formula for multiple regression is:

$$Y = a + b_1X_1 + b_2X_2 + \ldots b_nX_n$$

The number of independent variables used in each model depends on how many are needed to adequately estimate the Y value. Some equations may include more than 50 independent variables. However, in most forecasting situations involving a single product, the regression equation usually has fewer than ten predictor variables.

In simple regression, the resulting a and b values enable a line to be drawn (through the plotted data points) that minimize the sum of the squared deviations. In multiple regression, the number of axes will equal the total number of variables. Thus, instead of fitting a single line to all of those points, a multidimensional plane is needed.

Meaning of a and b Values

The a value in the multiple regression equation is still the value of Y (dependent variable) when all of the X values (independent variables) have a value of 0. Each b value (regression coefficients) measures the average change in Y for every one unit of change in that specific independent variable when the other independent variables are held constant.

Assume a regression model has the following parameters (constant and coefficients):

$$Y_c = 10.9 + .910(X_1) + .07(X_2) + 1.48(X_3)$$
Y = Sales of bathroom fixtures
X_1 = New housing starts (000s of units)
X_2 = Consumer price index
X_3 = Construction of new office space (millions of square feet)

The above model implies that bathroom fixture sales would be $10.9 million when all of the independent variables (X_1, X_2 and X_3) are zero. Also, for every one unit of change in X_1 (1,000 new housing starts), Y would change $910,000, assuming the values of X_2 and X_3 are held constant. This measures the net effect of X_1 and excludes the influence of the other two variables. The same interpretation applies to X_2 and X_3.

Selection of Computer Model

Most major statistical software packages include a multiple regression program. While the basic computations used to determine the regression coefficients are similar among these packages, each package provides a different set of "extras." Some provide a correlation matrix of all the variables, others provide an analysis of the residuals (autocorrelation tests), still others provide Durbin-Watson tests for the residuals.

Another major difference between computer packages is the general format used to evaluate each of the variables. One of three basic procedures is usually followed: stepwise regression, backward elimination, or total regression.

Stepwise Regression

In this package, one independent variable at a time is introduced into the equation. Each variable is brought into the model on the basis of how much of the variance in the dependent variable it explains. The variable that explains the greatest amount of variance (that is, has the highest r^2 value) is brought in first. The variable that explains the largest amount of the remaining unexplained variance is brought in second. This process continues until either all of the variables are included or those remaining outside the model do not meet some previously established minimum standards.

Backward Elimination

In this program, all independent variables are included at the outset, and then each variable is eliminated, one at a time, to determine the impact of its selection on the R^2 value.[1] This enables the forecaster to determine the value or contribution of each variable.

Total Regression Models

This program compares every possible regression equation that can be developed from the independent variables. The basis of this comparison is often the R^2 value but it could also be F values or some other criteria. While this procedure enables the forecaster to examine and compare all possible regression equations, it is an expensive and time-consuming approach.

Application of Multiple Regression–Stepwise Regression Model

The best way to describe the various aspects of multiple regression is to use the output from an actual regression model. For this example, the sales of a special diet drink are the dependent variable. Five independent variables affecting the sales of this product are tested in the model.

Y = Sales of the diet drink (hundreds of cases)
X_1 = Personal disposable income in the sales region
X_2 = Wholesale price per can
X_3 = Special promotional expenditures (hundreds of dollars)
X_4 = Advertising expenditures (hundreds of dollars)
X_5 = Supermarket sales of all diet-related foods (millions of dollars)

Quarterly data of the past eight years are used to compute the values of a and b. Thus, a total of 32 periods of data provide the information base. Since there is a total of five independent variables, this limited amount of data violates the "rule of thumb" of those statisticians who believe there should be at least ten periods of data for each independent variable, that is, five variables should have 50 periods of data. But, as stated earlier, there are also some statisticians who feel that five periods per variable are adequate, and our model satisfies that requirement.

Data for each of the five independent variables are contained in Table 7-1. These data were incorporated into a software package called SPSS (Statistical Package for the Social Sciences), which features a stepwise regression model. The results obtained from that model are used throughout the remainder of this chapter to illustrate various aspects of multiple regression.

As stated earlier, since the computations for determining b values can be quite complex and time consuming, these computations should usually be performed by a computer. The forecaster, or anyone else using multiple regression, does not really have to understand how the b values are derived. However, they should understand what the b values mean, along with the other data provided in most computer printouts. The remainder of this chapter covers some of the more important aspects of such printouts, using the data base found in Table 7-1.

Suggestion to Readers

Some readers of this book may only be seeking a broad understanding of multiple correlation and are not interested in some of the more esoteric material presented in computer printouts. Those readers can skip the next few pages and start reading the section titled "Adjustments to Regression Model."

Correlation Matrix—Multicollinearity

One of the first items provided by a stepwise regression model is the correlation matrix. This matrix (Table 7-2) identifies the correlation coefficient (r values) between all the variables in the model. Column 1 shows the degree of correlation between each independent variable and the dependent variable—unit sales of the diet drink. Thus, personal disposable income has a correlation coefficient (r value) of .746 with the diet drink. The variable with the next highest correlation with sales of the diet drink is X_5—general sales of diet foods (r = .696).

Table 7-1
Multiple Regression Model Using Quarterly Sales of Diet Drink as Dependent Variable

Period	Y Diet Drink Sales	X1 PD1	X2 Wholesale Price Per Unit	X3 Special Promotion $	X4 AD $	X5 Sales of All Diet Foods
1	2314	336	.59	30	40	213
2	2055	383	.60	45	32	201
3	2062	285	.63	28	12	176
4	2421	277	.62	76	68	175
5	2871	456	.65	144	52	253
6	2547	355	.65	113	77	208
7	2692	364	.64	128	96	195
8	2443	320	.66	10	48	154
9	2016	311	.67	25	27	181
10	2471	362	.67	117	73	220
11	2656	408	.67	120	62	235
12	2570	433	.68	122	25	258
13	2198	359	.69	71	74	196
14	2575	476	.71	4	63	279
15	2576	415	.69	47	29	207
16	2494	420	.70	8	91	213
17	2964	536	.73	127	74	294
18	2352	432	.73	50	16	245
19	2683	436	.73	100	43	276
20	2315	415	.75	40	41	211
21	2856	462	.73	68	92	283
22	2548	429	.74	88	83	218
23	3062	517	.74	27	75	307
24	2394	328	.77	59	87	211
25	2418	418	.78	142	74	270
26	2644	515	.77	126	21	328
27	2323	412	.78	30	27	258
28	2658	455	.78	18	95	233
29	3090	554	.81	42	92	324
30	2401	441	.80	22	50	267
31	2756	417	.81	148	83	257
32	2636	461	.83	17	91	265

Table 7-2
Correlation Matrix for Diet Drink Sales and Five Other Variables

		(1) Y	(2) X_1	(3) X_2	(4) X_3	(5) X_4	(6) X_5
Diet Drink Sales	Y	1.000					
Pers. Disp. Income	X_1	.746	1.000				
Wholesale Price	X_2	.396	.610	1.000			
Spec. Promotions	X_3	.344	.102	-.055	1.000		
Advertising	X_4	.529	.211	.312	.121	1.000	
Diet Food Sales	X_5	.696	.901	.635	.209	.137	1.000

In addition to showing the correlation among the dependent variable and the independent variables, the correlation matrix also identifies the degree of correlation among the independent variables. If two or more variables are highly correlated, then multi-collinearity exists (Columns 2 through 6 of the matrix, Table 7-2). For example, the correlation between wholesale price (X_2) and personal disposable income (X_1) is .610 (Column 2). When a high degree of correlation is found between two independent variables, multi-collinearity exists. (The negative values of Table 7-2 indicate negative or reverse relationships, that is, wholesale price and special promotions are related but in opposite directions.)

Multi-collinearity is quite common in regression models used for business forecasting since many of the independent variables have common links. (Education and income data of households, for example, are generally highly correlated.) When independent variables are highly correlated, they tend to explain the same variance in the dependent variable, making it very difficult to isolate the specific impact of each variable.

Table 7-2 discloses a high correlation between variables X_1 and X_5 $(r = .901)$. One of these two variables should be dropped because of this high multi-collinearity. The variable retained is usually the one with the highest correlation with the independent variable. In this case, variable X_1 has an r of .746 with the dependent variable, and variable X_5 has an r of .696. Thus, variable X_1 is retained.

Rule of Thumb: When is the multi-collinearity between two independent variables too high? Statisticians differ as to what is excessive multi-collinearity. Some feel any r greater than .8 is too high. Others are more strict and say an r of .6 or higher is too high. In this text, the cutoff point used for multicollinearity is: $r > .8$. In reality, any r greater than .5 indicates that a significant overlap is likely to occur between the variables' explanation of the variance.

Bringing in the First Independent Variable

Stepwise regression brings one independent variable at a time into the regression equation. Each variable is brought in on the basis of how much of the variance in the dependent variable it explains. The first variable entered into the model is X_1 (personal disposable income) since it has an r of .746 with diet drink sales (Column 1, Table 7-2).

The type of information provided by the computer on this first variable is found in Table 7-3. The following paragraphs explain each of these factors.

Multiple R

This is the correlation coefficient (r) between the dependent variable (Y) and the independent variable on which it is reporting; X_1 in the example shown in Table 7-3. In this first step, the multiple R is really a simple r value between sales of the diet drink and personal disposable income (.746). As additional variables are brought into the equation in later steps, this value becomes a "true" multiple R.

Table 7-3
Information Provided by Computer for Step One of Stepwise Regression Program

Variable Entered on <u>Step Number 1</u> X_1 PDI

Multiple R	.746
R Square	.557
Adjusted R SQ	.542
Standard Error	180.933

Analysis of Variance	DF*	Sum of Squares	Mean Square
Regression	1	1233554.727	1233554.727
Residual	30	982100.148	32736.672
Coefficient of Variability	7.1 Pct		

F	Significance
37.68	.000

*Degrees of freedom.

R Square

This is the coefficient of determination or the amount of the variance in the dependent variable explained by the independent variable in the equation at the time of the report. Thus, quarterly changes in personal disposable income explain .557 of the quarterly changes in the sales of the diet drink.

Adjusted R Square

This is an adjustment in the R square value based on the appropriate degrees of freedom.

Standard Error

This measures the accuracy of forecasts coming from the model at this particular step. The value (180.933) is the square root of the residual (982,100) divided by the degrees of freedom.

$$\sqrt{\frac{\text{Residual}}{\text{Degrees of Freedom}}} = \sqrt{\frac{982,100.148}{32 - 2}} = 180.933$$

The residual is the sum of the squared errors, or the sum of the dispersion of the actual Y values around the regression line. This is the standard error of the forecasted Y value, based on this one independent variable. This means, we are 95 percent confident that the actual sales of the diet drink lie within a range of plus or minus 354,560 cases (1.96 times 180.9) of the forecasted Y value. In some computer programs this value is labeled "standard deviation" or "standard error of estimate."

Sum of Squares Regression

This is the sum of the squared differences between the mean of the sum of all actual Y values $(\bar{Y})$ and each of the Y values predicted from the equation (Y_c).

$$\Sigma(\bar{Y} - Y_c)^2 = 1{,}233{,}554.7$$

Sum of Squares Residual

This is the difference between each actual Y and its forecast value when these differences are summed and squared. In reality, it is the sum of squares of the errors.

$$\Sigma(Y_c - Y)^2 = 982{,}100.148$$

Coefficient of Variability

This information is found in only a limited number of computer programs. It is determined by dividing the standard error of the forecast equation by the mean of the dependent variable.

$$\frac{180.933}{2{,}536.312} = 7.1 \text{ percent}$$

Since this value indicates the relative dispersion of the data series, the smaller the coefficient of variability, the better the fit between the regression model and the actual Y values. A coefficient of variability of less than 10 percent is considered to be a good fit.

Mean Square

The amount of variance explained by the regression line or, if more than one independent variable is involved, the amount explained by the regression plane. It is determined by dividing the sum of squares regression by the appropriate degrees of freedom.

$$\text{Mean Squares} = \frac{\text{Sum of Squares}}{\text{Degrees of Freedom}} = \frac{1{,}233{,}544.727}{1}$$

Mean Square (MS) Residual

The sum of squares of the residual divided by the appropriate degrees of freedom.

$$\text{MS Residual} = \frac{\text{Sum of Squares Residual}}{\text{Degrees of Freedom}} = \frac{982{,}100.148}{30} = 32{,}736.671$$

F Value

This is the ratio between the variance that is explained by the regression model and the variance that is unexplained. This determines the significance of the regression equation up to this point in the analysis. This computed F is then compared to a tabular F to determine whether it is significant.

$$F \text{ Value} = \frac{\text{Mean Square of Regression}}{\text{Mean Square of Residual}} = \frac{1,233,554.727}{32,736.671} = 37.68$$

The computer also provides information on the level of significance of this F value, that is, what the probability is of getting an F value of this size if the regression equation is not significant. In our example, the level of significance is .000, which means there is an infinitely small likelihood of getting an F value of this size (37.68) by chance. Thus, this is a significant equation. Since an .05 level of significance is typically used to evaluate the computed F, any significance value of .05 or greater suggests the regression equation is not effectively explaining the variation in the values of the dependent variable.

Additional Information in Printout

In addition to the basic information on the entire model found in Table 7-3, the computer printout also provides specific information about each variable at each step of the regression model. This information is found in Table 7-4.

Variables' Coefficient

This is the value of each variable in the equation at a given step; X_1 in the example shown in Table 7-4. In this case, the coefficient of X_1, personal disposable income, is 2.866 and the value of the constant (a) is 1,355.310. So at

Table 7-4
Information Provided by Computer for Step Two of Stepwise Regression Program

Variables in Equation				
Variable	B	Standard Error	F Significance	Beta
X_1	2.866	.457	39.33 .000	.746
Constant	1355.310	195.033	48.29 .000	

Variables Not in Equation				
Variable	Partial	Tolerance	F	Significance
X_2	-.112	.627	.370	.548
X_3	.404	.990	5.664	.024
X_4	.571	.955	14.081	.001
X_5	.082	.189	.197	.661

this juncture of the analysis, if a regression formula is used, it would be as follows:

$$Y = a + b(X)$$
$$Y = 1,355.310 + 2.866(X)$$

Standard Error B

This is the same concept (SE_b) discussed in Chapter 6. Because only 32 periods of data are being used to determine the actual value of X_1, allowances are made for sampling error. This value (.457) is the size of one sampling error for the B value of 2.866.

F Value and Significance of F

This measures the overall significance of the model at this point. Since only one independent variable has been included at this point, this F value is identical to the F value of the entire equation. However, as each additional independent variable is added, the F value represents the variance explained by adding that particular variable to the model.

The accompanying significance value (.000) determines whether this variable makes a significant contribution to explaining the remaining variance.

The F value for each variable is the square of the value obtained when a variable's B value is divided by its standard error:

$$F = \left(\frac{B}{SE_B}\right)^2 = \left(\frac{2.866}{.457}\right)^2 = 39.33$$

Beta Values

Regression coefficients (B_1, B_2, and so on) measure the net impact of each variable on the dependent variable. (Since many computer packages use upper case B values to identify the coefficients in multiple regression equations, the uppercase B will be used in the remainder of this chapter.) However, since these independent variables are often in different units (one variable may be in dollars, another in thousands of households), their B values can't be compared to determine the relative importance of each independent variable. Before a comparison can be made between these coefficients, they must be placed in similar formats, that is, normalized.

The beta value provides a normalized value of each coefficient. It is derived by multiplying the B value of each variable by the ratio of its standard deviation and the standard deviation of the dependent variable:

$$\text{Beta value for } X_1 = B\left(\frac{\text{Standard Deviation of } X_1}{\text{Standard Deviation of } Y}\right) = 2.866\left(\frac{69.61}{267.344}\right)$$

$$\text{Beta value for } X_1 = .746$$

Therefore, for each one unit increase in the standard deviation of X_1, the dependent variable increases .746 standard deviations. Beta values now enable a comparison to be made of the relative impact each independent variable has on the dependent variable. (The above standard deviation values are obtained from part of the printout that is not discussed in this section.)

Partials (Table 7-4)

Partial correlation values identify the potential contribution each of the remaining variables can make to the regression equation. Of the remaining four variables, X_4 will contribute most to reducing the unexplained variance since it has the largest partial correlation (.571). Thus, it is the next variable brought into the equation.

The remaining unexplained variance at this point is .443 $(1 - R^2$, or $1 - .557)$. How much will X_4 improve the R^2? A variable's contribution to the R^2 value is determined by multiplying the square of the variable's partial correlation by the unexplained variance.

Contribution of X_4 = Unexplained variance times the square of the partial correlation of X_4
$$= .443 \times .571^2$$
$$= .144$$

Therefore,
New R^2 = Original R^2 + Contribution of new variable
New $R^2 = .557 + .144$
New $R^2 = .701$

Tolerance Values

This measures the multi-collinearity of each variable outside the equation with variables already in the equation. Variable X_4 has a tolerance of .955. This means that over 95 percent of the variance in X_4 is not explained by the independent variable(s) already in the regression equation. The lower the tolerance value of any variable, the higher its correlation with variables in the equation. Thus, X_5, with a tolerance of .189, is highly correlated with X_1, a condition previously indicated in the correlation matrix.

F Values and Their Significance

This F value describes the contribution to the unexplained variance that each independent variable would make at this time. In the case of X_4, it will make a significant contribution, whereas the contribution of either X_2 or X_5 will be minimal.

Development of Entire Equation

Tables 7-3 and 7-4 depict the data the computer provides in the first step of stepwise regression. The program performs additional steps until all variables are

Table 7-5
Final Values of Five Independent Variables in Diet Drink Example

	Value	Standard Error	F Value (Significance)	Cumulative R^2	F Value Model
Constant	1629.91	293.62	-	-	-
X_1	2.140	.852	37.68 (.000)	.557	37.68 .000
X_4	4.294	1.017	14.08 (.001)	.701	34.09 .000
X_3	.985	.574	6.127 (.020)	.755	28.79 .000
X_2	-900.84	534.07	2.021 (.167)	.772	22.89 .000
X_5	1.438	1.438	1.001 (.326)	.781	18.51 .000

brought in, or until no additional variables can be brought in because they do not meet certain minimum standards. For example, if the forecaster set a minimum of 2.5 as the required ''F to enter,'' any variable with an F of less than 2.5 is not brought into the model.

Table 7-5 contains the final results for each of the independent variables being tested. These results indicate that variables X_2 and X_5 contribute little to the equation, since both have very low F values and their combined impact on the R^2 value was less than .026.

Although the model with all five variables has a significant F (18.51), it would be wise for the forecaster to exclude X_2 and X_5 since they contribute so little to the forecast. Thus, the final regression model is:

$$Y_c = a + B_1(X_1) + B_3(X_3) + B_4(X_4)$$

The actual coefficients used are those developed prior to the inclusion of X_2 or X_5. These values are determined in Step Three of the stepwise regression. Note that the coefficient values used in the final regression equation are not taken from Table 7-5 since they are based on the inclusion in the equation of all five variables. The coefficient values used are those computed at the end of Step Three, at which point only the values of X_1, X_4, and X_3 were in the equation.

The values of each variable at the end of Step Three are:

Constant $= 1,204.52$
B coefficient for $X_1 = 2.478$

B coefficient for X_4 = 3.673
B coefficient for X_3 = 1.328
Standard error = 139.180

Thus, the regression equation is:

$$Y_c = 1,204.52 + 2.478(X_1) + 1.328(X_3) + 3.673(X_4).$$

Assume the forecasted values for each of these variables are as follows for the first quarter of 1985.

X_1 = Disposable personal income = 482
X_3 = Special promotional expenditures = 101
X_4 = Advertising dollar = 95
Y_c = 1,204.52 + 2.478(482) + 1.328(101) + 3.673(95)
Y_c = 1,204.52 + 1,194.39 + 134.13 + 348.94
Y_c = 2,881.980

Sales of the diet drink in the first quarter of 1985 should be approximately 2,881,980 cases. The 95 percent confidence interval is:

$Y_c \pm$ 1.96 (SE_y)
2,881,980 ± 1.96 (139,180) or
2,609,000 to 3,155,000 cases.

This standard error value applicable to Y is the standard deviation value of the model at Step Three.

Analysis of Residuals

Another way to test the regression model is to analyze residuals. As you recall, a residual (or error) is the difference between the actual sales (Y), and the sales that were forecast using the regression equation (Y_c). If the residuals fall into a peculiar pattern, this suggests that some factor not included in the equation is influencing sales and may bias the results. (See discussion in Chapter 6.)

Most multiple regression models provide a computer printout of the actual residual values, as well as a graph of these values. An analysis of that information usually discloses whether problems exist.

In the example of the diet drink, when the residuals are plotted on a graph, they fall into a random pattern and the highest percentage of error for any one residual was 13 percent. (Residual divided by Y value equals percent of error.) The calculated Durbin-Watson score was 2.35, well within the range of values (1.5 to 2.5) that indicate the residuals are randomly dispersed.

ADJUSTMENTS TO REGRESSION MODEL

Quite often, the forecasting value of a regression model can be enhanced by making adjustments in the independent variables. In this section, three types of adjustments are described: lead-lag situations, dummy variables, and transformations.

LEAD-LAG SITUATIONS

The sales of the dependent variable may be associated with the occurrence of another event but on a delayed basis. In other words, the occurrence of a second event precedes the sales of a product. This is a very desirable situation for forecasters since it means actual (rather than forecast) data of the independent variable can be used in the regression model.

In an earlier example, sales of bathroom fixtures are closely related to the number of new housing starts. But the real demand for bathroom fixtures does not occur until sometime after the permits for new houses have been obtained. Thus, when forecasting sales of bathroom fixtures, recent housing starts can be used.

To make use of lead-lag situations, the data should be in monthly or quarterly time periods since the lead-lag impact is usually hidden in annual data. Therefore, the annual data contained in Table 6-1 is not useful for the purpose of developing a lead-lag model.

Table 7-6 contains monthly data of the regional sales of bathroom fixtures and new housing starts. Common sense suggests that new housing starts will precede or lead the sales of bathroom fixtures. But what is the length of this lead?

There are two ways to identify the nature of the lead-lag situation. The simplest method is to graph the value of both variables over a number of time periods and then line up their peaks and troughs. The amount of adjustment needed to match the profiles depicted on the graph by both sets of data indicates the length of time the independent variable leads the dependent variable. A second method of identifying the lead-lag relationship is to perform regression analysis using the independent variable at varying time periods. The highest r value identifies the appropriate lead-lag time period.

In performing such analysis, the dependent variable is usually kept in its actual time period, and the independent variable is moved forward n periods. Actually, the sales of the dependent variable lag behind changes in the independent variable but the time adjustments are generally built into the independent variable. In Table 7-6, the data on new housing starts is altered so that in Column 3, new housing starts lead fixture sales by one period and in Column 4 they lead by two periods.

Application of Lead-Lag Process

Regression analysis is performed on the information in Table 7-5, and r^2 values determined of each set of lagged housing starts.

Table 7-6
Using Lead-Lag Variable to Improve Regression Model (1981 sales)

	(1) Y Fixture Sales	(2) X_t Housing Starts	(3) X_{t+1}	(4) X_{t+2}
January	3.198	4.472	3.795	3.142
February	3.608	5.512	4.472	3.795
March	4.264	8.008	5.512	4.472
April	6.150	9.568	8.008	5.512
May	7.544	14.248	9.568	8.008
June	11.316	16.432	14.248	9.568
July	12.792	17.368	16.432	14.248
August	13.448	10.192	17.368	16.432
September	7.872	6.552	10.192	17.368
October	5.248	4.784	6.552	10.192
November	3.772	3.902	4.784	6.552
December	2.788	2.962	3.902	4.784
	$82 million	104,000 units		

r^2 value of X_t = .653
r^2 value of X_{t+1} = .960
r^2 value of X_{t+2} = .632

Thus, there seems to be a very close association with sales of bathroom fixture sales and the number of new housing starts in the preceding month, that is, April housing starts have a strong impact on May bathroom fixture sales. So the independent variable used in the equation is X_{t+1}. In this case, the regression equation is greatly strengthened by adjusting the time period of the independent variable.

In Table 7-6, the actual data of the independent variable are manually moved forward one and two periods. If there are a number of variables involved or a large number of time periods this can be quite time consuming. There are some computer programs that automatically lead or lag certain variables and incorporate them into the equation. One such program is Time Series Research (TSP), a program intended primarily for econometric analysis of time series data.

Don't Include Multiple Lead-Lag Periods for Same Variable

In the previous example, all three values of X (X_t, X_{t+1}, X_{t+2}) have respectable r^2 values. Some forecasters would include all three in a multiple regression equation. This is a questionable action since inclusion of the same independent variable at different time periods creates multi-collinearity. (In reality, this is autocorrelation rather than multi-collinearity since it is the correlation of a variable with itself at different time periods.) Because of this condition, it is not recommended that multiple time periods for the same variable be used in the regression equation even though it results in a high R^2.

DUMMY VARIABLES

A second way a regression model might be improved is through the use of dummy variables. A dummy variable is a substitute variable used in a regression equation to account for unusual events affecting the dependent variable. For example, an actual or threatened strike disrupts the normal sales pattern. Prior to the strike, demand may increase significantly as customers stock up on the product, whereas during the strike sales are non-existent. Conversely, competitors of the firm being struck also undergo temporary changes in demand, since their sales increase during the period the other firm is shut down.

When multiple regression is involved, these unusual events distort the "plane of best fit," weakening the models' forecasting efficiency. This impact is minimized with dummy variables.

A dummy variable is an independent variable. Values (usually 1 or 0) are subjectively assigned to the affected periods and are included in the regression equation.

Single Period Situation

If there is only one unusual period that must be acknowledged, a dummy variable of 1 is assigned to that period, with all other periods assigned a value of 0.

Multiple Period Situation

If the unusual event occurred over more than one period (strike, morale problems in company, delivery disruptions) then a 1 is assigned to each "unusual" period and a 0 assigned to each normal period.

The disruptions don't have to be one-time-only events; they can also be of a recurring nature. For example, a producer that occasionally offers middlemen "one case free for every three purchased," disrupts the normal sales pattern with such promotions. Sales increase significantly during these special promotional periods and will not be accounted for in the normal regression equation. Or an airline might offer specials in which "children under 10 fly free" for limited periods during a year and this affects the number of passengers. Dummy variables are the most effective way of dealing with such "special" events.

Assigning Values to Dummy Variables

Although the most frequent values assigned are 1 and 0, in some circumstances a variety of numbers are used. For example, a major retailer expanding its operations by continually purchasing other retail outlets, might use increasing values of the dummy variable to make allowances for the additional stores. In 1981, it purchased five stores, so the dummy variable introduced at that time might be .5 and later, when it purchased an additional eight stores, the dummy variable would be changed to 1, to acknowledge the larger number of stores.

Or values such as −1 could be used during a strike period, with a +1 used to designate the brief growth in sales prior to the strike. Such a pattern might look like this:

		Dummy Variable
April	Normal Period	0
May	Normal Period	0
June	Pre-strike Growth	+1
July	Strike Period	−1
August	Strike Period	−1
September	Normal Period	0
October	Normal Period	0

How Dummy Variables Work

The dummy variable is treated like any other independent variable. The new variable is created, and a value of the dummy variable is assigned to each period. The B coefficient for this new variable is then determined and added to the regression equation.

Assume X_4 = dummy variable and
$B_4 = .3210$
$Y = a + B_1X_1 + B_2X_2 + B_3X_3 + B_4X_4$

In those periods when the dummy variable has a value other than 0, this value is multiplied by .3210 and becomes part of the forecast. In those periods when it has no influence (0), it is not a factor in the forecast.

Remember, the advantage of using dummy variables is that they enable the other independent variables to account more accurately for the normal sales variances during unusual periods.

Diet Drink Example

The manufacturer of the diet drink uses a variety of media to advertise the product. The most effective media vehicle is *Reader's Digest;* because of its high cost, however, the company can afford to advertise in it only once or twice a year. To compensate for the increase in sales related to those ads, a dummy variable is introduced. The value of 1 is assigned to each month the ad is run in *Reader's Digest*, as well as to the month immediately following. A value of 0 is used for every other time period. The addition of this new variable (X_6) to the regression equation increases the R^2 from .755 to .830, a significant improvement.

TRANSFORMATION OF DATA

In some situations, the relationship between variables can be depicted more accurately if the data are altered or transformed. In some cases, such changes may be necessary because only limited data are available.

Examples

When an independent variable represents sales in current dollars and the dependent variable is in unit sales, it is often necessary to transform dollar sales into constant dollar values to compensate for inflation.

$$\text{Constant dollar} = \frac{\text{Current dollar value}}{\text{Price deflator}}$$

If too many independent variables are involved compared to the periods of data available, it could have a negative effect on the F value, or significance of the equation. The model can be enhanced by combining some of the independent variables, for example, combine health food sales of drug stores, supermarkets, and department stores into one category: "mass market sales of health foods."

Conversely, it may be necessary in some cases to disaggregate data to make the regression model more effective, for example, separate "total advertising expenditures" into TV and radio advertising, newspaper advertising, and magazine advertising.

Ratios can also be used to cut down on the number of independent variables. For example, instead of using both "number of households" and "advertising expenditures" for each territory, these two variables are combined into "ad dollar per household." A note of caution: If one variable is meaningful and the other is not, combining them will weaken the contribution of the meaningful variable.

In some cases, the model may provide a better fit if the data is transformed into logs. Or logs might be used to change non-linear data into linear data. A discussion of this action is beyond the scope of this text but it is a transformation that should be pursued if the forecaster is having difficulty developing a significant relationship in the regression equation.

OVERVIEW OF MULTIPLE REGRESSION

The best way to tie together the information provided in this chapter is to identify the key activities associated with using a multiple regression model and the sequence in which each should be performed. A brief review of each step follows:

(1) Identify possible predictor variables. Determine which are likely to be associated with changes in the dependent variable.

(2) Evaluate each variable on the basis of its potential contribution to the forecast using the following criteria:

    (a)   Available past data are adequate.

    (b)   Past data are in an appropriate time frame.

    (c)   Projections of its values are available.

    (d)   The variable's relationship to the dependent variable is likely to continue.

    (e)   The variable is linearly related to the dependent variable.

(3) Gather data on the variables to be included in the initial regression model. Seek out data and place it in the appropriate time frame (that is, if quarterly data is to be used, convert monthly data to quarterly format). You should also be reasonably confident the data available on each variable is accurate.

(4) Enter the data into the appropriate computer program. You may have to choose between a variety of general models: stepwise regression, backward elimination, or total regression.

(5) Evaluate each variable using the data provided in the computer printout.

    (a)   Review the correlation matrix to identify those predictors that are highly correlated with other predictors (multi-collinearity).

    (b)   Check the F value of each predictor to make sure it is significant at .05 or less.

    (c)   Check the F value of the entire equation to determine whether it indicates that the R^2 is significant.

    (d)   Review data on the residuals to determine whether they follow a random pattern and whether the Durbin-Watson value is acceptable.

    (e)   Drop those variables that don't make significant contributions to the equation.

(6) Determine whether additional adjustments can be made to enhance the equation, such as:

    (a)   Addition of dummy variables.

    (b)   Changing time periods of predictors that actually lead the dependent variable.

    (c)   Transformation of some data.

(7)Take the remaining coefficients (B values) and place them in the equation, add predictor values of the desired forecast period, and make the forecast.

Some Cautions about Regression Models

The availability of computers and a better understanding of multiple regression models have been instrumental in bringing about a greater use of this process or forecasting tool. The models, however, have some shortcomings.

The forecasts provided by the model are useful only if the estimated values of the predictors are reasonably accurate.

Multiple regression models are fairly expensive to use since they often require a great deal of data gathering as well as computer time. Thus, this technique is generally not economical for any firm trying to develop forecasts of a large number of products.

Finally, unless the user of this technique understands such concepts as multi-collinearity, residual patterns, F values, and so on, he or she can falsely assume that any equation resulting in a high R^2 means that it provides a useful forecast.

NOTE

1. When only two variables (one dependent and one independent) are involved in a correlation analysis, the symbol r^2 is used to represent the coefficient of determination. When more than two variables are involved, the symbol becomes R^2.

QUESTIONS AND EXERCISES

1. (a) Identify six possible prediction variables you might use in forecasting the sale of anti-freeze in the state of Iowa. We are interested in sales from September to December.

   (b) Once you have identified these six variables, apply the six key questions to them to see if they should be incorporated into the regression model.

2.

	Y	X_1	X_2	X_3	X_4	X_5
Y	1.00					
X_1	$-.37$	1.00				
X_2	.81	.34	1.00			
X_3	.54	.42	.89	1.00		
X_4	.53	.05	.52	.59	1.00	
X_5	.12	.21	.36	.21	.80	1.00

Use the above correlation matrix to answer these questions:

   (a) Which independent variable has the highest correlation with the dependent variable?

   (b) Which variables should probably be eliminated due to high multi-collinearity?

   (c) If stepwise regression was used, which variables would be entered into the equation first?

   (d) What does the negative sign with X_1 tell you?

3. Following is information that might be found on a computer printout using step-wise regression. Use the data in this printout to answer the questions.

Variables in the Equation

Variable	B	Standard Error	F
X_2	4.81	.369	13.03
			.01
Constant	1,200.15	95.60	22.50
			.00

Variables Not in the Equation

Variable	Partial	Tolerance	F	Significance
X_1	$-.45$	.72	10.68	.050
X_3	.20	.15	.48	.399
X_4	.61	.89	33.69	.001
X_5	.06	.33	.29	.548

(a) What is the regression equation at this point?

(b) What will be the next variable entered into the equation?

(c) What will be its contribution to R^2? What will the R^2 be?

(d) What does the tolerance value for X_3 indicate?

(e) Which variables should not be brought in to the equation?

4. Assume multiple regression is used to forecast each of the following types of sales. Give some examples for each situation where a dummy variable might be needed.

(a) Supermarket sales.

(b) Sales of Firestone tires.

(c) Tylenol sales.

(d) Ticket sales for Continental Airlines.

(e) Lift ticket sales for Vail, Colorado.

5. Use the following set of data to develop a regression equation for estimating sales of video cassettes.

City	$ Sales per Store (000s)	Buying Power Index	$ Appliance Sales (millions)	Number of Autos per Household
	Y	X_1	X_2	X_3
1	5.1	.435	475	1.4
2	5.8	.361	510	1.8
3	6.5	.484	530	2.1
4	7.0	.572	670	1.8
5	5.9	.482	580	2.1
6	4.8	.292	460	2.4
7	6.2	.490	700	1.7
8	7.0	.504	684	1.5
9	6.5	.483	605	2.2
10	5.9	.412	537	1.6
11	6.1	.437	529	1.8
12	6.2	.392	542	2.1
13	5.6	.404	489	2.1
14	6.2	.444	505	1.8
15	5.2	.371	534	2.3

(a) Evaluate all the B values. Should they be retained in the equation?

(b) What is the 95 percent CI for the Y value?

(c) Is there multi-collinearity between any independent variables?

(d) Is the R^2 value significant?

(e) Make a forecast when $X_1 = .486$; $X_2 = 601$; $X_3 = 2.4$. Use 95 percent CI.

8

Judgmental Methods

INTRODUCTION

Time series models use the past values of a variable to forecast its future value. In causal models, a forecast of the variable is based on its past association with other predictable factor(s).

There are numerous situations where either past data of a variable does not exist or its value cannot be tied directly to the occurrence of some other event. In these situations, forecasts are based primarily on the judgment or best estimates of people believed to be knowledgeable about the behavior of the variable. Forecasts obtained in this way are called "subjective" or "judgmental" forecasts, because they rely heavily on such intangibles as intuition, past experiences, instinct, and so forth.

Judgmental methods should not be viewed as "last resort" techniques, however, since in many situations they can provide more accurate forecasts than those derived from sophisticated mathematical models. Their strength is that they capitalize on the experience and savvy of people who are in a position to evaluate accurately both what is presently happening and what is likely to happen in their particular area of specialization.

The next two chapters describe some of the more frequently used judgmental methods. Also included are some simulation models, such as the Monte Carlo method and the Markov Chain process. In each instance, the technique is discussed in the context of sales.

SALES FORCE COMPOSITE

Many decision makers believe the best source of estimates of a firm's future sales is its own sales force. Salespeople are in frequent contact with customers and potential buyers and thus have first-hand knowledge of present market conditions and buying intentions.

Procedures

Salespeople are asked to estimate future sales by product, by geographic area, or by type of customer. Such estimates may be obtained on a fairly frequent basis (monthly or quarterly) or less frequently via annual reports.

A standard reporting form is usually provided and, in some cases, extensive historical sales data are included to refresh the salesperson's memory and thus improve forecasts. Some firms pose different scenarios (for example, an overall industry slowdown of 10 percent or a 20 percent increase of industry sales) and ask salespeople to provide a forecast under each of these circumstances. In firms where the majority of sales come from only a small proportion of customers (80-20 Principle), the salespeople may be asked to estimate sales to their major customers only.

Each salesperson's forecast is usually sent to his or her immediate sales manager for adjustment, if necessary. The sales manager combines the forecasts and sends them to the next level of management, if one exists. A composite forecast is then derived, based on the input from the entire sales force.

Strengths and Drawbacks of Technique

Strengths

- Uses input from those people closest to actual markets.
- Enables reasonably detailed forecasts to be derived, that is, by product, customer, and territory.
- May enhance morale of sales force if their input is used to guide company decisions.

Drawbacks

- Salespeople may continually underestimate sales if they suspect their forecast is being used to set sales quotas.
- Can take excessive amounts of a salesperson's time if required to provide estimates too often.
- Salespeople usually lack the background to evaluate the total macro (economic) situation and how it might affect their future sales.

Overview

Results indicate that the short-term (two to three months) forecasts of salespeople tend to be significantly more accurate than their annual or long-range forecasts. This forecasting procedure also provides best results when each salesperson has relatively few customers.

SURVEY OF BUYERS' INTENTIONS

With this approach, the firm asks key customers to identify their buying plans. Such data, if obtained from just a few of the firm's key customers, can provide solid information about future sales.

Procedures

The firm's present (and in some cases, potential) customers are queried about their intentions to buy the firm's product over some future time period. The information may be obtained either by mail or telephone survey; or the firm's own sales staff may call on customers and solicit such information. The various responses are consolidated to provide an overview of the buying attitudes and intentions of customers.

In selecting the persons to be interviewed, it is important that they be knowledgeable about and heavily involved in their firm's buying decisions. The persons often contacted for such information are the firm's purchasing agents. One note of caution about purchasing agents: in spite of their title, they may not play a key role in their firm's buying decisions. In many firms, a purchasing agent is merely the office through which a firm's purchase orders are placed, and they know little about purchase intentions. Thus, the purchasing agent's role in each firm should be fully understood before they are used as the major information source.

Strengths and Drawbacks of Technique

Strengths

- Forecasts are based on customers' buying plans.
- Contacts with customers can also provide feedback about possible problems with the company's products.
- Can be relatively inexpensive if only a few customers are involved.

Drawbacks

- Situations can change abruptly and intentions may never culminate into actual purchases.
- Some firms may be unwilling to disclose buying intentions, especially if they are not regular customers.

Overview

This method can also provide customers' appraisals of future business conditions. In fact, the overall outlook and attitudes of customers may be more meaningful to forecasters than their stated buying intentions. Firms that have solid customer relationships will usually benefit most from this method.

In addition to the firm's own surveys, there are surveys conducted regularly by both *Business Week* magazine and the Department of Commerce on the buying intentions of selected industries. There is also an "Index of Consumer Attitudes" published annually by the Institute of Social Research at the University of Michigan. This study is based on findings from consumer surveys and describes the buying attitudes that are expected to prevail among consumers.

JURY OF EXECUTIVE OPINIONS

One of the shortcomings of obtaining forecasts from the firm's own sales force is that most salespeople make their forecasts from fairly narrow perspectives. They do not fully understand the impact of such factors as general economic conditions or general industry conditions on sales. The "jury of executive opinions" overcomes this shortcoming.

This approach combines input from a variety of the firm's key decision makers. The participants are usually higher echelon executives or managers representing such functional areas as finance, production, purchasing, sales, and so on. They usually have the background to integrate macro-based data into their forecasts. Unlike the salespeople, however, they are not in constant contact with the marketplace nor are they able to provide forecasts down to the disaggregated level (by territory, customer) as salespeople can.

Procedures

Participating executives meet as a group on a quarterly or semi-annual basis to monitor present sales and forecast future sales. The group usually comprises three to ten people. In some firms, the group is initially given some forecast figures about which they exchange ideas. The discussion ends when the executives arrive at a consensus forecast. In other firms, each group member is asked to provide a forecast along with the reasoning behind it. Again, based on a lengthy exchange of ideas, a final consensus forecast is developed.

Strengths and Drawbacks of Technique

Strengths

- Provides input from representatives of the firm's key functional areas.
- Executives usually have a solid understanding of broad-based factors and how they affect sales.

Drawbacks

- May require excessive amounts of time from executives.
- Some executives (finance, personnel) may not really understand the firm's sales situation.
- Most executives are quite removed from the actual marketplace.

Overview

This procedure seems best suited to situations in which forecasts have already been developed by others and the executives merely identify major factors that they believe affect sales and the extent to which these factors influence future sales. This enables them to provide input from their area of strength—a broader, or macro perspective.

DELPHI METHOD

One of the main shortcomings of having people express opinions in a group setting is that the opinions of the group may be unduly influenced by one or two individuals. This may occur because of the dominant person's position (president of the firm), alleged expertise in an area (marketing manager viewed as authority on sales), or personal magnetism. Also, in group settings, early majority opinion may prevent fringe opinions from being voiced (the bandwagon effect). The purpose of the Delphi method is to obtain a consensus from a group of experts in such a way as to control intra-group influences.

This is accomplished by questioning "experts" individually at separate locales while still allowing them to receive input and feedback from other group members. Although the Delphi method is used in any situation in which a group consensus is sought, in this book it is presented as a sales forecasting technique.

Procedures

The Delphi process is handled by a coordinator in a totally objective manner in the following sequence:

Step One—A panel of experts is selected based on their perceived knowledge of the variable to be forecasted, sales in this case. The size of the group can be from 4 people to as many as 500 people, although large groups become quite cumbersome and require a great deal of coordination. They may all be from the same firm or from a variety of firms scattered geographically. In some cases, each participant is given background information about the product or situation for which a forecast is sought.

Step Two—An initial set of questions is sent to all participants, who are asked to respond in terms of one or more of the following:

(a) The probability that a given event or amount of sales will occur.

(b) The date on which a certain level of sales might be achieved.

(c) Maximum and minimum sales for a product.

The respondents are also asked to provide reasons for assigning these values.

Step Three—The responses are returned to the coordinator who tabulates the results and, where appropriate, develops a median value or an inter-quartile range (an interval containing the middle half of the responses).

Step Four—The results are returned to each participant along with anonymous statements provided by the participants to justify their estimates. After seeing these figures and the accompanying statements, each participant may modify his or her initial response.

Step Five—A second round of responses is provided by each participant and mailed back to the coordinator who again tabulates and summarizes them.

The process is continued until little or no change occurs in the responses, that is, a consensus is reached. Figure 8-1 illustrates questions and results from two rounds of questioning. The entire process can take anywhere from two months to more than a year to complete.

Advantages and Shortcomings of Delphi Method

Advantages

- Eliminates the need for committee or group meetings.
- Eliminates the major shortcomings associated with group decision making, such as specious persuasion, bandwagon effect.
- Enables participants to receive the input of other "experts" but in an isolated environment.
- Allows participants to change their minds anonymously.

Drawbacks

- Participants are often selected more on the basis of their willingness to participate and their accessibility than on their real knowledge or representativeness.
- Can take a great deal of time to arrive at a consensus.
- Process may suffer because of high dropout rate of participants.
- Many business people are not familiar with the method and may be reluctant to participate.

TECHNOLOGICAL FORECASTING

The judgmental forecasting techniques discussed in the previous sections are primarily intended to provide forecasts for a three-month to two-year period. Technological forecasting, on the other hand, is concerned with identifying (predicting) technological developments that could possibly affect the firm's long-term future activities. Not only are possible technological changes identified, but estimates are made as to when such changes are expected to occur. For the most part, technological forecasting does not lend itself to the use of mathematical models.

Approaches to Technological Forecasting

Two different approaches are usually followed in technological forecasting: exploratory and normative. In the exploratory approach, existing technology is projected into the future to determine how it may be applied and how the firm will be affected by the applications.

Round One		Primary Reason for Answer
By what year do you feel at least 15% of homes in Colorado will have some type of active solar system?	______	
What percent of the homes in Colorado will have a solar hot water heating system by 1990?	______%	
What will be the average price of a solar hot water system in Colorado in 1985?	$______	

Round Two	Your Original Answer	Median Group Answer	Major Ranges	Your New Answer	Reasons Your Answer Differs from Median
By what year do you feel at least 15% of homes in Colorado will have some type of active solar system?	1987	1990	1986-1992	☐	
What percent of the homes in Colorado will have a solar hot water heating system by 1990?	20%	15%	13-17	☐	
What will be the average price of a solar hot water system in Colorado in 1985?	$2,000	$2,400	$2,100-$2,700	☐	

Figure 8-1
Two Rounds of Delphi Method

Example: What will educational facilities be like in the 1990s?
Predict role of computer in education
Predict role of cable television
Predict physical structure of classrooms

Example: What will the "food-away-from-home" industry be like in the 1990s?
Predict restaurant motifs
Predict self-service versus full service facilities
Predict types of foods served

In the normative approach, the firm's own long-range goals and objectives are identified first followed by the technologies required to achieve them.

Example

Firm A is a major producer of business textbooks. Its goal for 1990 is to supply at least 10 percent of all the educational material used by business colleges. Since computers and cable TV are expected to play an important role in education, Firm A will have to develop educational materials compatible with individual learning through either or both of those technologies if their goal of 10 percent of educational material is to be reached.

The normative approach places the emphasis on what the firm can do to achieve certain goals and thus effect technological changes, whereas the exploratory method emphasizes how technological changes will likely affect the firm.

Of the two, the exploratory approach is used more frequently by business firms because it is easier to take an existing technology and project its effect on the company than it is to devise ways for the firm to bring about technological change.

Present Use of Technological Forecasting

Technological forecasting is used primarily by firms involved with products of a technical nature and that have the financial and personnel resources to engage in such a program. It is also widely used by government agencies. In 1974, the Office of Technology Assessment was created by Congress to aid legislative policy makers anticipate and plan for major changes and to examine ways in which the changes could affect the lives of their constituents. Special "think tank" groups such as the RAND Corporation also perform technological forecasting.

Techniques Used for Technological Forecasting

(1) Trend Extrapolation

In this technique, expected changes in a particular technology are tied to the pattern of its past changes.

Example: The expected speed and size of commercial airplanes by 1990 is related to the rate of such change over the past 30 years.

Example: The average educational level of American adults by 1995 is related to the changes that took place from 1960 to 1980.

Example: The average life of automobile batteries in 1995 is based on improvements since 1950. (This assumes batteries will still be used in cars by 1995.)

(2) Precursor Events

These are situations in which the technological progress of one product lags behind, but is closely tied to, the changes in another product. The expected speed of commercial airplanes at some future time, for example, is related to the changes in speed achieved by military aircraft (the precursor).

(3) Scenarios

Dramatic situations are created for which members of a panel are asked to identify a variety of technological changes that may result.

Example: What if, by 1990, air pollution in Los Angeles were so extreme that all gasoline-powered vehicles had to be banned?

Example: What if America's natural gas supplies were depleted by 1995?

(4) Morphological Analysis

All possible means or techniques to a given end are identified and placed in some type of matrix. Then all possible combinations of these techniques are used to arrive at some solution. Figure 8-2 illustrates the use of morphological analysis in developing alternative possibilities for manually propelling a small boat.

(5) Delphi Method

This method, discussed in an earlier section of this chapter, is frequently used for technological forecasting because it enables the exchange of ideas among experts without the drawback of having some participants directly influence the input of others.

Parameters Design Characteristics and Requirements	Ideas Design Alternatives					
Input Motion	Rotating	Oscillating	Linear	Reciprocating	Etc.	
Input Source	One Hand	Two Hands	One Foot	Two Feet	Hand & Foot	Etc.
Input Device	Crank	Turnstile	Pedals	Lever	Treadmill	Etc.
Output	Propeller	Paddle	Paddle Wheel	Fin	Screw	Jet	Etc.
Mechanism	Gears	Chains	Belts	Pump	Linkage	Piston	Etc.
Operator Position	Sitting	Standing	Kneeling	Straddling	Etc.	

Figure 8-2
Using Morphological Analysis in the Design of a Manual Propulsion System for a Small Boat

Source: L. Harrisberger, *Engineermanship* (Belmont, CA: Wadsworth
          Publishing Co., Inc., 1966).

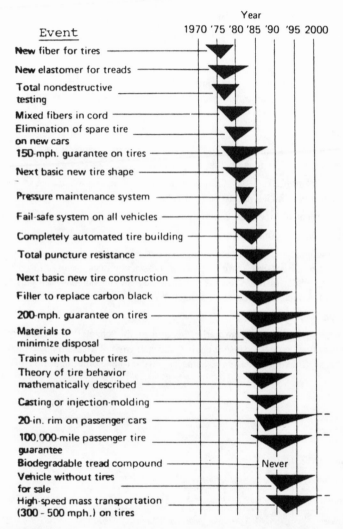

Figure 8-3
Year in Which an Event Has at Least a 50 Percent Chance of Occurring

Source: F. J. Kovac, "Technological Forecasting--Tires," Chemical
         Technology, January 1971, p. 22.

Figure 8-3 illustrates the results of Goodyear's use of the Delphi method to identify future technological breakthroughs in the tire industry.[1] Each "expert" was asked to identify changes that would occur in the industry in the next 25 years. Those changes that were most frequently mentioned were then placed on a list, and each expert asked to identify when that event had at least a 50 percent chance of occurring. Those events for which there was greatest agreement were placed on another list (with the times they were expected to occur), and the experts were asked to reassess these times. This was repeated until the list was narrowed and there was wide agreement as to the probable time of their occurrence.

Participants in Technological Forecasting

Because technological forecasting is still fairly new and used by only a limited number of firms, no one group of persons has emerged as the most effective type of participant. Following are the types of persons that have been used most frequently.

Scientific Advisors

A scientific advisory committee consisting of eminent people from industry, government, and academia which meets annually or semi-annually to introduce new ideas that are either within or outside the scope of company's present operations.

Company Personnel

A technological forecasting group composed of company personnel, usually those who hold key positions and who have shown evidence of reasonable foresight and an understanding of the industries in which the firm competes. They go by such names as "Program Evaluation Group," "Long-Range Planning Group," "Opportunity Seeking Group," or "Commercial Intelligence Group."

"Wild Man" or "Iconoclast"

One or two imaginative persons from within the company. The assignment usually goes to those who are viewed as "kooks" by others because of their fertile imaginations and unusual perspectives.

Limitations

Attempting to forecast technological change is a precarious activity. Dramatic breakthroughs in other areas (computer chips, laser beams) can raise havoc with present technologies. Often, these breakthroughs are totally unexpected since many firms are highly secretive about them. Unforeseen legislative changes also can take place that radically affect a technology—banning of certain chemicals, bottle bans in certain states, banning of aerosols, and so on.

If technological forecasting is to be an effective tool, management must be convinced that it is a worthwhile undertaking and that the firm will benefit from it. Because it is so difficult to assign a dollar value to the contribution of technological forecasting, it is not uncommon for firms to discontinue it after a few years if no significant benefits are identified.

ANALOGOUS (SURROGATE) DATA

A new product does not have a past sales record that can be used as a guide to a sales forecast. But there are some situations in which data about another product already on the market (surrogate) can be substituted to forecast a new product's expected growth pattern. This procedure is generally viewed as a judgmental method, because a subjective decision is made as to which existing product has a sales pattern similar to the new product.

Such a procedure was used by several television manufacturers in the early 1960s to estimate the sales potential of television sets in the 1970s. They tied sales of TV sets to the sales of radios during similar time periods in their life cycles. A "sales per household" ratio was established for the initial growth period of radios. This ratio was used to estimate television sales under different rates of growth: (a) TV sales growing at three times the rate of radio sales per thousand households, (b) TV sales growing at the same rate as the sales of radios, and (c) TV sales growing only three-fourths as fast as radio sales. The forecaster experiments with such scenarios to derive the most realistic estimate.[2]

Using a similar approach, the sales pattern of video recorders during the 1980s could be related to the sales pattern of color television sets from the late 1960s to the mid-1970s. Estimated sales of microwave ovens into the 1980s could be developed from the sales patterns of electric dishwashers through the 1960s.

Successful application of this approach depends upon the establishment of a logical connection between the sales patterns of the two products involved. The availability of accurate and comprehensive data of the surrogate product is also essential.

A firm such as Proctor and Gamble with many similar product offerings in a given product category (for example, detergents) can use the sales records of its existing products effectively to forecast sales of a new detergent.

Overview of Method

The "analogy" process is generally not accurate for short-range forecasting or for identifying expected turning points in a new product's sales. However, it can be an effective method for intermediate and long-range forecasting, especially if a logical match exists between the products. At least five to ten years of sales data of the analogous product is required.

NOTES

1. J. P. Martens, "Technological Forecasting for the Chemical Process Industries," *Chemical Engineering* (December 27, 1971), pp. 54–62.
2. Lester C. Sartorius and N. Carrol Mohn, *Sales Forecasting Models: A Diagnostic Approach,* Research Monograph No. 69, College of Business Administration, Georgia State University, 1976, pp. 211–213.

QUESTIONS AND EXERCISES

1. Identify four situations where forecasts are needed and which judgmental method would be the most likely technique to use.

2. What can the sales manager do to increase the likelihood that the sales estimates provided by his or her salespeople are reasonably accurate?

3. What factors weaken the findings from such surveys as "Consumers' Buying Intentions" or "Industrial Firms' Buying Intentions"?

4. (a) What is the Delphi method and what are its strengths and weaknesses as a forecasting tool?

   (b) Develop a Delphi method that could be used to determine the future impact of visual or picture telephones (that is, where caller and receiver can see one another).

5. Use morphological analysis to identify possible ways for cleaning rugs.

6. What analogous products might you use to aid in forecasting the demand for:

   (a) Personal computers?

   (b) Solar hot water heaters?

   (c) A new fad item for children?

   (d) A "flotation" tank center in which people come and float in a salt water tank to relax?

9

Additional Judgmental and Simulation Techniques

INTRODUCTION

In the preceding chapter, it is stated that judgmental forecasting models rely on the input of people deemed knowledgeable about a product or industry. Their expertise enables them to estimate the future value of a variable such as sales of a product or an industry or predict the occurrence of an event(s) that is likely to affect that variable. As stated in Chapter 8, judgmental models are used because little or no past data exists or because long-term forecasts that require subjective judgments are desired.

This chapter also deals with techniques that rely on the subjective input of experts but the forecasts generally cover shorter time periods. In addition, some simulation models that also can be used for short-term forecasting are described.

JUDGMENTAL METHODS USING PROBABILITIES

Levels of Knowledge about Future Events

Forecasting is a difficult task because of the many internal and external factors that affect people and events. Some level of uncertainty exists in any forecast since no one can have perfect knowledge of future events. The degree of uncertainty, however, can vary greatly among different forecasting situations.

In some cases, solid information exists about past sales and can be used to lessen the uncertainty of future sales significantly. For example, the past bread sales of an established supermarket provide a pretty good indication of its future bread sales, at least over the short term.

In other situations, only limited information exists but it still provides enough insight into a future outcome to change a situation of great uncertainty to one of "risk." This is best illustrated by weather-related events. Coffee sales at a football game are directly related to weather conditions on the day of the game; attendance at a ski area depends on the amount of snow and the outside temperature. Past weather records are used to predict the likelihood of certain weather conditions and thus lower the uncertainty surrounding a forecast.

A third type of situation is one in which little or no information exists to estimate future events. Forecasting under these conditions is usually viewed as mere speculation.

The following continuum illustrates the various situations in which forecasts must be made:

Certainty	Risk	Uncertainty
(Complete Knowledge)	(Some Knowledge)	(Little or No Knowledge)

Risk versus Uncertainty

The forecaster must generally perform his or her activities under conditions of either risk or uncertainty. In a risk situation, it is possible to assign probabilities objectively to different events because historical data exist that enable estimates to be made on the likelihood of different outcomes.

A condition of uncertainty exists when there is little or no information available about which of a number of possible events will occur. Forecasts under that condition must be based largely on subjective or highly speculative assessments.

A firm introducing a dramatically new product (Rubik's Cube, for example) that has not been test marketed must rely on highly subjective estimates as to its expected sales during the first six months.

Use of Probabilities

The previous section on risk and uncertainty describes the different conditions a forecaster (or decision maker) faces when trying to determine the likelihood of different events. A series of decision models has been developed in which probabilities are assigned to various outcomes. "Expected payoffs" or "values" are determined on the basis of these probabilities. These models are known by such titles as "decision tree analysis," "decision theory," or the most specialized form, "Bayesian decision theory."

Simplified versions of probability models are discussed in this chapter; if they seem appropriate for the reader's forecasting needs, he or she should consult other texts that describe the procedures in greater depth.

Regardless of whether the probabilities are objectively or subjectively assigned, two conditions must be satisfied. First, all possible outcomes or events must be included. In other words, the sum of the probabilities for each outcome must sum to the value of 1. When rolling a die, only one of six outcomes can occur: 1, 2, 3, 4, 5, or 6. In a fair die, each side has an equal chance (one-sixth) of occurring, and the sum of all possible outcomes equals one.

A second requirement is that the probability assigned to any outcome being considered must be greater than 0, but can never exceed 1. A value of 1 or 0 implies certainty.

Example of a Risk Situation

The SPIRO Vending Company is one of many companies that will bid for the rights to the food and drink concessions for the "Dubuque Days" celebration to be held on July 4 and 5 in Dubuque, Iowa. The celebration is sponsored by the Chamber of Commerce and only one vendor will be allowed to sell food and drinks on the grounds during the event. The primary factor in the selection of this vendor is the dollar amount of the bid.

The two owners of SPIRO Vending have to decide what dollar bid (if any) they should submit. They know the amount of money they make on the festival depends primarily on two things: the size of their bid (since this is an expense item) and the weather conditions during the time of the festival (since this affects total revenue).

Thus, their first task is to determine the amount of money they expect to net (excluding the cost of their bid), and this is tied directly to different weather conditions.

Condition 1: Hot, dry weather—if this type of weather occurs, SPIRO estimates they can net $160,000 over the two-day event.

Condition 2: Mixed weather—part of the time the weather is very good and at other times it might be rainy or cool. If this weather condition occurs, SPIRO estimates they will net $100,000 over the two-day event.

Condition 3: Bad weather—rainy or cold weather holds down the crowd both days. The net to SPIRO under these conditions would be $30,000.

SPIRO must make its bid six months prior to the actual event and thus has to estimate the likelihood of these three different weather conditions. SPIRO can objectively assign probabilities to each of these conditions by studying the recorded weather for Dubuque, Iowa, on previous fourths and fifths of July. A study of the weather for the preceding 100 years indicates that good weather occurred 50 times on both dates, mixed weather 25 times, and poor weather 25 times. Thus, the probability of Condition 1 (good weather) is 50 percent, Condition 2 (mixed weather) is 25 percent, and Condition 3 (bad weather) is 25 percent. SPIRO uses these probabilities to determine the expected revenue for each condition, as well as for all three conditions.

Expected value for an event equals probability of the event occurring times the potential revenue associated with that event ($EV_1 = P_1 \times R_1$) (see Table 9-1).

The data and calculations in Figure 9-1 indicate that the overall value of Dubuque Days to SPIRO is $112,500. The reader must recognize, however, that in reality only one of these weather conditions will occur, and under the worst condition, a net (before the bid expense) of only $30,000 is realized.

Table 9-1
Expected Value to SPIRO under Different Weather Conditions

Event	(1) Probability	(2) Potential Revenue from Event	(3) Expected Value (1) x (2)
Condition 1	.5	$160,000	$ 30,000
Condition 2	.25	$100,000	$ 25,000
Condition 3	.25	$ 30,000	$ 7,500
		Total Expected Values to SPIRO:	$112,500

This is a "risk" situation because the probabilities are objectively assigned on the basis of historical data.

Example of Uncertainty

SPIRO's estimate of expected revenues under three possible weather conditions suggests this could be a worthwhile venture. Now they must decide what dollar bid to submit to the Chamber of Commerce.

Based on past bidding experiences and estimates as to what other firms may be bidding, SPIRO derives the following probabilities on the likely acceptance of three different bids (only three possible bids are used to simplify the example).

SPIRO believes that if they bid $90,000, they will have at least a 90 percent chance of winning the exclusive vending rights; if they bid $70,000, they will have a 50 percent chance of winning; if they bid $40,000, they will have only a 20 percent chance of winning. Which amount should they bid? Remember, the size of the bid is an actual expense to them, so the higher their bid, the less money they make. Figure 9-1 contains the possible outcomes for SPIRO.

Thus, based on expected payoffs from the three different bids, SPIRO seemingly should enter a bid of $70,000 since it has the highest probable payoff ($26,250). But note the uncertainty with such a bid (50 percent chance of acceptance) compared a 90 percent chance of acceptance associated with the $90,000 bid. Many people looking at these alternatives might select the alternative with the greatest chance of acceptance—Bid number 1, despite its lower payoff. The selection of any of the alternatives implies that a great deal of certainty surrounds the probabilities assigned, which may not be true. Remember, these are subjectively assigned probabilities.

Two Approaches for Assigning Probabilities

The value of any probability model depends completely on the appropriateness of the probabilities it uses, that is, how close are they to the true probabilities? If

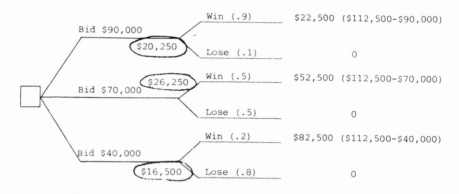

In each bid situation, the payoff figures was determined by taking the total expected value to SPIRO based on the three possible weather conditions--$112,500.

Figure 9-1
Payoffs to SPIRO from Three Bid Possibilities

these models are to be useful, acceptable methods for assigning subjective probabilities must be followed. Two different approaches for making such assignments are (a) assigning events to a set of probabilities and (b) assigning probabilities to events. An example of each approach is now presented.

Assigning Events to Probabilities

This approach would be used when an event has a variety of possible outcomes. "Experts" are given a set of probabilities and asked to identify which outcome they believe conforms most closely to a given probability, that is, what do they believe is the highest possible mortgage rate that will exist at April-May 1987? (There are 99 out of 100 chances the real rate will fall below this rate.)

A series of similar questions using different probabilities force the expert to describe additional outcomes relative to a list of probabilities. Thus, the expert derives high, low, and mid-values through a bracketing process. The group's responses are combined and mean values are identified for different probabilities.

Mortgage Rate Example. The River City Board of Realtors wants to project new housing starts for June of 1987. They believe the critical factor in determining these housing starts is the existing mortgage rate around April-May of 1987. To get an estimate of this rate they contact ten people (in banking, economics, or government) believed to have a reasonable insight into expected mortgage rates.

Each expert is sent a survey asking him or her to provide five possible mortgage rates for the April-May 1987 period. The questions are phrased as follows:

(1) What do you believe is the highest possible mortgage rate for April-May 1987? There are 99 out of 100 chances the real rate will fall below this amount.

(2) What do you believe is the lowest possible mortgage rate for April-May 1987? There is only 1 out of 100 chances the true mortgage rate will lie below this rate.

(3) Based on the range derived from your answers (1) and (2), what mortgage rate do you believe would have a 50-50 chance of having the true mortgage rate fall below or above it?

(4) Based on the range developed from your answer to questions (2) and (3), what mortgage rate do you believe would have a 25 percent chance of being the true mortgage rate for April-May 1987?

(5) Based on the range developed from your answers to questions (1) and (2), what mortgage rate do you believe would have a 75 percent chance of being the true mortgage rate in April-May 1987?

The results from the ten experts are tabulated and a mean mortgage value derived for each of the five values (Table 9-2). To save space, actual data from only three of the ten respondents' responses are included in the table.

Thus, the mid-point estimate of the ten experts for mortgage rates in April-May 1987 is 9.75 percent. Further statements that could be made based on the data in Table 9-2 are: (a) there is a 75 percent chance that mortgage rates will be 12.67 percent or less and (b) there is only a 1 percent chance that mortgage rates will be less than 7.00 percent.

Assigning Probabilities to Events

Another way to derive probabilities is to ask people to identify the likelihood of each of a number of different events. This is the opposite of the technique in the previous example in that respondents are asked to assign probabilities to given events, whereas in the previous technique (Table 9-2) they are asked to assign events to probabilities.

Table 9-2
Delphi Method Responses of Experts to Questions about Expected Mortgage Rates in April-May 1987

Respondent	1%	25%	50%	75%	99%
1	7.5	8.5	9.5	12.0	14.0
2	7.0	8.75	9.25	13.5	15.5
3	6.5	9.0	10.25	12.5	13.5
X =	7.25	8.5	9.75	12.0	14.25
Cumulative Probability	1%	25%	50%	75%	99%

Table 9-3
Experts' Assignment of Probability to Given Events

Mortgage Rate	Expert 1 Probability	Expert 2 Probability	X̄
Between 7-8.5%	_____	_____	_____
Between 8.6-10%	_____	_____	_____
Between 10.1-11.5%	_____	_____	_____
Between 11.6%-12%	_____	_____	_____
Between 12.1-13.5%	_____	_____	_____
Greater than 13.5%	_____	_____	_____
	1.00	1.00	1.00

Using the mortgage example again, each expert is asked to assign probabilities to each event so that his or her total probabilities sum to 1. Means are derived for each range and then adjusted so they total 100 percent or 1. Thus, a probability for each range emerges based on the input of experts (Table 9-3).

Assessing the Results

If one particular technique is used on a regular basis with the same group of experts, it is usually worthwhile to compare each person's estimates with what actually occurred so that "fudge factors" can be used in the future to compensate for a person's tendency to be either overly optimistic or pessimistic.

For example, assume salespeople are asked for quarterly estimates of sales in their territory. The estimates from salesperson X over the last two years were as follows:

Forecast	Actual	Ratio Actual/Forecast
130	140	1.08
145	150	1.03
150	147	.98
150	160	1.07
155	157	1.01
155	162	1.05
150	148	.99
150	155	1.03
		$\bar{X} = 1.03$

Salesperson X tends to underestimate when forecasting and a compensation factor of 103 percent should be applied to each of his or her forecasts (1.03 × salesperson X's forecast).

Cross-Impact Technique

The probability that a particular event (Event A) will take place at some future time is usually directly related to the occurrence or non-occurrence of other events. For example, the future of "gasohol" as a major fuel for automobiles depends on such conditions as the future price of gasoline, the passage and enforcement of more stringent pollution controls, the prices of certain grain products, and so forth.

Suppose a decision maker was seeking input for the following scenario: "What is the probability that, by 1988, at least 20 percent of U.S. automobile fuel needs will be supplied by gasohol?" In deriving the requested probability figure, estimates would also have to be made on the likely occurrence of the impacting events (that is, increased pollution controls, price of grain).

Cross-impact analysis is a technique for examining the likely impact of related events upon one another. This enables the forecaster to refine the probability of a particular event occurring by acknowledging its relationship with other events.

Application of Cross-Impact Technique

Through the Delphi technique or some other process where experts can provide input, a list of the key conditions or developments related to a particular event are identified. These developments are then placed in a matrix and an evaluation made of their impact upon one another.

To illustrate the process, an updated example from Jain's text, *Marketing Planning and Strategy*, will be used.[1] The following cross-impact analysis is used to aid in the forecast of future gas consumption by automobiles in the United States. It was determined that these four key events will impact on each other and on the future consumption of gas:

(a) Safety standards for automobiles are passed that increase the weight of an average U.S. car by 260 pounds.

(b) A relaxation of the 1978 emission regulations.

(c) The retail price of gasoline is $1.40 per gallon.

(d) U.S. automakers introduce cars that will achieve at least 40 miles per gallon under normal driving conditions.

These events are placed in a matrix (Figure 9-2) and assessments are made about their expected impact on one another. If Event A occurs, this will likely create pressure on regulatory people to relax enforcement of emission regulations

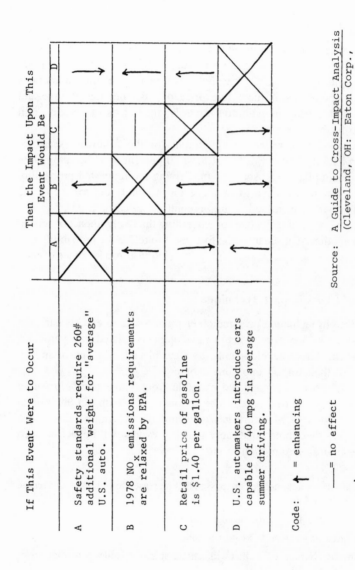

Figure 9-2
Basic Format for Cross-Impact Matrix

(Event B). This is considered an "enhancement" effect, that is, occurrence of Event A enhances the likelihood of the occurrence of Event B. An enhancement situation is represented by an arrow pointing upward.

The passage of the safety standards (Event A) is not expected to have any effect on the price of gasoline, so this "neutral" effect is denoted by a horizontal line. If the occurrence of one event is believed to make the occurrence of a second event less likely, this is considered an "inhibiting" effect and is denoted by an arrow pointing downward. It is felt that the occurrence of Event A makes Event D less likely to occur. Once the initial cross-impact matrix is developed, the ensuing steps of the analysis vary depending upon the type of information sought. What usually happens is that an attempt is made to "fine tune" the relationships. What impact will Event A's occurrence have on the likelihood that Event B will occur (Figure 9-3)?

In this example, scales of 0 to +8 and 0 to −8 are used, with 8 representing the most critical impact. (The scale actually used varies among analysts since some use a scale of 0 to 5 and others use a scale of 0 to 10.) Thus, a +4 indicates that while Event A has a reasonably important positive impact on the occurrence of Event B, it is not essential to Event B's occurrence. Conversely, Event A's occurrence would make Event D less likely to occur (−4).

For some situations, these two steps (Figures 9-3 and 9-4) may provide all the information needed to assess the cross impacts. But usually a third step is also taken, wherein the previous relationships are quantified further into probabilities (Figure 9-4).

The probability of each event's occurrence is identified first and then altered on the basis of the identified cross impact. For example, Event A is assigned a 70 percent chance of occurring and Event B an 80 percent chance (Column 2, Figure 9-4). It is believed that the occurrence of Event A will enhance the chances of Event B. Thus, the probability of Event B's occurrence is increased to .9 if Event A occurs. Probability figures are assigned to each cell depending on whether an event has a positive or negative effect. For example, since Event B has no impact on Event C, the occurrence of Event B will not alter the likelihood of C's occurrence.

Knowing the effects of these cross impacts can help decision makers (in this case the gas industry) determine which events they should attempt to influence. For example, if the occurrence of Event D is desired, attempts should be made to bring about Event B, since B's occurrence increases the likelihood of D's occurrence.

The preceding coverage of cross-impact analysis is at a fairly simple level. A number of firms that use cross-impact models use much more complicated equations, simulating numerous levels of interactions.[2]

SIMULATION MODELS

Simulation models attempt to re-create or simulate real business situations to prepare a forecast. In reality, most forecasting techniques are simulation models

If This Event Were to Occur

Then the Impact Upon This Event Would Be

If This Event Were to Occur	A	B	C	D
A Safety standards require 260# additional weight for "average" U.S. auto.		+4	0	-4
B 1978 NO_x emissions requirements are relaxed by EPA.	+2		0	+4
C Retail price of gasoline is $1.40 per gallon.	-4	+4		+2
D U.S. automakers introduce cars capable of 40 mpg in average summer driving.	+2	-2	-2	

Source: A Guide to Cross-Impact Analysis (Cleveland, OH: Eaton Corp., no date).

Figure 9-3
Cross-Impact Matrix Showing Degrees of Impact

If This Event Were to Occur	Having This Probability of Occurrence	Then the Impact Upon This Event Would Be			
		A	B	C	D
A Safety standards require additional weight for "average" U.S. auto.	0.7	✕	0.9 immed.	0.5	0.4 immed.
B 1978 NO$_x$ emissions requirements are relaxed by EPA.	0.8	0.8 immed.	✕	0.5	0.7 +2 yrs
C Retail price of gasoline is $1.40 per gallon.	0.5	0.6 +1 yr.	0.9 +1 yr.	✕	0.7 +2 yrs
D U.S. automakers introduce cars capable of 40 mpg in average summer driving.	0.5	0.8 immed.	0.6 immed.	0.4 +1 yr.	✕

Source: A Guide to Cross-Impact Analysis (Cleveland, OH: Eaton Corp., no date).

Figure 9-4
Cross-Impact Matrix Showing Interactive Probabilities of Occurrence

175

since they are based on the premise that past relationships will continue into the future, that is, the future imitates its past.

Simulation models usually involve time compression techniques in which alternative future activities are simulated to determine their likely impact on a firm. Although simulation is primarily used to project production and inventory control activities, some models are also used by sales forecasters. In this section, two such techniques are presented—Monte Carlo and the Markov Chain process.

Monte Carlo Method

Marketing managers use test markets to determine the sales associated with alternative marketing actions. However, these field tests are time consuming, expensive, and can be informative to competition. It is often preferable, therefore, to construct a model that simulates the marketplace to evaluate different strategies. The Monte Carlo process is frequently used for such simulation activities.
The Monte Carlo process is frequently used for such simulation activities.

Example: Acme Airlines is contemplating using a promotional campaign in which they state: "We pay 10 percent of your ticket if you have to wait in line more than five minutes." Is this promise realistic considering Acme's present facilities and personnel? Before they can approve this ad campaign, they need to know how many Acme customers may have to wait more than five minutes to be ticketed assuming a typical Acme ticket counter, staffed by three people.

Poisson Distribution

In some situations, the probability of an event's occurrence can be easily determined. For example, if each of six events has an equal chance of taking place, the number of events is divided into 1 to derive a probability for the occurrence of each event (16.7 percent). In most situations, however, it is rare that each event has an equal chance of occurring, so it is necessary to assign probabilities. One procedure that could be used is the Poisson process. This process bases the probability of a future event on strong evidence about the past occurrences of that event. The formula for assigning Poisson probabilities is:

$P_{(k)} = \frac{m^k}{k!} e^{-m}$
P = Probability of particular event occurring
k = Number of times an event might occur
m = The average occurrence of that event in the past
e = 2.7 (a constant; always this value)
! = Factorial (for example 4! = 4 × 3 × 2 × 1, or 24).

In some texts, the above application of the Poisson process is called a "queuing" or "waiting line" model.

Application to Acme Airlines Example

Step One—Apply historical data to develop probabilities for the occurrence of all possible events. In our example, the Poisson process will be used to derive these probabilities.

Extensive studies over the preceding three months show that on the average, one customer per minute appears at Acme's ticket counter. By applying the Poisson model, the probabilities for different numbers of customers arriving per minute can be ascertained.

Example: What is the probability that two customers will arrive during one minute given that historically, only one customer arrives per minute?

$$m = 1, \ k = 2$$

$$P_{(2)} = \frac{1^2}{2!} 2.7^{-1} = .18$$

The Poisson process is then used to derive probabilities for the occurrence of all possible events (Table 9-4). The probability of more than four customers arriving per minute is extremely small (less than one percent).

Step Two—Develop probabilities related to the second critical action—time needed to serve a customer. Past studies indicate that the length of time required to serve a customer has an equal chance of being anywhere between one to five minutes. In other words there is a 20 percent chance it will take one minute to serve a customer, a 20 percent chance it will take two minutes, and so on (see Table 9-5).

Step Three—Simulate the number of customers arriving each minute over a 16-hour period (Acme's customer service counter is only open 16 hours a day) for several consecutive days and the amount of time needed to serve each customer. A table of random numbers is the basis for replicating these events.

Example: The first number selected from the table of random numbers is 47. This is compared with numbers in the cumulative probability column and their associated event (Table 9-4). Thus, one customer arrives the first minute. A second random number is selected to determine how long it takes to serve that first customer. In this case, the number 67 was selected, which falls in the range of 60–79 (Table 9-5), so it takes four minutes to ticket that customer.

The second minute is then replicated. The number 32 is randomly chosen and compared to the appropriate cumulative figures in Table 9-4 (00–36). This indicates that no customers arrive during that minute.

This procedure is continued for each minute of the 16-hour period, enabling a count to be made of the number of people who had to wait in line more than five minutes. (Remember, there are three employees working at the ticket counter.)

This procedure is quite time consuming if done manually. There are numerous

Table 9-4
Likelihood of Various Numbers of Customers Arriving Each Minute

Event	Probability	Cumulative Probability
0 customer per minute	.37	00 - 36
1 customer per minute	.37	37 - 73
2 customers per minute	.18	74 - 91
3 customers per minute	.06	92 - 97
4 customers per minute	.02	98 - 99

Table 9-5
Likelihood of Time Needed to Service a Particular Customer

Event	Probability	Cumulative Probability
1 minute to service	.20	00 - 19
2 minutes to service	.20	20 - 39
3 minutes to service	.20	40 - 59
4 minutes to service	.20	60 - 79
5 minutes to service	.20	80 - 99

computer models that can handle such queuing problems. In the Acme example, a computer model indicated that a total of 42 people per week would have to wait in line more than five minutes to be serviced at a typical Acme ticket counter. This means the campaign promise of "10 percent off the ticket price" to those waiting more than five minutes would be too costly for Acme, when only three persons staffed a typical ticket booth.

Markov Chain Model

The Markov Process is used to simulate the impact that a firm's present marketing activities will have on its future market share.[3] Its usefulness as a forecasting model is that it can forecast a firm's sales at a specific future time if the total sales of a market for that period can be reasonably estimated.

The premise of this model is that three factors interact to determine a firm's market share at some future date.

(a)   The rate at which the firm retains its present customers (retention rate).

(b)   The rate at which its present customers switch to competitors (switching-out rate).

(c)   The rate at which competitor's customers switch to the company's product (switching-in rate).

By assessing the present interaction of all three rates, a firm's future market share can be predicted. A major assumption of this model is that the customers' purchase behavior in the last time period will continue to be the same in the forecast period. It also assumes a fairly constant market size with no new competitors.

Thus, if these conditions can be accepted, the Markov process provides the following information:

1.   A firm's market share at some future time.

2.   The point in time when market equilibrium will be reached among competitors.

3.   A firm's gain or loss of market share based on the impact of its marketing efforts.

The following example illustrates how each of these three events are determined using the Markov Chain model.

Dairy Example

There are three dairies serving River City, supplying all of that city's milk. Customers switch from dairy to dairy over time because of promotions, dissatisfaction with service, and so on. One of these dairies, Golden Glow, wants to determine what its future market share would be under its present promotional programs as well as under alternative programs. The dairy hires a market research firm to collect information on the brand loyalty and brand switching of River City milk customers. The researchers provide the following information:

Dairy A—Golden Glow: Retains .8 of its customers, loses .1 of its customers to Dairy B, and loses .1 of its customers to Dairy C.

Dairy B: Retains .9 of its customers, loses .07 of its customers to Dairy A, and loses .03 of its customers to Dairy C.

Dairy C: Retains .85 of its customers, loses .083 of its customers to Dairy A, and loses .067 of its customers to Dairy B.

Column A of Table 9-6 indicates that Dairy A retains 80 percent of its customers, gains 7 percent of Dairy B's customers, and gains 8.3 percent of Dairy C's customers during a given time period.

As previously stated, it is assumed brand switching by customers follows a fairly consistent pattern, so that future switching patterns mirror the past patterns. The research also disclosed that during the most recent period (July), the

Table 9-6
Customer Gains and Losses of Three Dairies

Firms	A	B	C	
A	.8	.1	.1	= 1
B	.07	.9	.03	= 1
C	.083	.067	.850	= 1

Gains from ↓

⟶

Loses to

market shares of the three dairies were: Dairy A, 22 percent; Dairy B, 49 percent; and Dairy C, 29 percent.

Dairy A (Golden Glow) wants to determine what its market share will be on August 1, assuming the present brand-switching pattern continues and no dairy changes its promotional efforts or its pricing policies. The results are obtained by multiplying the figures in the matrix by present market shares (see Table 9-7 for calculations).

Table 9-7
Firm A's Market Share for August 1

$$
\begin{pmatrix}
 & A & B & C \\
A & .80 & .1 & .1 \\
B & .07 & .9 & .03 \\
C & .083 & .067 & .85
\end{pmatrix} \times \quad .22 \quad .49 \quad .29
$$

Multiplication is as follows:

(A's rate of retention of its customers x its share of the market)	.8 x .22	= .176
(A's attraction of B's customers x B's share of the market)	.07 x .49	= .034
(A's attraction of C's customers x C's share of the market)	.083 x .29	= .024
	Sum =	$\overline{.234}$

Table 9-8
Firm B's and Firm C's Market Shares for August 1

.1 x .22 = .022	.1 x .22 = .022
.9 x .49 = .441	.03 x .49 = .015
.067 x .29 = .020	.85 x .29 = .246
———	———
B's Share = 48.3%	C's Share = 28.3%
August 1	August 1

A's share of the market on August 1 should be 23.4 percent. The same procedures are followed to derive the August 1 market share of Dairy B and Dairy C (see Table 9-8 for calculations).

Multiple Period Estimates

If on July 1 Dairy A wanted to determine what its September 1 share would be, two methods could be used: (a) The brand-shifting matrix could be squared or (b) the market share for August 1 (which was just computed) could be determined and this new market share substituted into future computations. Squaring a matrix is a complex procedure involving many calculations, so whenever possible a computer should be used with this procedure.

Table 9-9 shows the computations for deriving September 1 market shares for each dairy, based on their estimated August market shares using technique (b).

Equilibrium Points

A second benefit of the Markov process is its ability to determine points of equilibrium, that is, the time period when market shares for all competitors no longer change because the number of customers leaving various dairies equal the number they attract from other dairies. (Again, this assumes no action is taken by any of the dairies to affect the brand-switching matrix.)

Equilibrium points are determined by continuing the computations (shown in Table 9-8) through additional months until changes in each firm's market share become infinitely small. In the dairy example the equilibrium points are: Dairy A, .272; Dairy B, .456; and Dairy C, .272. These are the market shares each dairy will retain if their present marketing programs are continued.

Analysis of Marketing Activities

The third benefit of the Markov process is that it can be used to analyze various marketing activities and determine the likely impact of each on market

Table 9-9
Market Shares for September 1 Based on Estimated Shares for August

```
                                      Estimated New Shares (Aug. 1st)

      .8        .1        .1              A      B      C
   /                         \
  (  .07       .9        .03  )      x   .234   .483   .283
   \                         /
      .083      .067      .85

A

.8 x .234   = .187    (Retained share)

.07 x .483  = .034    (Share from B)

.083 x .283 = .023    (Share from C)
              ____

              .244 = A's probable share on September 1

              .477 = B's probable share

              .279 = C's probable share
```

share. Following is a brand-switching matrix of the same three dairies that is different from the one used earlier:

```
A      .2      .6      .2
B      .1      .5      .5
C      .2      .3      .5
```

If the marketing strategies of each firm does not change, at the point of equilibrium A should have .156 market share, B .434, and C would have .410. In light of the above possible outcome, Firm A is considering two strategies to improve its market share.

Strategy 1. Firm A attempts to retain more of its own customers. By constant advertising to their present customers through handbills left with products, they think they can increase their retention to .4 from the current .2 and they believe most of the customers retained will come at the expense of Firm B. The new matrix is:

```
.4      .4      .2
.1      .5      .4
.2      .3      .5
```

The market shares at equilibrium become: A, .2; B, .4; and C, .4. Although A's efforts are directed mainly at Firm B, under this strategy Firm C also is affected because it now gets fewer customers from B since B's total share is smaller.

Strategy 2. As an alternative, A directs its marketing efforts toward obtaining a larger share of Firm C's customers. Firm A plans to entice more of those who switch from Firm C to buy from them rather than B. Assume switchers from Firm C are seeking better service, thus Firm A will heavily promote this aspect of its operation. Under this strategy, its new brand-switching pattern might be:

.2	.6	.2
.1	.5	.4
.4	.1	.5

Note the large amount of C's customers obtained by A. The new equilibrium market share is: A, .233; B, .391; and C, .376.

Assuming both strategy 1 and strategy 2 cost about the same amount of money to carry out, strategy 2 would be used because in the long run it would provide Firm A with a larger market share. (This assumes no counter actions are initiated by B or C.)

Additional Uses of Markov Model

The previous examples dealt only with brand-switching aspects. The Markov model also is used to forecast the impact of population shifts and personnel turnover. Also, the preceding description of the Markov process is fairly low level since a number of assumptions about competitors' actions (or lack of same) had to be made to allow the model to work. There are higher-order Markov models that can handle less restrictive conditions and still simulate expected changes. Such models are found in advanced statistics texts.

OVERVIEW OF MODELS

Some forecasters and decision makers question whether most of the models described in this chapter are really forecasting techniques. Many managers are reluctant to use forecasts derived from someone assigning probabilities to the likelihood of an event occurring. Many business people believe true forecasting models are based either on past data (time series) or tied directly to other events (causal models). They look upon simulation and probability models as techniques to be used only as a last resort.

This writer disagrees with such assessments. The judgment and simulation models described in this and the preceding chapter are legitimate tools for a forecaster. They require those people providing input to give extensive thought to all events possibly affecting a firm or industry. They enable decision makers to use additional variables, other than just past sales, in estimating future sales. So these techniques, if properly applied, can increase decision makers' understanding of forces that have an impact on their product or industry.

The phrase, "if properly applied," should be emphasized. If probabilities are assigned in a haphazard way or if little discussion or thought is given to their selection then the resulting models will, at best, be only of limited value and, at worst, dangerous tools. Therefore, all parties involved must be made aware of how important it is to devote the time and energy needed to provide their best estimates of certain events.

When simulation models are involved, the users of the model's output must be made aware of the inherent limitations of each model. But here too, by studying the data used in the model, the decision maker is going to learn a great deal about the factors affecting his or her firm's sales.

These models can also be very effective tools when used in conjunction with causal and time series models. Forecasts from the different models can be compared and, where major differences exist, decision makers and forecasters can explore reasons for the variations. The result should be that all parties emerge with a better understanding of their respective markets.

NOTES

1. Subhash C. Jain, *Marketing Planning and Strategy* (Cincinnati: Southwestern Publishing Co., 1981), pp. 490–496.
2. For an expanded discussion of this simulation process see William Sullivan and W. Wayne Claycombe, *Fundamentals of Forecasting* (Reston, Va.: Reston Publishing Co., 1977), pp. 164–189.
3. The Markov process was named for a Russian mathematician who used this process to predict the behavior of gas particles in a closed chamber.

QUESTIONS AND EXERCISES

1. The Wildcat Oil Company must decide whether to drill for oil on newly leased federal land in Wyoming. They use soil tests to give them some idea about the general underground structures they will have to drill through to reach oil. They have historical data that indicate the likelihood of certain underground structures with certain types of soil. The soil test in tract Y indicates the likelihood of the following ground structures:

   Underground structure A has probability of .6.

   Underground structure B has probability of .3.

   Underground structure C has probability of .1.

   Underground structure A usually indicates only limited oil deposits (potential payoff of $500,000). Structure B indicates better oil deposits (potential payoff of $1 million), and structure C indicates big oil payoffs (potential payoffs of $4 million).

   (a) Based on this information, what is Wildcat's expected oil payoff from this tract of land?

(b)   The total estimated costs for drilling in that tract of land is $800,000. Should they drill?

(c)   Is this a situation of risk or uncertainty?

2.   Frill Tool Company asks each of its sales staff to estimate sales for their territory in the coming year. Shirley Jones is the salesperson in District 5. She has been making forecasts for six years and her forecasts, along with actual sales, are now provided.

Year	Jones' Forecast	Actual Sales
1	103	101
2	110	107
3	126	118
4	132	131
5	125	119
6	135	131

(a)   Based on Jones' past performance what type of "fudge factor" would you assign her forecast?

(b)   Her forecast for this year is 137 units. How would you adjust that forecast?

3.   The Third National Bank of Toledo, Ohio presently has two drive-up windows to serve customers. A recent survey of their customers indicates that a sizable number feel they have to wait too long in these drive-up lines, especially during rush hours. The president of the bank believes that if more than 10 percent of the customers using drive-up windows have to wait in excess of five minutes, a third drive-up facility should be built. Observations of customers and their service times are made for three days. That information indicates the following probabilities for service time.

Service Time in Minutes	Probability
2 minutes	.2
3 minutes	.3
4 minutes	.3
5 minutes	.15
6 minutes	.05

The observations also indicated that two cars per minute arrive at each drive-up window. Using this information, simulate a typical 15-minute time period for each of the drive-up windows. Based on these results, is a third window needed? (Recognize that in real situations, a 15-minute simulation is certainly not long enough to make such a decision.)

4.   There are three major supermarkets serving Forest City, Georgia: (a) Southern Belle, (b) Albright's, and (c) Rhett's. A survey of consumers in Forest City indicate the following store switching patterns.

	A	B	C		
A	.75	.15	.10	=	1.00
B	.05	.85	.10	=	1.00
C	.10	.10	.80	=	1.00

The current market share of each of the three supermarkets is:

Southern Belle	.30
Albright's	.30
Rhett's	.40

(a) If each supermarket's present marketing program is continued into the next period, what will the market share be for each of the three stores?

(b) What would their market shares be at the end of period 2?

(c) Based on the original market shares and brand-switching figures, what marketing actions should Southern Belle take to improve their sales position in the community?

5. Use the cross-impact technique to derive probabilities for the occurrence of the following events:

(a) Prices of natural gas and oil increase dramatically.

(b) EPA increases pollution standards for coal- and wood-burning devices.

(c) Government drops its tax credit program for energy conservation devices.

(d) Prices of solar equipment decline 20 percent.

10

Selecting and Monitoring Forecasting Techniques

INTRODUCTION

In the preceding chapters, descriptions were provided of forecasting techniques that presently have the widest application among business firms. But it is not enough merely to understand how these techniques work, it is also necessary to know (1) which model is most appropriate for a particular situation, (2) how to evaluate the accuracy of different models, and (3) if and when to alter a forecast. These three aspects of forecasting are covered in this chapter.

SELECTION OF THE FORECASTING TECHNIQUE

In Chapter 1, nine factors to consider when selecting a forecast model were identified. At that time, only a brief discussion of each factor was provided since the forecasting models themselves had not as yet been covered. Now that the reader is acquainted with the purposes and procedures of a number of forecasting techniques, more extensive coverage on the subject can be provided.

Key Factors to Consider

Of the nine factors identified in Chapter 1 as influencing the selection of a forecasting technique, six are of major importance:

(1) Length of the forecast period (forecast horizon).
(2) Pattern of data.
(3) Cost of using each technique.
(4) Types of data available.
(5) Complexity of the forecasting technique.
(6) The technique's accuracy (size of error).

Length of Forecast Period

A forecast may cover one of three time periods: (1) short term, the next three months; (2) medium term, four months to two years; and (3) long term, more than two years.

Short-Term Forecast. These forecasts are generally used to guide decisions involving inventories of raw materials and components, work schedules for production personnel, cash flows, sales performance of people and/or products. Extreme changes in the value of a variable in the short term are generally caused by a unique, unforeseen event (that is, unusual weather conditions, wildcat strikes, major catastrophes). Short-term forecasts are usually the easiest to make and, generally, are more accurate than either medium- or long-term forecasts.

Since seasonal fluctuations and randomness are the major influences on sales in the short term, the most effective forecasting methods are those that incorporate seasonality into the forecast (decomposition, Census II and the Winter's method), keeping in mind that three or more years of past data are required to compute the value of seasonality. If there is little or no seasonal impact and only minimum trend exponential smoothing and moving averages are appropriate.

Medium-Term Forecast. These forecasts cover a period of from four months to two years and are used to guide such decisions as equipment needs, promotional activities, hiring of personnel, and addition or deletion of products or brands.

Because of the length of time involved, these forecasts should make allowances for such variables as expected economic conditions (unemployment, interest rates), competitive conditions, and population changes. Since both cyclical change and trend are important factors in this time frame, regression, decomposition, Winter's method, and Box-Jenkins are efficient techniques for medium-term forecasts.

Long-Term Forecast. This covers a time period at least two years into the future and is generally used to guide long-term business decisions, that is, capital equipment needs, building needs, possible product acquisitions, and significant product changes. Major considerations must be given to expected trends, economic conditions, and competitive situations; all of which are events that often can only be estimated subjectively. Therefore, judgmental methods such as expert opinions, simulation, and technological forecasting are most useful for long-term forecasting.

Pattern of Past Data

If the forecast is to be for an existing activity, for example, a mature product, the pattern of its previous data is usually a major factor in determining the most appropriate forecasting technique. Past sales data can possess both a major pattern and a "sub-pattern." The major or primary pattern is the general trend of past sales. Is this overall trend linear, curvilinear, or stationary, that is, essentially one of no growth? Sub-patterns take place within a given year—seasonals, cyclicals, and short-term changes.

If only annual data are used in the forecast, it is not possible to isolate seasonal influences and it is also difficult to determine cyclical changes. The smaller the time unit used (monthly, weekly), the more sub-patterns that can be identified. Decomposition and the Winter's method can both identify seasonal influences, and the Census II technique goes one step further by including the number of work or business days or weeks in a month as a factor.

If the general trend of the data is stationary, moving averages and exponential smoothing are recommended. Regression methods handle linear growth patterns and special versions of regression models can be developed to handle curvilinear patterns.

Since the pattern of past data is so crucial to the selection of the proper model, it is a good idea initially to graph the data to identify both its general pattern and underlying sub-patterns. It may be necessary to apply autocorrelation analysis to non-stationary data to allow the sub-patterns to emerge.

Cost of Technique

There are three categories of costs that should be considered when selecting a forecasting technique:

(a) Collecting the data.

(b) Developing and using the model.

(c) Monitoring and updating forecasts.

Collecting Data. Data collection costs may be insignificant when only a single product is involved and a time series model is used. The firm's own records can usually provide all of the historical data needed for most time series models.

However, when a model uses external data it may be necessary to conduct a major search for data on potential independent variables; industry sales data, demographic data, retail sales data on competitive or complementary products. This may necessitate a costly search of government or trade association publications.

Obtaining data can also be fairly costly when judgmental methods are used. A great deal of time may be required of those experts asked to provide estimates. This is especially true when numerous meetings are needed to arrive at a consensus forecast.

If input-output or econometric models are used, the costs of obtaining data can be quite high, especially if the firm develops its own unique model. Input-output models depend upon a transactions table that simulates the flow of income, goods, and services through the economy. In some cases, such transactions can be derived from existing government input-output models but it is often necessary to obtain some primary data to depict unique inter-industry relationships.

Cross-impact models may also require a great deal of primary data. Like input-output models, they are based on a realization that a great deal of inter-dependence exists between firms and industries. Equations are developed to show these relationships and are then used to derive probabilities or forecasts. The key task is to identify and quantify the relationships, a task that can result in huge data-gathering costs.

Costs of Developing and Using the Forecast Model. The second set of expenses associated with forecasting is the costs of using the model. These costs apply primarily to situations where a computer model is involved and are basically of three types:

(1) Development costs.

(2) Data storage costs.

(3) Computer usage costs.

Development activities include writing the program for a forecast model and testing and modifying it. This includes costs for both human and computer time. Today, a large number of software forecasting packages are available, so the only development costs may be the purchase price or leasing expense of such a package. Often, these packaged programs must still be fine-tuned to the firm's unique needs.

Storage costs include the cost of storing the program and the data to be used. Box-Jenkins and Census II have high data storage requirements.

Although the computer costs per run are fairly small, certain models require a number of iterations (exponential smoothing, adaptive filtering). Other models such as Census II and Box-Jenkins require fewer program runs, but each run is quite expensive.

In most cases, however, the cost of computer time is not great enough to be a major factor in the decision of which model to use. The major cost element is usually the development cost.

Costs of Monitoring/Updating the Forecasts. In a later section of this chapter, coverage is provided on the importance of properly monitoring forecasts to see whether corrective actions are needed. Such monitoring is performed manually or by computer. If computer models are used, upper and lower limits should be established for the forecast. If actual outcomes differ from the limits, a warning is given. Monitoring is an important component of any forecasting activity and usually does not involve significant dollar outlays.

Updating the forecast involves constantly feeding the most current data into the model. The time and expense associated with obtaining this data is greatly reduced once the information sources have been identified. Generally, updating is not an expensive activity.

Overview of the Cost Factor

Today, with the widespread availability of computers and their increased capabilities in terms of speed, storage, and software packages, costs are usually no longer a critical factor in the selection of a sales-forecasting model.

This does not mean that there are not significant differences in the overall development costs of various models. But since numerous forecasting software packages exist that can be purchased for reasonable fees, firms usually no longer need to incur the costs of developing their own forecasting models from scratch.

Type of Data Available

A fourth factor influencing selection of a model is the nature of data available. Oftentimes, the data needed for a particular forecasting model are not available in the desired time frame or format. For example, a great deal of government and industry data are available only in quarterly or annual formats. Thus, a firm wishing to build a multiple regression model using its own product's monthly sales as the dependent variable, will often have a difficult time obtaining monthly data on some of the intended independent variables (industry sales, industry advertising expenditures).

Or a firm may wish to use an input-output model but the necessary transactions ratios are either outdated or non-existent. Since gathering of the required data in these two examples is very expensive, a model better suited to available data would be chosen.

Time series models usually do not pose this problem since most firms have disaggregated data on each of their activities except in cases of new or fairly new products.

Complexity of the Forecasting Technique

A fifth consideration in selecting a forecasting technique is its complexity. Do the parties involved understand how the technique works? This understanding must exist among both the forecaster and his or her primary user. In some cases, both parties are the same person, for example, a sales manager who forecasts his or her company's sales and makes decisions based on the forecast. But in many situations the forecaster and the user are different people and usually differ in their comprehension of the techniques.

A full-time professional forecaster has a strong quantitative background and usually feels comfortable with such complex techniques as Box-Jenkins and econometric models. This is usually not the case for the users, however. It is important that users understand the underlying concepts of the forecast technique so that they also can feel comfortable with its results. The user may know that the Box-Jenkins model generally provides the most accurate forecast of all time series models, but will still be reluctant to use its output unless he or she has at least a basic understanding of its procedures.

Various studies have shown that the most widely used forecasting techniques among business firms are jury of executive opinions, sales force composite, regression, and moving averages. Their wide use is not because they are cheaper to use or provide the most accurate results. Rather, they are used because their procedures are fairly easy to understand by all parties involved. Thus, if a forecaster believes a complicated model is the most appropriate one for a firm, a special effort should be made to educate users on the general philosophy of the model and how it basically works.

Accuracy of the Forecast Model

The crucial question for a forecast model is: How close are its forecasts to actual outcomes? This is usually the single most influential factor affecting the choice of a forecasting technique.

Some techniques for measuring the model's accuracy are covered in Chapter 2. Now that the reader is familiar with a variety of forecast models, it would be beneficial to deal briefly with that topic again.

The Inherent Problem—Prediction versus Forecast

Many forecasters have learned through bitter experience that a forecast model that seemed well suited to historical data does not necessarily provide the best forecast. In spite of this situation, most tools for assessing the accuracy of models are based on how well the model fits historical data.

Sartorius and Mohn make a distinction between a prediction and a forecast to illustrate this dilemma.[1] They view a prediction as identifying the sales that would occur using historical data. The model, which is developed from past data, is merely applied to this same past data. A prediction should be fairly accurate, therefore, since the model is built from the same data it is predicting.

A forecast, on the other hand, is the calculation of a value of some future period. Although forecasting is the real reason for developing these models, selection of the "best" model is usually based on its relative success in predicting. We assume the best predicting model will also be the best forecasting model.

Thus, the three dominant methods for measuring forecasting accuracy—mean absolute percentage error (MAPE), mean absolute error (MAD), and mean squared error (MSE)—are really assessing a model's accuracy in predicting. (See Chapter 2 for a discussion of these three methods).

Reliance on Predictive Accuracy

The primary reason that the accuracy of predictions rather than the accuracy of forecasts is the selection criterion is that information about the success of a forecast can only be obtained after the actual results (outcome) are in. Thus, the forecaster is caught in a "catch-22" situation. Once a model has been chosen, however, there will be opportunities to evaluate it since a record of its accuracy will begin to emerge over time. But this is generally too late, since the damage from a bad forecast will already have been done.

Data Splitting

Although the selection of a model must often be based on how well it predicts the data from which it is originally developed, data splitting can be used to overcome this drawback partially. One strategy frequently used is to include only half of the data in developing the model and the other half to test the model's accuracy. Some data-splitting strategies even divide the data into two sub-sets with a model developed from the first set of data and used to forecast the second set. Then the process is repeated with the second sub-set used to develop the model and the first sub-set to test its accuracy.

The effectiveness of data splitting depends on the total number of data points available for the analysis as well as the length of the forecasting period.

Tests Used

The method used to test a model's accuracy depends on the forecast accuracy desired. If management is not overly concerned with consistent small errors ($\pm$ 5 percent) but rather wants to minimize the occurrence of a major error, then a test should be used which severely penalizes large forecast errors. Mean squared errors is such a test. If the unit or dollar value of past data are fairly large, the mean absolute percentage error test is used since percentages are more meaningful. If there is concern about all errors, regardless of whether they are in the positive or negative direction, then mean absolute errors should be evaluated.

There are additional tests such as Thiel's U coefficient,[2] directional error analysis,[3] or coefficients of determination for time series data,[4] which also could be applied if the forecaster wants to apply a full complement of tests.

Overview

This portion of the chapter has dealt with the factors that should be considered when selecting the forecast model. All six of the factors covered will likely have an impact on model selection. The key criterion, however, is accuracy, or the size of error.

MONITORING FORECASTS

Once the technique is chosen and forecasts are developed, the forecasted sales and actual sales should be monitored on a regular basis to see whether corrective action is needed. Even if sales forecasts are made only on an annual basis, it is necessary to monitor actual sales at least quarterly to determine whether any major deviations are occurring.

Extreme Types of Monitoring

Monitoring often suffers from two major forms of misuse. At one extreme are those firms that monitor sales weekly and constantly revise the forecast upward or downward based on the most recent week's sales. They fail to recognize that many discrepancies are merely short-term disruptions resulting from competitors' actions (a special sale) or weather problems (blizzard hampers truck transportation) and do not require a major overhaul of the forecast.

At the other extreme are those firms that wait too long to alter their forecasts. Even six or seven months into the year they are reluctant to alter what appears to be an errant forecast, seeking even more concrete evidence.

Whereas all firms should monitor forecasts, the actual impact of errant forecasts will vary among firms. Firms that can expand or contract their production activities on short notice or can fill their raw material needs rather easily will not suffer as much from an errant forecast as those that must make long-term capital and personnel commitments to meet production schedules (car manufacturers, heavy equipment producers, seasonal goods makers that produce four to six months in advance of holidays).

Identifying Reasons for Forecast Error

Once it has been confirmed that the forecast is in error, it is crucial that the factors causing this error be identified. Before a forecast can be revised, it is necessary to understand why it differed from actual results. Why are actual sales 20 percent higher than forecasted sales? Why are unit sales 1,000 less than the forecast? Is the basic forecast technique at fault or have some unusual events taken place that raised havoc with the forecast?

Factors Causing Major Errors

There are numerous factors that can cause a forecast to be in error. Some of the more common ones are:

(1) Relationships in the model change. In a multiple regression model, the influence of one or more independent variables may change and no longer are accurately represented by the existing regression coefficients (b values). When people became accustomed to high interest rates, the rates no longer were a major deterrent to buying.

(2) New explanatory variables emerge. New energy tax credits dramatically changed demand for home insulation.

(3) Inaccurate data exists on "predictors." Since forecasts of independent variables are used to forecast the dependent variable, inaccuracies in these predictors will distort the forecasts of the dependent variables.

(4) Changes occur in data pattern. Seasonal patterns can change or the rate of growth from period to period changes. Unless the model is self-correcting (adaptive filtering), these changes require alterations in the basic model.

When to Revise Forecasts

Since the impact of an errant forecast varies among firms, each firm must establish its own signals that warn when a forecast should be revised. Following are some examples of such signals (it is emphasized that these are merely examples and are not intended to be rules of thumb for firms):

(1) Error is in excess of 10 percent three forecast periods in a row.
(2) Error is in the same direction three consecutive periods.
(3) The pattern of present data is significantly different from the pattern in comparable periods of previous years.

Temporary disruptions in the marketplace occur frequently. It is important, therefore, to distinguish between such disruptions and real forecast errors. The previously cited signals are ways of making such distinctions.

Again, it is emphasized that each firm must develop its own criteria as to when to review a forecast and when to revise it. A multi-product firm may even have to establish different criteria for each product or product category.

Methods for Monitoring Forecasts

Monitoring compares actual sales with forecasted sales over consecutive time periods. But there is no one "best" way to monitor forecasts. The method used depends on such factors as seasonality, the growth pattern of the entire industry, how often the forecast is to be monitored, and a company's adjustment capability.

Dollar Sales versus Unit Sales

Multi-product firms such as supermarkets and drug stores generally use dollar sales as the dependent variable because they carry many products offered at a variety of prices. In such cases, a comparison of overall unit sales from one period to another is meaningless, because the use of dollar sales introduces the problem of sales distortion due to changes in prices. Thus, even though dollar sales may increase, unit sales could decline.

The advantage of using unit sales is that price changes do not distort results. Assuming no changes occur in product size, the differences in unit sales from period to period are real changes. Therefore, whenever possible units should be used in the analysis rather than dollars, especially in sales forecasting.

Using Actual Sales Data

Table 10-1 contains both the actual and forecasted sales of Acme Productions. A forecast of the entire year was made ($730,244) and apportioned to the individual months based on seasonal values.

Seven months have passed, and it appears that there are no major disparities between the forecasts and actual sales. The firm's management is willing to accept monthly differences of ± 5 percent. One disturbing factor is that the forecast seems to be constantly underestimating actual sales and the amount of this difference seems to be increasing (Column 5). An analysis should be per-

Table 10-1
Acme Productions (sales in dollars)

Month	(1) Seasonals	(2) Forecast	(3) Actual	(4) Difference	(5) Difference (%)
January	6.8	49,604	50,091	+ 487	+1.0
February	8.1	59,154	58,922	- 232	- .4
March	9.2	67,188	68,732	+1544	+2.2
1st Quarter	24.1	175,946	177,745	+1799	+1.0
April	9.5	69,379	70,621	+1242	+1.8
May	10.3	75,221	76,681	+1460	+1.9
June	9.1	66,457	68,297	+1840	+2.7
2nd Quarter	28.9	211,057	215,599	+4542	+2.1
July	7.8	56,963	58,842	+1879	+3.2
August	6.3	46,009			
September	6.2	45,279			
3rd Quarter	20.3	148,251			
October	7.9	57,694			
November	9.0	65,727			
December	9.8	71,569			
4th Quarter	26.7	194,990			
Total	100.0	$730,244			

formed to determine the reasons for this continual disparity. If it is due solely to higher prices caused by inflation, a "fudge factor" for inflation should be built into the forecasts of the remaining months.

Using Cumulative Sales Data

Temporary disruptions in the market often occur. A firm should be able to distinguish between these disruptions and real forecast errors. One way of doing this is to use cumulative sales in the monitoring process. Table 10-2 contains 12 months of cumulative unit sales of Johnson Sewing Machines, Inc.

Column 1 contains the accumulated sales at the end of each period. Column 2 contains the cumulative portion of each month's sales based on past seasonal performances. Column 3 is a projection of annual sales based on actual sales.

The original sales forecast for the year had been for approximately 60,000 units. Management can live with a variation of ± 3 percent of the forecast (58,200 to 61,800).

After the first four months, unit sales are slightly lower than the annual amount forecasted, but within the acceptable range. Thus, no major change is needed in the firm's production activities. At about mid-year, a significant increase in unit sales occurred and continued through the end of October.

Table 10-2
Cumulative Monthly Unit Sales of Johnson's Sewing Machines

	Cumulative Monthly Sales (1)	Cumulative Proportion of Annual Sales (2)*	Projected Annual Sales (1) ÷ (2)
January	3,811	.064	59,547
February	7,892	.138	57,188
March	12,664	.218	58,092
April	18,025	.307	58,713
May	24,100	.406	59,360
June	29,320	.507	57,830
July	35,326	.594	59,471
August	41,347	.687	60,185
September	48,854	.784	62,314
October	54,935	.871	63,071
November		.948	
December		1.000	

* One method for deriving this value is to divide each month's seasonal index by 12, i.e.

January Seasonal Index = .768   (from earlier calculation)

Therefore, .768 ÷ 12 = .064

At that point, the cause of the change should be determined and a decision made as to whether the forecast should be revised for November and December.

Monitoring Patterns of Variation

A variable may historically experience greater variation in some periods than others. Thus, a variation of 6 percent for June, a normally unstable month, may not cause as much concern as a 4 percent disparity in the February forecast, a month that usually has little variation from year to year.

So in monitoring forecasts, it may be necessary to use different acceptable error ranges for each time period. Table 10-3 shows how such values are determined. Standard deviations for each specific month are used to develop acceptable error ranges.

Table 10-3
Sales of Audio Heaven's Stereo Units, 1975–1982, for February and June (in thousands of units)

Year	Forecast	Actual Sales	Deviations	Squared Deviations
February				
1975	425	417	− 8	64
1976	452	468	16	256
1977	461	447	−14	196
1978	471	489	18	324
1979	482	487	5	25
1980	487	479	− 8	64
1981	497	486	−11	121
1982	503	514	11	121
				$\Sigma = 1171$

$$\text{Standard Deviation} = \sqrt{\frac{\Sigma \text{ Deviations}^2}{n-1}} = \sqrt{\frac{1171}{7}} = 12.9$$

Year	Forecast	Actual Sales	Deviations	Squared Deviations
June				
1975	531	501	−30	900
1976	562	602	40	1600
1977	579	589	10	100
1978	594	572	−22	484
1979	597	612	15	225
1980	612	600	−12	144
1981	618	637	19	361
1982	631	607	24	576
				$\Sigma = 4390$

$$\text{Standard Deviation} = \sqrt{\frac{\Sigma \text{ Deviations}^2}{n-1}} = \sqrt{\frac{4390}{7}} = 25.1$$

If plus or minus two standard deviations are considered an acceptable difference from the forecast, February sales could differ by 25,800 units (2×12.9) from the forecast before a significant error is assumed. June sales, on the other hand, could vary from the forecast by $\pm$ 50,200 units and the forecast model would still be acceptable.

Statistical Criteria

When regression models are involved, a standard error of the forecast (SE_y) is statistically derived. It is the criterion for determining whether there is a critical difference between actual and forecast values.

For example, if the standard error is 2,107 and the actual sales forecast derived from the regression equation is 37,102, the actual sales should fall somewhere between 32,888 and 41,316 ($\pm$ 2 SE_y). If they don't, the model would seem to be in error.

Although statistically defensible, most decision makers would find the error range of 8,428 units in the previous example too large, and would likely set a confidence interval that included fewer units.

Which Products to Monitor

The costs of monitoring sales must be offset by the savings resulting from more accurate forecasts. For many low cost, low volume products, the costs of monitoring and adjusting forecasts may not be justified. Thus, it may be necessary to categorize products according to the Pareto principle, or ABC analysis.[5] (Marketers call this the 80-20 principle, whereas production people use the term Pareto principle.)

This principle states that in most firms, a small number of the firm's products provide the largest portion of its sales. Therefore, in monitoring sales, these products should be separated into three groups—A, B, and C.

A items are those with a higher turnover rate, relatively few in number (10 to 20 percent of total) and account for 70 to 80 percent of annual sales. It is crucial that effective monitoring be used with these items so that changes in demand can be detected early.

B items are relatively important to the firm, but forecast errors with them will not drastically hurt the firm. Monitoring is needed, but it doesn't have to be as sophisticated as the monitoring procedures for A items.

C items are not nearly as important as A or B items. They represent only a small portion of the firm's annual sales and it is not practical to monitor them closely. Some firms may not even maintain specific inventory records on these items; they merely attempt to have a small surplus on hand at all times.

Thus, a firm should use sophisticated monitoring methods with A products, moderate monitoring with B products, and little or no monitoring of C products. In fact, sales of C items are usually forecasted only on an annual basis.

Overview of Monitoring Activities

The success of a forecasting model must be continually evaluated. If major disparities occur between actual and forecasted outcomes, steps must be taken to alter the situation. The first step is to set standards that signal when a significant error has occurred. Once a significant error has been identified, the cause of the error must be determined. Identifying the cause determines two things: (1) whether the disturbance is permanent or temporary and (2) whether the error is inherent in the model or due to extraneous factors.

Once the cause of the error is determined, a decision can be made to either make minor adjustments to certain data in the model or use a different forecasting model. Some combination of these two might even be needed.

Forecasters and managers must work together in these monitoring and control activities. Managers should not assume an advocacy position in which they blame forecasters for all errors. Rather, they should recognize the difficulties associated with forecasting and accept the fact that there are times when major alterations in forecasts are needed. If they accept this philosophy, managers will be able to aid the forecaster in determining the causes of forecast errors.

NOTES

1. Lester C. Sartorius and N. Carroll Mohn, *Sales Forecasting Models: A Diagnostic Approach*, Research Monograph No. 69 (Georgia State University: Publishing Services Division, College of Business, 1976), pp. 236–238.
2. Spyros Makridakis and Steven C. Wheelwright, *The Handbook of Forecasting: A Manager's Guide* (New York: John Wiley & Sons, Inc.), pp. 460–461.
3. Sartorius and Mohn, *Sales Forecasting Models*, pp. 239–241.
4. D. A. Pierce, "R^2 Measures for Time Series," *Journal of American Statistical Association*, vol. 74 (1979), pp. 901–910.
5. C. D. Lewis, *Demand Analysis and Inventory Control* (Lexington, Mass.: Lexington Books, 1975).

QUESTIONS AND EXERCISES

1. Why are short-term forecasts usually more accurate than medium- or long-term forecasts?
2. What is usually the most important factor when selecting a forecasting technique?
3. Why is cost becoming less important as a factor in the selection of a forecasting model?
4. What is the difference between a prediction and a forecast? Why is the prediction usually fairly accurate?
5. List some conditions that could cause major error to occur in the forecasts of:

    (a) Passenger miles flown on United Airlines in the past six months.

    (b) Sales of 1984 Toyotas.

    (c) Christmas toy sales at Sears.

    (d) Sales of personal computers.

11

Acquiring the Needed Data

INTRODUCTION

Forecasters, analysts, and market researchers share a common characteristic: they are major users of quantitative data. Therefore, the people in these positions must be knowledgeable about the types of data available and the most effective ways of obtaining that data.

Primary versus Secondary Data

People often mistakenly distinguish between these two types of data on the basis of who gathers the data. If I gather the data, they are primary data; if someone else gathers the data, they are secondary data. This is an erroneous interpretation since it is the origin of the data, not who gathers them, that distinguishes secondary data from primary data.

Primary data originate with the specific research being undertaken. Secondary data are data that have been gathered for some other purpose but are applicable to this specific study.

Primary Data Usage

The need for primary data often arises when judgmental techniques are involved, such as technological forecasting, the jury of executive opinion, and delphi. These techniques require an original base of information to help participants develop their estimates.

A description of the actual procedures to follow when gathering primary data is better handled in a marketing research text since surveys and observation procedures are such an important part of that activity.

This chapter concentrates on sources of secondary data since they are of major importance to most forecasters.

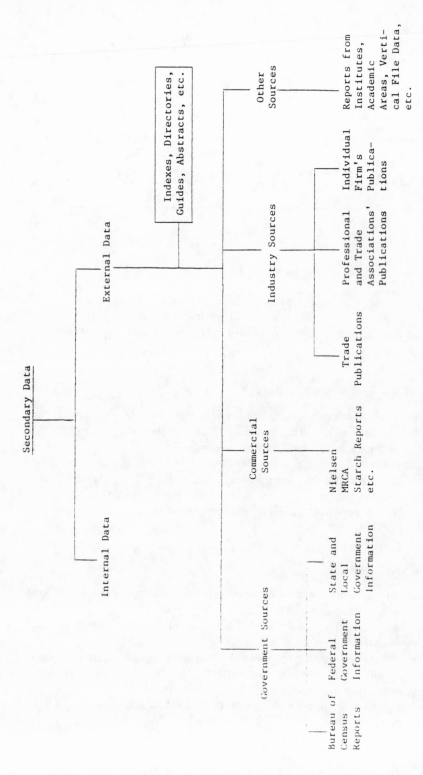

Figure 11-1
Secondary Sources of Business Information

CATEGORIES OF SECONDARY DATA

From the perspective of individual firms, there are two broad groups of data—external and internal (see Figure 11-1). Internal data is compiled by a firm in its normal business operations and include such information as sales figures, raw material expenditures, inventory records, and payroll data. External data come from a myriad of sources outside the firm and comprise the majority of secondary data.

Because such an immense volume and variety of external secondary data is available to the business community, it is necessary to separate it further into categories. This author uses four broad classifications to identify each source of "external" secondary data: government, commercial, industry, and "other." These categories are discussed more fully later in this chapter.

Internal Data

In many firms the internal data is gathered in such an unorganized manner that there is little knowledge even among a firm's own departments about the actual types of information being compiled. This confusion has led many forecasters to go outside the firm for data already existing within the company. For example, Company X manufactures metal casters. The firm's corporate forecasters believed they needed sales information on its chief competitors. Questionnaires were sent to a variety of potential customers inquiring about the brands of metal casters being used. The forecasters weren't aware that the firm's own salespeople had market-share data and sales data on customers and potential customers for the past three years. Surprisingly, this lack of communication between departments seems to be the rule rather than the exception.

Almost as great a sin as not knowing what information exists in the firm is passing up opportunities to obtain additional information that could be useful to decision makers. Many firms could restructure their sales receipts so that they would provide more specific information about customers. Accounting records could be structured in such a way that expenses and revenues could be more accurately assigned to products, customer groups, salesmen, and territories.

There is growing awareness among firms that greater interdepartmental cooperation is needed if everyone is to obtain maximum value from internal data. This realization has led to the development in many firms of a formal information system.

Information Systems

A firm's information system can be broadly described as an organized system of people and/or equipment designed to provide the orderly collection and dissemination of information obtained from both primary and secondary sources. Ideally, such a system would be similar to an intelligence center that accumulates

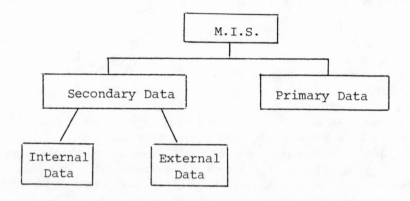

Figure 11-2
Ideal Relationship between Information System and Data Sources

and generates all data (secondary and primary) of potential use to the firm's decision makers (Figure 11-2).

Most firms that claim they have an information system are really talking about a system in which managers regularly receive computer printouts of internal data (sales, production, receivables, and so on) but have little knowledge about the types of external data or primary data available in the firm. Figure 11-3 is a more realistic depiction of the typical information system of firms. Most of the external data and almost all of the primary data, regrettably, remains in the private domain of the person or department that originally requested it.

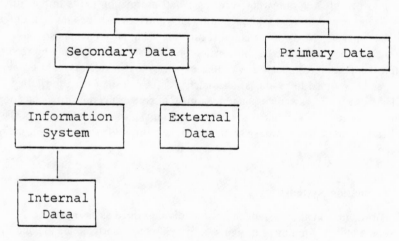

Figure 11-3
Typical Relationship between Information System and Data Sources

External Data

These data come from a huge number of data sources outside the firm. In a typical year more than 40,000 books are published just in the United States, and 90 percent of these are non-fiction. There are over 55,000 periodicals presently published throughout the world. The *Monthly Catalog of U.S. Government Publications* has almost 32,000 listings annually which is only a fraction of our government's total output.[1]

The various sources of external data are so numerous that to use them effectively, a forecaster or analyst must be a skilled user of indices, abstracts, and directories. If such skill is lacking, much time will be wasted in information searches and a great deal of secondary information will never be found.

As stated earlier, this author has chosen to divide external business data into four categories based on the type of agency or firm providing the data: (a) government sources, (b) commercial sources, (c) inter- and intra-industry sources, and (d) a catch-all category for those sources not fitting into the other three. The remainder of this chapter is devoted to a presentation of external data sources and how to use them effectively. This is not meant to minimize the value of internal data but it is assumed most managers and forecasters already have reasonable knowledge of their own firm's data and how to gain access to them.

SEARCHING FOR EXTERNAL DATA

The procedures used to search for external data depend upon the general nature of the data sought. In those situations where very specific data are sought, only a brief search may be needed. For instance, you may just want information on the annual sales of florists in the state of New York from 1978 to 1983. If you know the specific data source, you can go directly to it and obtain the needed information. In this case, the Society of American Florists' annual report provides the desired information.

Oftentimes, the forecaster or analyst will not be aware of a specific information source so some type of organized search procedure must be initiated. A pet food manufacturer may want to know the number of dogs and cats in the Rocky Mountain region. Or a producer of a plastic wrap may desire data on packaged meat sales in five midwest states over the past five years. What is the starting point for such searches?

Systematic Use of Aids

When gathering information, it is important to make effective use of indices, abstracts, directories, and other aids available in libraries. Abstracts present the basic contents of a publication in capsule form, whereas indices present only minimum data about the publication—author, publisher, date of publication.

The starting point is to identify the topic for which you are seeking information. List all the possible categories or headings under which the topic might be discussed in secondary sources. If the topic is defined too narrowly and information is only pursued on a single subject, a lot of useful information may never be tapped. For example, a forecaster seeking information on dog food sales should also search for articles under such headings as "pet food"; "pets, feeding of"; "meat by-products"; or even "animal feeds."

The broader the vantage point taken when seeking secondary data, the better the chances of covering all possible data sources. It is important to have a number of these possible subject headings in mind prior to the information search so that you won't have to continually return to the references because you thought of a new subject heading.

Once the possible subject headings have been established, attention can be turned to aids that will direct the research toward the desired information. The first step is to determine whether a bibliography on the subject already exists. The publication, *Bibliographies Index: A Cumulative Bibliography of Bibliographies,* published by the H. W. Wilson Co. in New York, should be consulted. This lists various books, periodicals, and other publications pertaining to identified subjects. If the desired subject heading is listed in that book, a large bibliography might be provided.

If the subject is somewhat unique, a bibliography will probably not already exist so one must be developed. Different aids can be used for developing such a list from books, periodicals, newspapers, and government publications.

Aids for Books

Persons seeking secondary data from books can use the following aids to find the ones most appropriate to their needs.

(a) *Card Catalog*—This is a file kept in each library listing its offerings and should be the starting point for most library research. Most card catalog systems present information on books in at least two ways: an author-title section for those seeking a particular book or the works of a particular author and a subject section that lists the books on the basis of its general subject matter.

(b) *Publishers Weekly*—A journal for the book trade that provides a complete record of American books published during given weeks and includes brief descriptions of the subject matter of each book.

(c) *Book Review Index*—Published monthly by the Gale Research Company in Detroit. It provides an index of book reviews that have appeared in hundreds of periodicals and annually covers over 8,000 books.

(d) *Cumulative Book Index*—Monthly index, by subject, of books published throughout the world. Books are also listed by author and title.

(e) *Economic Abstracts*—This is a semi-monthly review of abstracts of books and reports on economics, finance, management, real estate, and so on.

(f) Book review sections in journals such as the *Journal of Marketing and Journal of Consumer Research* provide lists of recent books that might contain useful information.

Aids for Periodicals

The large number of existing periodicals and their wide variety of articles mean that analysts must rely heavily on indices in their search for appropriate data. Most of these indices are found in the reference areas of libraries.

(a) *Business Periodicals Index*—Lists articles by subject headings from approximately 150 business-oriented periodicals. *Forbes, Business Week, Fortune, Harvard Business Review, Management Review, Industrial Marketing,* and *Journal of Business* are just a few of the magazines indexed in this aid.

(b) *Predicasts Index*—This is the successor to the F & S Index. It provides information about companies, industries, and products from over 750 financial publications, business-oriented newspapers, trade magazines, and special reports. It is the most detailed index available on business-related subjects and is updated quarterly. The information is arranged by industry and product codes as well as by company name.

(c) *Readers' Guide to Periodical Literature*—Indexes articles from magazines of a more general nature: *Newsweek, Time, Saturday Review, U.S. News and World Report.*

(d) *Applied Science and Technology Index*—An index of approximately 200 periodicals from the fields of automation, chemistry, engineering, and physics as well as other technical fields frequently researched for business purposes.

(e) *Ulrich's Periodical Directory*—Covers over 20,000 current foreign and domestic periodicals. It is published by R. R. Bowker Company in New York.

(f) *Public Affairs Information Services Bulletin (PAIS)*—Although it overlaps somewhat with the *Business Periodicals Index,* it includes more foreign publications. It also indexes, by subject, many books, government publications, and even more non-periodical publications.

Aids for Government Publications

The Department of Commerce maintains excellent reference libraries in field offices located in 35 major U.S. cities. The Small Business Administration also maintains field offices in 54 cities. Following are some aids for tracking down government data.

(a) *Monthly Catalog of U.S. Government Publications*—A monthly list of all federal publications published by the U.S. Superintendent of Documents. It is probably the most useful tool available for identifying government publications. Throughout the country there are libraries designated as "depository libraries" that hold a collection of major government documents. A list of these depository libraries is given in each September issue of the catalog. But even these libraries will not have every publication designated for depositories. A heavy black dot placed next to an entry in the catalog identifies those items available at depository libraries.

(b) *Monthly Checklist of State Publications*—Records those state documents received by the Library of Congress.

(c) *Government Statistics for Business Use*—Hansen and Leonard's book provides a great deal of information about the sources of federal information.

(d) *Guide to U.S. Government Publications*—A book by John Andriot that describes government periodicals by issuing agency, title, or document number.

Miscellaneous Aids

(a) *American Doctoral Dissertation Index and Dissertation Abstracts*—A service of the Microfilm Library Service, Ann Arbor, Michigan, that contains abstracts of many of the dissertations written by Ph.D. candidates. A lot of valuable information is found in these publications, and much of it has never been disseminated to the general public.

(b) *Index of University Publications of Bureau of Business and Economic Research*— This publication from the Bureau of Business Research at the University of Oregon lists the articles and papers published by the various Bureaus of Business Research on university campuses.

Directories as Aids

Directories can serve a dual role. Some are guides to information on available services, associations, and specialists. Others provide company names and addresses, information on company operations, and detailed information about a firm's product.

(a) *Poor's Register of Corporations, Directors, and Executives*—An annual directory of manufacturers and suppliers in which firms are classified by products and arranged geographically. It also lists the firm's products, address, and capital ratings.

(b) Two Dun and Bradstreet publications: *Middle Market Directory*—An annual directory listing approximately 33,000 U.S. companies with indicated worth of $500,000 to $999,999. It lists key company personnel, standard industrial classification data, sales and number of employees. *Million Dollar Directory*—Similar to the above directory except that it provides information on 31,000 U.S. companies with an indicated worth of over $1 million.

(c) *Moody's Manual of Investments*—Published by Moody's Investors Service, Inc., in New York, this aid contains historical and operational data on selected firms as well as their income accounts, balance sheets, and dividend records for the most recent five years.

(d) *Ayer Directory of Publications*—List of American newspapers and periodicals arranged by state and city. It also has an alphabetical list of trade, technical, and professional journals, which is especially valuable for identifying the trade publications of various industries and product categories, such as pet foods, dry cleaners, and so forth.

(e) *Encyclopedia of Associations*—Published by Gale Research, this publication provides information on the size of associations and their officers and publications. This is another excellent source of sales data of specific industries.

Specific Aids for Obtaining Statistics

Numerous firms and agencies publish statistics. A major problem for forecasters is identifying the types of statistics available and locating the publications containing them. Following are some sources that can aid in locating the desired statistics.

(a) *American Statistics Index*—Published by the Congressional Information Service, it is a comprehensive guide and index to the statistical publications of the U.S. government.

(b) *Statistics Sources*—A monthly publication of Gale Research that identifies sources of statistical data from government, business, and international sources.

(c) *Statistical Reference Index*—Published by the Congressional Information Service, Washington, D.C., this is a guide to statistical publications from non-government sources such as trade and professional organizations.

(d) *A Handbook for Business on the Use of Government Statistics* by Eleanor G. May (Charlottesville, Va.: Taylor Murphy Institute, 1979)—Provides a series of brief case studies demonstrating how problems can be solved using government statistics.

(e) *Guide to Foreign Trade Statistics*—Issued periodically by the Bureau of the Census (Government Printing Office), it provides a guide to foreign trade statistics.

Computerized Search Systems

The tremendous variety of secondary data presents a search problem for even the most highly trained information specialist. The recent availability of computerized searching systems has enabled information to be retrieved in a more efficient manner. Such computerized searches are available from several government agencies and commercial firms. The commercial firms generally lease or buy groups of data bases containing bibliographic references filed on magnetic tapes. Each data base stores thousands of citations, containing the title, author, publisher, and, in some cases, even an abstract of the work.

Bibliographies are usually accessed through certain key words that identify the types of information desired. For example, assume the subject area to be researched is "market and sales potential for soft drinks in Rocky Mountain region." Some key words that would be used in the search could be: soft drinks, sugar-free drinks, non-alcoholic beverages, and carbonated drinks.

The total cost of the above search would be $30 to $40 and would likely result in 30 to 35 printed citations. Names of commercial information retrieval firms in the United States can be obtained from the Information Industry Association in Washington, D.C.

Human "Aids"

Anyone searching for secondary data should be aware of the potential contribution of reference librarians. They are knowledgeable about their libraries' resources and if a business or economics specialist is available, he or she can probably provide the researcher with a number of new sources. In fact, because of their potential contribution, these specialists should be contacted immediately after the list of potential subject headings has been developed.

SOURCES OF SECONDARY INFORMATION

This section describes the actual types of secondary information available to business. As indicated in Figure 11-1, these data can best be presented by using four categories based on the source of the data.

GOVERNMENT SOURCES

The federal government develops and circulates more data than any other agency in the world. A wide variety of useful data also comes from state and local governments. Following are examples of some of the most widely used government publications.

Bureau of Census Reports

The Bureau of the Census is a general purpose, statistical agency whose primary function is to collect, process, compile, and disseminate statistical data for use by the general public and government agencies.

The primary job of the Bureau is to set up and carry out the eight major census studies. Table 11-1 shows the titles of these studies, the frequency with which they are carried out, and the year of the most recent study.

Updating of Census Data

Because of the length of time between census studies (five to ten years), the Bureau publishes updated census reports. For example, in conjunction with the *Census of Business,* more timely but less detailed information is collected by

Table 11-1
Description of Eight Census Studies

Census Title	Frequency of Study (years)	Last Census	Next Census
Population	10	1980	1990
Housing	10	1980	1990
Agriculture	5	1979	1984
Business	5	1982	1987
Manufacturers	5	1982	1987
Mineral Industries	5	1982	1987
Transportation	5	1982	1987
Governments	5	1982	1987

surveying a small sample of retail, wholesale, and selected service operations. These survey findings are released in a series of weekly, monthly, quarterly, and annual reports. Similar studies are carried out in the other census areas and result in such publications as "Annual Survey of Manufacturers," "Current Industry Reports," and "Current Population Reports." Anyone seeking updated census data should use the *Monthly Catalog of U.S. Government Publications* to find which studies have been performed.

Drawback of Census Data

The major shortcoming of census data is the length of time between the collection of the data and its release to the public. It was almost 30 months after its collection that most of the detailed information from the 1980 Census of Population and Housing was made available to the general public. By the time it is released, much of the data is already outdated.

Special Federal Government Information

Various federal government agencies also provide reports of possible use to forecasters. The Department of Agriculture is especially prolific in the number of its reports. This Department's research efforts in the growing, canning, and preparation of food products provide a wealth of statistics for food processors, wholesalers, and food retailers. Once again, the old reliable—*The Monthly Catalog of U.S. Government Publications*—is the best source to use to track down these publications.

Information Coming from State and Local Government Agencies

The majority of this information is really "registration data." This is data collected as part of legal requirements—records on births, deaths, marriages, sales tax payments, auto registrations, new home starts, property improvements, and so on. These data are collected at the local level and passed on to state agencies where they are accumulated and published in a statistical summary for the state.

The county recorder's office, the motor vehicles office, the county planning office, as well as their municipal counterparts are the main sources of the registration data useful to business. For example, the motor vehicles division has information on the number and make of new cars sold weekly within the city as well as the transfer of ownership of secondhand cars.

In addition to registration data, state and local agencies compile data needed for their everyday activities. The city engineering office, in its studies for traffic lights and stop signs, collects information on the traffic flow past various locations. This type of information is useful to firms selecting new sites for plants or distribution centers.

Certain state and city commissions, as well as Chambers of Commerce, publish information booklets wherein they proclaim their virtues and give reasons why people or industries should choose a particular locale. While much of this descriptive information is quite biased, these reports also contain useful statistics about population, average temperatures, types of employers, that can be of use to forecasters or market analysts.

COMMERCIAL SOURCES

In 1980, there were well over 1,200 firms in the United States that collected data, either on a subscription basis or as a one-time-only research project. Included are such well known firms as A. C. Nielsen, Audits and Surveys, Selling Areas—Marketing Inc. (SAMI), National Family Opinion (NFO), and Market Research Corporation of America (MRCA). Because of the nature of the data they provide, these firms generally are of greater value to market analysts and researchers than to forecasters.

Some commercial firms maintain large macro-economic models and supply clients with both historical sales data and forecasts. Four firms dominate the field of economic forecasting: Data Resources, Inc. (DRI); Wharton Economic Forecasting Association, Inc.; Chase Econometrics; and Merrill-Lynch Economics, Inc. Each uses an econometric model of the U.S. economy with over 800 equations, incorporating such factors as interest rates, auto sales, and business investment rates. Clients receive general macro forecasts as well as more specialized forecasts of their specific industry or variables. The clients may even submit a variety of scenarios and have forecasts prepared of each.

A number of other commercial firms and academic agencies have developed macro- and micro-forecasting models and provide results to the public or clients. Some of the better known of these are General Electric's MAPCAST Group, Citibank Economics, National Bureau of Economic Research, University of Michigan, Claremont College, University of North Carolina, and Kent Economic and Development Institute, Kent, Ohio.

There are also consulting firms that provide more specialized forecasting services. They might develop a forecasting system for a firm to use on its own premises. Or they can provide computer time-sharing linkages so that clients can receive forecasts directly from the consultant.

A third possible offering is the sale of a general forecasting package that the firm can use on their in-house computer. (SIBYL/RUNNER is such a software package.) Numerous software forecasting packages are available for mini- and micro-computers.

INDUSTRY SOURCES

This category includes information sources that exist primarily to serve an industry, firms, or a firm's shareholders. Publications range from general industry articles in trade magazines to annual reports of individual firms.

Trade Publications

Each major industry has one or more magazines specifically aimed at its member firms. An index titled *Business Publication Rates and Data*, published monthly by the Standard Rate and Data Service, Inc., will be of great help in identifying these publications. The previously cited *Ayer Directory of Publications* will also help.

Professional and Trade Association Publications

Professional and trade associations are also good sources of forecasting data. *The Encyclopedia of Associations*, published by the Gale Research Company of Detroit, lists associations' names, addresses, number of members, and most important, their publications.

Publications of Individual Firms

Most large business firms furnish financial reports to the public. These annual reports are prepared primarily for stockholders or potential stockholders and can be obtained from the firm's home office. In addition, many firms have in-house publications intended primarily for their own employees.

OTHER SOURCES

This is a "catch-all" category since it covers those data sources that can be useful to forecasters and analysts but don't fit neatly into any of the three previous categories. These include reports prepared by institutes and research centers, as well as academic research projects (theses, dissertations, and monographs).

Indices for these sources were presented earlier in this chapter but it would be well to repeat some of the more important ones. The *American Doctoral Dissertation Index* is a yearly publication that includes abstracts of recent doctoral dissertations. The *Index of University Publications of Business and Economic Research* is the best source of reports published by some of the academic affiliated bureaus.

Libraries also receive published material such as charts, reports, pamphlets, and monographs that generally do not have wide appeal. Most libraries keep these materials in a collection called the "Vertical File Index." The library usually does not keep a precise record of these materials, although there is a Vertical File Service Catalog in most libraries which lists some of these materials by subject headings.

KEY SOURCES OF STATISTICS

The previous sections described the general types of data available to forecasters and analysts as well as the sources of this data. This section lists 18 major publications containing statistics. They are probably the ones most frequently used by forecasters and market analysts.

(a) *Statistical Abstract of the United States* (Government Printing Office)—This annual publication is the best single source of government statistics. It provides statistics on a wide variety of social, industrial, and governmental subjects. It should be in the personal library of every forecaster and one of the first sources to use when business-related statistics are needed.

(b) *County and City Data Book* (Government Printing Office)—This is a supplement to the *Statistical Abstract* and contains around 200 categories of statistics of counties, standard metropolitan areas, and cities. The categories include population data, employment data, housing data, retail and wholesale sales data, and so on.

(c) *Business Conditions Digest,* Bureau of Economic Analysis, Department of Commerce (Government Printing Office)—This monthly publication contains numerous indicators of current business activity and is useful for developing and updating industry and company forecasts.

(d) *Economic Indicators,* Council of Economic Advisers (Government Printing Office)—A monthly publication providing statistical data on the key indicators of general business conditions such as gross national product, personal consumption expenditures, and so forth.

(e) *Federal Reserve Bulletin* (Federal Reserve System Board of Governors)—This monthly publication contains financial data on banking activities, savings, interest rates, credit, and domestic non-financial statistics; an index of industrial production; and some statistics on international trade and finance.

(f) *Handbook of Basic Economic Statistics* (Economic Statistics Bureau)—Annual, plus monthly supplements. This publication is a compilation of statistics collected by federal government agencies dealing with all areas of the national economy.

(g) *Monthly Labor Review*, Bureau of Labor Statistics (Government Printing Office)—Presents current data and related articles on employment, earnings, wholesale and retail prices.

(h) *Predicasts Forecasts and Predicasts Basebook* (Predicasts, Inc.). *Predicasts Forecasts* is a quarterly publication that provides short- and long-range projection data of economic indicators, products, and industries. It is also a guide to other statistics since the source of the data (trade journal, newspaper, government reports, or other publication) is given with each entry. *Predicasts Basebook* is a second publication of value to forecasters. It contains more than 28,000 sets of data in a time series format.

(i) *Statistical Service* (Standard & Poor's Corporation)—Presents current and historical statistical data covering banking and finance, production and labor, price indices, income and trade, transportation and communication, and some major industries.

(j) *Survey of Current Business*, Bureau of Economic Analysis, Department of Commerce (Government Printing Office)—A monthly publication that provides over 2,600 current statistical series such as indicators of general business, domestic trade, industry statistics, personal consumption expenditures, earnings and employment by industry.

(k) "Survey of Buying Power" (*Sales and Marketing Management Magazine*)— This annual publication of the magazine, usually the July issue, contains valuable information on markets by state, county, and Standard Metropolitan Area. Statistics are provided on population, household incomes and retail sales. A "Buying Power Index" is also determined for each geographic area.

(l) "Survey of Industrial Purchasing Power"—Another annual publication (April) by *Sales and Marketing Management Magazine*. It provides sales data on industrial firms and is especially useful for developing sales and market potential for industrial products.

(m) *A Graphic Guide to Consumer Markets* (National Industrial Conference Board)—Contains statistics on population, income, expenditures, advertising, prices, and production.

(n) *Consumer Buying Indicators*—Issued quarterly by the Bureau of the Census, contains 6-month and/or 12-month expected purchase estimates (in units) of automobiles, homes, furniture, carpets, major appliances, and home improvements, with a 24-month projection of home purchases also included. These estimates, which are seasonally adjusted, cover all of the major areas of consumer durable expenditures.

(o) *Economic Prospects* (Commercial Credit Company)—Based on the data provided in the Census Bureau's surveys, the Commercial Credit Company develops dollar purchase estimates for new homes, automobiles, appliances, and other durable goods. The seasonally adjusted projections are for the quarter in which the report is issued as well as the following two quarters.

(p) *County Business Patterns* (Government Printing Office)—Annual individual reports of each state provide data on employment and payroll figures based on different SIC categories for each county and SMA.

(q) *American Statistics Index* (Congressional Information Service, Inc.) A comprehensive guide to the statistical publications of the U.S. Government, it lists and indexes all federal government publications containing statistics of probable significance to researchers or forecasters.

SHORTCOMINGS OF SECONDARY DATA

Anyone using secondary data must remember that it is not developed for a specific project. Users should, therefore, be aware of conditions that may impair its usefulness.

Heterogeneous Data. The existing statistics might not be useful because of differences in definitions. The forecaster might be dealing with sales of chain food stores and would like to use some of the sales data found in various issues of *Chain Store Age.* However, the forecaster defined a chain as comprising 11 or more stores, whereas *Chain Store Age* views two or more similar stores as a chain operation and bases its statistics on this definition.

A market analyst seeks secondary data comparing retail opportunities in two cities—Dubuque, Iowa, and Waterloo, Iowa. The most recent income and population data come from each city's Chamber of Commerce. However, since Waterloo's income data are broken down on the basis of households and Dubuque's are in terms of families, the data can't be merged.

Out-of-Date Information. A person projecting new housing starts for 1985 could really be in error if the forecast were based solely on data from the 1980 Census of Housing. There is no rule of thumb as to when information becomes obsolete but the analyst should realize that in these volatile times, data more than five years old is of questionable value.

Inaccuracies in Secondhand Information. "Secondhand" information is data found in a paraphrase or quotation of the study report. The Bureau of Business Research at the University of Iowa does an in-depth study on the average debt of farmers in five selected Iowa counties. The information is published in a report by the Bureau and when incorporated into a newspaper story by the *Denver Post* it becomes secondhand data.

The major problem associated with secondhand data is the inaccuracies arising when statistics are transferred from one report to another. The figure $2,345 can easily become $3,245. Thus, whenever possible, the forecaster or analyst should bypass secondhand data and seek the original source to make sure he or she is not building a study on somebody else's mistakes.

Bias of Gathering Source. The user of secondary information should always be cognizant of the intent of the original study and judge the validity of the results accordingly. Depending upon the whims of the person or firm gathering and using the data, results can be twisted to defend almost any side of an argument. In their continuing debate, the tobacco industry and the American Cancer Society cite statistics that defend their respective positions.

Time Frame and Aggregation of the Data. A frequent shortcoming of secondary data is that it is not in the proper time frame. The forecaster wishes to use monthly appliance sales as an independent variable in a regression model but only quarterly sales data exist.

In this same vein, the data may be in an aggregated format that weakens its value. The forecaster may wish to use monthly sales of sit-down restaurants as an independent variable in the regression model but the only sales data available also include fast-food operations. There is no logical basis to disaggregate this data into two categories. Thus, the forecaster must either include the aggregated data or discard it.

Sales Results May Not Be Tied to Correct Periods. Some firms, when reporting sales, identify the month in which the original sale was made; some when the merchandise is paid for, and others when it is shipped. Thus, Firm A might sell 20 units in February and record them in that month; Firm B also sells 20 units in February, but records them in April sales, the month in which they are paid for; Firm C records them in March, the shipment month. This dramatically alters the combined sales figures of the three companies and really raises havoc with regression models that incorporate aggregated sales data.

SUMMARY OF SECONDARY DATA SOURCES

The huge amount and variety of secondary data make it essential that forecasters be familiar with the major sources of secondary data and, more importantly, know how to effectively search out these data.

Secondary data come either from within the firm (internal data) or from some outside source or agency (external data). The continual development of marketing information systems will provide firms with greater access to internal data. The bulk of secondary information though, is the external data, coming from government agencies (federal, state, and local), as well as commercial, industry, and academic sources. To use external data successfully, the researcher must know how to systematically use the various indices, directories, abstracts, and guides that identify these data.

The biggest collector and disseminator of information is the federal government, with its major data gathering agency being the Bureau of the Census. Registration data coming from state and local governments provide information of a more localized nature.

Businesses can also fill some of their information needs with data from their industries' trade publications. Commercial firms syndicating data for a fee can be valuable sources to clients needing regional and national information.

While secondary information can usually be obtained quickly and at little expense, the user should also be cognizant of some key limitations: inaccuracies may exist; the data may be dated; or it may not fit the specific information needs of the study.

STANDARD INDUSTRIAL CLASSIFICATION

Although the Standard Industrial Classification System (SIC) is not a secondary data source comparable to those already presented in this chapter, forecasters and analysts should understand its purpose and coverage. Thus, this special section is intended for those with little or no knowledge of the SIC.

The SIC was developed in 1945 under the sponsorship and supervision of the Office of Statistical Standards of the Bureau of the Budget. The system facilitates the collection, tabulation, presentation, and analysis of data relating to various business establishments. It also enables the various statistical data collected by governmental agencies, trade associations, and private research organizations to be assembled and presented in a uniform manner.

Makeup of the SIC

The SIC is a system that separates the total economy into industry segments. Each business establishment is assigned to a segment on the basis of its major line of business. Industry segments are identified by a numbering system of from two to seven digits, depending upon how fine a breakdown is desired. The assigned numbers are referred to as the "SIC code."

The two-digit code is designated as a "major group" breakdown, and is the foundation of the entire system. It starts at 01 and presently goes up to 94. For example, major group 08 covers forestry; major group 31 covers leather and leather products; major group 50, wholesale trade; major group 82, educational services; and major group 94, international government. There are presently (1985) more than 80 major group classifications.

The third digit separates a major group into more homogenous segments. While major group 50 identifies wholesale trade, the number 501 identifies the motor vehicle and automotive equipment segment of wholesale trade and 504 identifies the grocery segment. Major group number 32 identifies the stone, clay, and glass products industry and 325 identifies structural clay products.

The fourth digit is an even more finite classification. The number 5014 identifies establishments primarily engaged in the wholesale distribution of rubber tires and tubes for passenger and commercial vehicles, while 5043 identifies those establishments primarily engaged in the wholesale distribution of dairy products. The number 3253 identifies establishments primarily engaged in manufacturing ceramic wall and floor tile, while 3255 identifies those establishments manufacturing clay firebricks.

The listings in SIC manuals do not go beyond the four-digit code. The fifth, sixth, and seventh digits, where used, identify products and groups of products within an industry. At present, very little published data are available to this degree of refinement, although the code framework does exist and will probably be used in the future.

A company with multiple plants, each producing different products and services, is assigned a different SIC number for each of its establishments. If a firm performs two or more distinct activities at the same physical location, each activity might be listed as a separate establishment. This assumes that they prepare separate reports on salaries, output, purchases, and so on for each activity area.

Use of SIC

Dun and Bradstreet uses the SIC in its descriptive coverage of firms. For instance, in the *Dun and Bradstreet Million Dollar Directory*, five SIC numbers are assigned to the Sheller-Globe Corporation of Ohio (3069, 3429, 3714, 3461, 2522) to identify the firm's various operations. In this era of consolidations and mergers, a firm's name is not necessarily an accurate indicator of its actual lines of business but its SIC identification pretty well pins down its operations.

Many government publications use the SIC code to arrange their data. *County Business Patterns* groups every business establishment in the U.S. by its SIC number. It provides information on types of businesses conducted within the boundaries of each county, number of employees per type of business, and company payrolls. These statistics can be used for developing market and sales potentials, studying a region's industrial structure, assigning sales quotas, and as independent variables in regression equations.

NOTE

1. Emory C. William, *Business Research Methods* (Homewood, Ill.: Richard D. Irwin, Inc., 1976), p. 178.

QUESTIONS AND EXERCISES

1. Why is so much internal data wasted or, even worse, duplicated?
2. You have been asked to compile a bibliography of articles pertaining to "the impact of solar energy on the heating industry in 1986." Develop a list of possible topic headings for your library search. Develop a list of the trade magazines most likely to carry articles on solar energy for heating buildings.
3. Which of the following secondary sources would be used to answer each of the following questions?
    Statistical Abstract of the U.S.
    American Statistical Index
    Encyclopedia of Associations
    Standard & Poor's Industry Survey
    Survey of Buying Power
    Monthly Catalog of U.S. Government Publications
    Census of Retail Trade
    Editor and Publisher Market Guide

Predicast's Index
Business Periodicals Index
Standard Rate and Data Service

(a) What was the per capita consumption of refined sugar in the United States in 1983?

(b) What is the projected growth for the copying and duplicating equipment industry over the next five years?

(c) What is the buying power index for the San Diego metropolitan area?

(d) In 1981 the Department of Commerce published a document on marketing in Sweden. Where would information about this document be found?

(e) What articles have appeared in newspapers about Shell Oil Co.?

(f) How many retail bakeries are in the Standard Metropolitan Statistical Area of Topeka, Kansas?

(g) What are the principal shopping days in Fort Collins, Colorado?

4. What is the SIC code for retail bakeries? For athletic clubs? For manufacturers of steel girders?

5. What conditions could negatively affect the quality or value of the following secondary data?

(a) "Growth Potential Reports" issued by the Denver, Colorado Chamber of Commerce.

(b) A study on the relationship between smoking and cancer, published by the American Tobacco Industry.

(c) Sales data about the soft drink industry published in a newspaper article.

(d) Sales data for specific SIC industries.

(e) A figure identifying the sales potential for microwave ovens in Madison, Wisconsin based on demographics from the 1980 Census of Housing.

12

An Overview of Forecasting

INTRODUCTION

This final chapter deals with three key issues related to forecasts: (1) how to develop the formal forecast, (2) how to get the forecast used within the firm, and (3) the role of forecasting in future years.

DEVELOPING THE FORMAL FORECAST

In Chapter 1 the major steps in the sales forecasting process are discussed. It illustrates that forecasting is a multi-step process that includes both initial and formal forecasts. However, the chapter provides only a broad view of the forecasting process; it does not cover the specific activities involved in developing initial and formal forecasts. It is now time to look at those activities.

Why is coverage of these basic activities postponed until this final chapter? It was felt readers would better understand and appreciate these activities after they had been exposed to some forecasting techniques.

Step One—Determine Purpose of the Forecast

Why is the forecast needed? How will its results be used? Answers to these questions might seem obvious to the reader but that is because much of this book's emphasis has been on one specific type of forecast—the sales forecast. But forecasts are also used to determine personnel needs, raw material needs for production purposes, inventory requirements, and so on.

Example: General Appliance, located in Ohio, is a mid-size manufacturer of major appliances. Its management desires a forecast of refrigerator sales for the next year, the next five years, and the next ten years. These forecasts will be used to (a) develop a raw material purchase plan, (b) provide a basis for union contract negotiations, (c) determine whether to enter into an agreement to produce private brands of appliances for a major retailer, and (d) provide the basis for future marketing efforts. Items (b) and (c) go beyond what is viewed as the normal role of a sales forecast.

Step Two—Choose Specific Item(s) to Be Forecast

Once the general purpose of the forecast has been determined, the specific item(s) to be forecast can be selected. In the General Appliance example, it is clear that even though refrigerator sales are the items to be forecast, additional decisions are still needed. Do we want to forecast refrigerator sales in general or just sales of household refrigerators? Refrigerator sales for the entire United States, or just those regions served by General Appliance? In our example, the forecast will include sales of household refrigerators for a 12-state area in the midwest.

Step Three—Determine Key Elements of the Forecast

Steps Two and Three are closely related. In Step Two, the specific item(s) to be forecast is identified and in Step Three, additional elements to be included in that forecast are determined.

(a) What forecast period is desired—short term (three months or less into the future), medium term (three months to two years), or long term (more than two years into the future)?

(b) What specific time frames will be used for the data in the forecast? Will the data be in a weekly, monthly, quarterly, or annual format?

(c) What specific aspects of the subject will be forecast? Will it involve total unit sales or will it be by type of customer (chains versus independent)? Will the forecast be in dollars or units?

General Appliance's management wants two types of forecasts—a forecast of monthly sales for the coming year and longer-term forecasts for the next five and ten years. They want the forecast in unit sales and by geographic territory. They want forecasts of household refrigerator sales for the industry as a whole and for General Appliance in particular.

Step Four—Identify Key Forces Affecting the Forecast

Once the specific item(s) to be forecast has been determined, it is necessary to identify the forces likely to have an impact on that item during the forecast period. Two general sets of forces will affect any item to be forecast—external (factors outside the firm) and internal forces (factors within the firm's control). A discussion of these forces was presented in Chapter 1.

If the forecaster and user are different individuals, it is critical that they work together on this step. The user will likely have greater knowledge of the internal forces, whereas the forecaster should have more insight about macro forces. By sharing their expertise, a more precise picture is obtained of the overall impact of both sets of forces.

Example: The forecaster for General Appliance believes three key external forces will affect the sales of refrigerators over the next few years: (1) mortgage rates will drop to 10 percent, leading to an increase in housing starts; (2) unemployment will decline to 8 percent, having a positive effect on purchases of major appliances; and (3) the number of one-person households will continue to increase and the average size of families will continue to decrease, leading to an increase in the overall demand for refrigerators, especially for smaller-sized models.

The marketing manager of General Appliance believes raw material prices will stay about the same over the next year and there won't be any major model changes in the refrigerators themselves. No major price changes are expected for General Appliance's products or those of its competitors.

When these "impressions" are tied together, they provide a general assessment of the forces affecting overall refrigerator sales and the sales of General Appliance refrigerators in particular.

Step Five—Choose the Forecasting Technique(s)

Factors affecting the selection of a specific forecasting technique were discussed in Chapters 1 and 10.

The selection of the forecasting technique is based on available past data and the forecast needs of the firm. This emphasizes a point that is sometimes missed by both users and forecasters. The objective of the forecast and the conditions surrounding that forecast dictate which forecasting technique should be used. Too often the reverse seems to occur; the forecasting technique is selected first, and the objectives and forecasting conditions then become secondary issues.

Example: Both the forecaster and the marketing manager for General Appliance believe the most effective model would be a time series technique that can make allowances for seasonal impacts and trend. The Winter's method is selected since at least ten years of monthly sales data are available on both the industry and the firm.

Step Six—Make the Initial Forecast

The initial forecast using the Winter's method indicates that industry sales of home refrigerators for the coming year in the 12 midwest states will total 1.7 million units and General Appliance's refrigerator sales will be 153,000 units. Sales forecasts are also made for each month of the coming year. Subjective assessments are then made on the expected rate of growth in new housing starts five and ten years into the future. A growth rate of 5 percent per year is assumed and sales are adjusted upward by this 5 percent to derive the five- and ten-year forecasts.

Step Seven—Relate Initial Forecast to Firm's Goals

Users take the initial forecast and relate it to their future expectations for the product. A firm may seek to increase its market share by a total of 10 percent over the next five years, starting with a 3 percent increase in the coming year. Or it may decide to deemphasize this particular product, choosing instead to devote more attention to other products with higher profit margins. They might even view this initial forecast as reasonable and design their marketing activities to achieve these sales.

Example: The initial forecast (Step Six) indicated General Appliance refrigerator sales in the coming year would be around 153,000 units. Management established a goal for the coming year of 165,000 units and an eventual market share of 14 percent by 1990. This disparity between forecasted sales and desired sales means a change must be made in future marketing activities.

Step Eight—Coordinate with Marketing Plan

Steps Seven and Eight involve decisions that are closely entwined. Once future sales goals are determined, the firm must develop marketing plans that will enable these goals to be achieved. Will changes in pricing or promotional procedures be necessary? Will distribution channels have to be altered? What about packaging or other design aspects of the product? In-depth coverage of such activities is beyond the scope of this book but is provided in most marketing management texts.

Example: The management of General Appliance believes that their desired increase in market share can best be accomplished by switching from newspaper ads to co-op radio ads and by providing larger margins to retailers. With these actions in mind, they develop a specific marketing plan for the next year and tentative plans for the next five to ten years. These plans are distributed to selected lower level managers to obtain their reactions. If major disagreements arise about either the planned marketing activities or projected sales, it will be necessary to make some revisions.

Step Nine—Make the Formal Forecast

This step is merely a formality since the actual forecast decisions were made in steps seven and eight. What remains is to project formally expected sales for selected future periods based on the final marketing plan. This forecast information should be shared with all parties in the firm who will be directly affected by such sales—purchasing agents, production managers, personnel directors.

Roles of Users and Forecasters in Forecasting Process

Throughout this book it has been emphasized that effective communication must exist between forecaster and user. This section identifies the roles of both parties in the development of the formal forecast and the importance of their communicating at every stage of the forecasting process.

Users must participate in the first three steps because it is in those steps that the specific nature of the forecast is determined. Thus, users and forecasters should work together to identify the purpose of the forecast, the item(s) to be forecast, and key elements of the forecast.

Each party will make unique contributions toward identifying the forces likely to affect the forecast (Step Four). Forecasters will usually have a better feel for macro aspects (future interest rates, expected level of unemployment), whereas users will have a better understanding of the micro or internal forces. Combining the insights of both parties should enhance the quality of the initial forecast.

Although the specific forecasting technique usually will be chosen by the forecaster, the user should be given the opportunity to approve the choice. Remember, the user's willingness to accept a forecast figure is based on the confidence he or she has in the technique used to derive that forecast. Citing historical evidence that shows the success of Box-Jenkins models won't eliminate the apprehension of a user who doesn't understand those models. Thus, if the forecaster strongly favors a certain forecasting technique, he or she should attempt to educate the user about the workings of that technique.

Once the initial forecast has been developed, the users will compare that figure to their future expectations for the product. Assume the initial forecast indicated sales of around 153,000 units. The user believes next year's sales should be higher, which would indicate a change in future marketing efforts. These changes are identified in a marketing plan.

Most of the decisions and activities involved in converting the initial forecast to a formal forecast will be performed by the user. The forecaster should be consulted, however, about the appropriateness of the "formal" forecast. Although forecasters may lack marketing expertise, they usually have enough of a feel for the marketplace to assess the reasonableness of the formal forecast.

In summary, if the forecaster and the user are distinct parties, their respective inputs will differ during the various steps of the forecasting process. However, neither party should take total control of any step without some type of feedback from the other.

GETTING THE FORECAST USED

Any firm that devotes the time and manpower needed to develop formal forecasts should also establish an environment that will entice their decision makers to use those forecasts. Some suggestions for creating such an environment are now presented.

Have Forecast Available When Needed

The forecast has to be available prior to the time decisions based on them are to be made. For example, a forecast that is not available until September may be too late to guide raw material purchases for the coming spring season. Or, a September forecast might not provide enough lead time to purchase advertising space in spring editions of magazines.

Thus, forecasters should be aware of the dates at which key decisions must be made and have their forecasts available early enough to be incorporated into such decisions.

Have Forecast in Useful Format

Should the forecast be in dollars or units? Should the forecast be broken down by product, by territory, or by customer? Is weekly, monthly, or quarterly data most useful? Since a number of different decision makers may be using the forecast, a variety of formats for the forecast may be needed to effectively serve their diverse needs.

Provide Different Forecast Scenarios

The formal forecast is usually the scenario most likely to occur. It will enhance the value of forecasts, though, if "worst case" and "best case" situations are also included. The inclusion of extreme scenarios will not only provide forecast ranges for decision makers, it will also alert them to the fact that such extremes can occur.

Make Sure User Understands the Forecasting Technique

The user or decision maker must feel comfortable with the technique used to derive the forecast. In addition to explaining the technique to the user, information about the major assumptions used in the generation of the forecast also should be provided. For example, in deriving the forecast for General Appliance's refrigerator sales, it was assumed mortgage rates would drop below 11 percent in 1985. In addition, assumptions were made about the likely level of unemployment, the number of new households, and the expected actions by competitors. All such assumptions should be identified for the user.

The forecast's limitations should also be identified to alert users to conditions that could possibly affect its accuracy. Examples of such limitations would be: "This time series model was based on only 25 months of data and therefore lacks historical strength"; or "The projected unemployment figure for 1986 used in this model was made by the government prior to the economic recovery of 1983."

Make Forecast Available to All Users

A forecast can only be used by decision makers if they have access to it. Don't assume that providing forecast data to one person in the managerial hierarchy will ensure its distribution to others needing it. A copy of the forecast report should be available to every decision maker likely to need such data.

Provide Accurate Forecasts

Probably the most critical factor determining whether a forecast is used in the decision-making process is the faith that users have in its accuracy. None of the previous five actions will have much impact if decision makers don't have confidence in the forecaster and such confidence is contingent on the forecaster's past performance.

FUTURE DIRECTIONS OF FORECASTING

It is only proper that a book about forecasting conclude by assessing the future of its own discipline. This assessment focuses on five major factors the author believes will have a significant impact on forecasting over the next five to ten years.

Role of Computers

The factor that will affect forecasting most in the coming years is the increased role of computers. Their widespread availability along with increased memory and analytic capabilities will dramatically influence forecasting activities. "They will be mainly interactive; they will cover the full range of forecasting methodologies; and they will be packaged in a form that provides a convenient interface between formal forecasting methods and judgmental inputs."[1]

Increased competition will force software producers to market their packages more effectively, resulting in software packages that are both easier to use and more versatile. Software producers will place increased emphasis on such tools as seminars, demonstrations, manuals, and so forth to show how various forecasting techniques work and when they should be used.

Computers not only will have a major impact on the analytic aspects of forecasting, they will also affect the information gathered by firms. Large amounts of both internal and external data will become accessible on short notice through computerized information systems. Each firm will have greater access to data on its own products and their linkages with commercial information gathering firms will make more external data available.

The present situation in which managers are frequently overwhelmed by huge computer printouts will be replaced by systems that provide data tied to the specific needs of the decision maker, for example, "sales of 17-inch color TV sets in July 1984 in Larimer County, Colorado."

This access to increased amounts of data will be especially beneficial to firms using regression and input-output models. A major limitation of these models has been the lack of data on the independent or influencing variables and these expanded information systems will greatly reduce that restraint.

Competitive Environment

What will the marketplace and competitive environment be like in future years and how will each have an impact on future forecasting activities?

The length of the typical product's life cycle will continue to shorten due to two key factors: (1) competition will be able to duplicate new products more quickly, meaning products will have much shorter introduction and growth periods and (2) there also will be increased emphasis on changing product offerings more frequently, either by developing new products or altering existing ones. Both conditions will result in greater emphasis on more accurate short-term forecasts.

The present emphasis on increased productivity will continue. Thus, manufacturers will strive to have their production outputs more closely match the actual demand for their products. Continual increases in the costs of raw materials, transportation, and storage will provide major rewards for those firms able to make accurate forecasts.

Another set of expected conditions, at first glance, seems to be contradictory. Firms will become more specialized and firms will become more diversified. This situation can best be illustrated at the retail level where there will be increased numbers of specialty stores such as women's shoe stores, accessory stores, and so on. When firms become this specialized, their forecasting tasks become easier because they are dealing with a narrower range of products.

At the same time that specialization is occurring, there also will be an increase in the number of giant "one-stop shopping" outlets. These super stores will sell everything from groceries to clothing and automobile supplies. This proliferation of products makes the forecasting tasks for such stores more difficult.

This same (seemingly) contradictory environment—greater specialization and greater generalization—will occur at wholesale and manufacturing levels, resulting in forecasting problems similar to the ones described for retailers.

Users of Forecasts

A major hurdle to wider use of some forecasting models has been the inability of users to understand these models. For example, many decision makers don't understand multiple regression and thus are reluctant to use forecasts based on such models.

In the future, increasing numbers of users will have the quantitative skills needed to understand more complex models. These quantitative skills will be the result of two factors: (1) increasing numbers of decision makers will have had contact with statistics and math courses in their college years and (2) numerous educational programs and seminars will be sponsored by computer firms for the purpose of increasing awareness of their packages.

Thus, reluctance to use quantitative models will be less of a factor in future years. This means a wider variety of forecasting techniques will be employed and users will be more willing to experiment with a number of different models rather than continue to rely on a single technique.

Forecasters

The quantitative skills of forecasters will also increase. This will be especially true among those people who develop forecasts as just one part of their overall job activities (sales managers, owners of small firms, product managers).

The reasons for their increased quantitative skills are basically the same two factors raising the skill levels of users—stronger quantitative backgrounds and more educational materials on forecasting methods.

Full-time forecasters will also benefit from advances made in computer technology, especially the improved information systems. They will have access to more data on a wider variety of variables, a condition that will increase their use of multiple regression models. There will also be more current data to update the coefficients for input-output models. This combination of events will provide an impetus for increased usage of econometric models.

Another likely change will be an increase in the number of private firms that, for a fee, provide forecasts for individual business firms. They will not only provide macro forecasts, but will also develop specific micro models depicting sales for products, firms, and industries.

Techniques

The increased capabilities of computers, along with the higher quantitative skills of users and forecasters, suggests that there will also be major advances in forecasting models. Although some breakthroughs no doubt will occur, especially among models for handling non-linear sales data, it is unlikely that any dramatically different techniques will be discovered.

What will likely occur is that there will be continual refinements of existing techniques such as what took place with exponential smoothing models, where Holt's two-parameter models, triple exponential smoothing, and Winter's method were developed. Such refinements will be especially prevalent among individual firms, where general models will be adapted to a firm's own competitive environment.

Summary

The 1980s, labeled by many as "the decade of the computer," hold great promise for forecasting. Computers will make greater amounts of data accessible to forecasters. In addition, the increased availability of forecasting software will promote wider use of the sophisticated forecasting techniques.

These two factors—more data and better techniques—should improve the overall accuracy of forecasts. But the more intense competitive environment of the 1980s, along with shorter product life cycles, will lead to more volatile markets, increasing the difficulties forecasters already face.

Regardless of what advances are made in computer software or hardware, there always will be a need for an "intuitive feel" of the market that most successful forecasters possess. The successful forecaster will continue to be the person who can merge computer forecasts with his or her personal insights of the marketplace.

NOTE

1. Spyros Makridakis and Steven C. Wheelwright, *The Handbook of Forecasting: A Manager's Guide* (New York: John Wiley and Sons, 1982), p. 559.

Appendix

Determining Market and Sales Potentials

INTRODUCTION

In Chapter 1, some of the key terms associated with measuring markets were defined. At that time it was stated that two terms—market potential and sales potential—were often erroneously viewed as meaning the same thing as a forecast. This appendix shows how "potentials" differ from forecasts and describes some methods for their development.

Forecasts versus Potentials

Market potential is the total demand opportunities that exist for a category of products or services. It is the maximum number of units that could be demanded in a given area, during a given time period, assuming industry marketing efforts are completely successful. It is what "could be" sold under ideal conditions. A market forecast, on the other hand, identifies what is "expected to be" sold based on the industry's proposed marketing efforts.

Whereas the market potential describes the number of units that could be sold by the entire industry, a sales potential figure identifies what one particular firm could sell if it applied maximum marketing effort. A sales forecast (as opposed to a market forecast) is what a specific firm expects to sell at some future time under a given marketing plan under given market conditions.

Why Cover Potentials?

Market and sales potential figures establish maximum parameters for the forecast. They provide the forecaster with a feel for the size and scope of the market, enabling him or her to assess better the reasonableness of the forecast. Because of their common tie to the future and to markets, this author believes market potential and market measurement should be included with the coverage of forecasting. This material is presented in an appendix, rather than a regular

chapter, so as not to interfere with the flow of the book's central topic—
forecasting.

Contribution of Market Potentials

In addition to being useful to forecasters, market and sales potential figures
provide management with valuable information for various types of planning.

1. *Aid in determining territories and quotas for salespeople.* Market potential figures
   can be identified for specific geographic regions. Based on these figures, the
   manager can determine the number of salespeople each territory should be able to
   support, the amount of sales that could be expected from these salespeople, and the
   relative performance of different territories and different salespeople.

2. *Aid in determining trade channels.* Will a territory support the firm's own salespeople, or should some type of middleman be used? Should a long or short trade
   channel be used?

3. *Aid in selecting sites for plants, sales branches, warehouse locations.* The high
   cost of transportation makes it increasingly desirable to locate closer to large
   groups of customers. In the case of industrial products, fast delivery is a critical
   factor in the selection of suppliers, emphasizing the importance of locating near
   customers.

4. *Aid in allocating promotional efforts.* Most firms base their promotional efforts on
   the size of the potential market, spending more in those markets with higher
   potential.

5. *Aid in determining which products to introduce and which to withdraw.* Firms
   attempt to add to their profits by regularly adding new products. Market and sales
   potentials help determine which products hold greatest promise. Potential figures
   are also used to identify when products are in the decline stage of their life cycle
   and should be withdrawn from the market.

6. *Aid in making acquisition decisions.* Firms whose products have limited potential
   may be planning to acquire other firms in higher growth industries. Through the
   use of market potentials, high-growth industries can be identified more easily.

Components of a Market

A market for a product comprises people or firms, with a present or future use
for the product and the ability to buy it. A fourth criterion frequently included is
"desire for the product." Many marketers, however, believe that this fourth
condition is not necessarily an original component of market potential because
the "desire" element can come later due to the firms' promotional efforts.

Another reason for downplaying the "desire to buy" aspect is that it is so
difficult to quantify. A piano manufacturer can identify the number of households in the United States with children between the ages of 8 and 15, but can't
determine what portion of those households have a real desire for a piano for

their children. Surveys might be used to derive a desire factor but such undertakings are fairly expensive, especially when a firm has a large number of products.

Thus, market potential figures are usually derived from the first three elements: people or firms with a potential use for the product and the ability to purchase it.

Industrial versus Consumer Markets

A number of different techniques can be used to determine a product's market potential but each technique is not equally appropriate for every product. The technique used has to fit the general type of market the product is intended to reach. Is it meant for the consumer market or the industrial market or both?

Industrial markets comprise those firms that buy goods to aid in the production of other goods or assist in their eventual sale. There are major differences between industrial markets and consumer markets and some of the more critical ones are now listed.

1. *Fewer Industrial Customers.* Whereas there are over 230 million consumers and more than 80 million households in the United States, the industrial market numbers only about 15 million units (470,000 of which are manufacturing operations).

2. *Industrial Customers Tend to Be Clustered.* More than half of the industrial firms are located in seven states and are clustered by type of industry. For example, the steel industry is heavily concentrated in the Pittsburgh, Gary, and Chicago areas; whereas the computer industry is heavily concentrated in California's "Silicon Valley."

3. *Demand from Industrial Market Is More Volatile.* The demand for industrial goods is largely derived from the demand for consumer goods. Tied in with this derived demand aspect is the fact that changes in demand for consumer goods often result in even greater changes in the demand for industrial goods—the "acceleration principle." Thus, a 10 percent increase or decrease in demand for refrigerators will often lead to an even greater percentage change in the demand for the equipment used to produce those refrigerators.

4. *Purchase Process Differs.* In the consumer market just one person frequently makes the decision to buy and that decision is made fairly quickly. In the industrial market, since significantly more dollars are involved in the typical purchase, more people are involved in the decision-making process. This results in a longer time period for the buying decision.

MARKET POTENTIAL TECHNIQUES FOR CONSUMER MARKETS

This section describes those techniques most widely used to determine market potential for consumer products. A later section identifies techniques for industrial markets. Some of the techniques (with slight modifications) are similar for both types of markets.

Chain Ratio Method

This technique is also called the "top down" or "funneling" method since an initial, large group of customers is narrowed down to a smaller group that more accurately depicts the potential users.

Example: A new, more efficient solar panel has been developed by Acme Solar Inc. This panel does not require as much sunlight as existing panels, thus providing more and longer periods of solar power for the user. However, this new panel costs about 30 percent more than existing panels. What is the market potential in the United States for this type of product among single family residences? (We are not concerned with the apartment or commercial market at this time.)

The starting point would be to identify the number of owner-occupied households in the United States. That figure is 54.3 million units.[1] Since the product is practical only in areas of high sunshine, the number of households in areas with at least 200 days of sunshine per year should be ascertained. Information from the *Statistical Abstract* indicates that those states contain 24 percent of U.S. single-family households.

Other factors also significantly affect potential demand and should be used to refine this potential figure further. Since the panels are fairly expensive, it is assumed potential households would likely have an annual income of at least $30,000. Size of fuel bill is another factor. To make an investment of this sort (+$12,000) the household should have an annual heating bill of at least $700. This means size of home (number of rooms) and geographic location need to be considered. Finally, since the tax credits associated with solar products significantly affect their potential demand, the solar tax credits of states should be factored into the model.

Assuming an average of 128 square feet of solar panels per potential household, the following model is used to estimate the potential for this solar panel: solar panel market potential = total U.S. households × percentage of homes with 200+ days of sunshine × percentage of homes with seven or more rooms × percent of households with incomes of $30,000 or more × 128 square feet. (The tax credit factor would have to be figured in on a state-by-state basis.)

Potential = 54.3 million × .24 × .21 × .16 × 128 sq. ft.
Potential = 56,048,000 square ft of panel

Users of this method should realize that errors can occur if an association exists between two or more of the model's components. For example, in our model both income and number of rooms in the home are used. There is a close relationship between these two factors since higher-income households usually also have bigger homes. Thus, the percentage of those households with +$30,000 in the United States when multiplied by the number of rooms factor is distorted because the same factor is considered twice. This shortcoming can be offset somewhat by using census data in which both factors (income and number of rooms) have already been combined.

Build-Up Method

This method first divides the market for possible users into meaningful segments and then estimates the sales to each segment. Results for each segment are then added together. If this method was used to develop the potential for solar panels, the segmentation would most likely be done on a geographic basis, that is, state by state. For other types of products, the segmentation might be based on frequency of usage (regular versus occasional), nature of purchase (new versus replacement), or even the population's ethnic makeup, if this is a factor in the use of the product.

The build-up method will be discussed more thoroughly in the industrial products section since it is more widely used for determining potential for that category of products.

Single Factor Index Method

This is a fairly simple technique to understand and apply since it ties a market potential to a single factor that an area possesses relative to other areas. For example, Dubuque, Iowa has a population of approximately 94,500, which is 3.2 percent of the state's entire population of 2.9 million. Thus, a firm selling a consumer product throughout Iowa would expect approximately 3.2 percent of that state's sales to be in Dubuque.

The major drawback of this technique is that it identifies potential in percentages, not actual units. In the above example, Dubuque should have 3.2 percent of potential sales for a product in Iowa but no estimate of actual unit sales is provided. Thus, this method's primary value is that it enables a total market potential figure to be apportioned among smaller areas. For example, if the market potential for soft drinks for the state of Iowa in 1986 was believed to be 580 million cans, then Dubuque's potential would be 3.2 percent of that total, or 18.6 million cans.

The procedure could also be reversed by first developing a market potential for a small area and then using the factor index to make projections for larger areas. An in-depth survey could be used to identify potential soft drink consumption in Dubuque, Iowa and this figure could then be projected to the entire state. For example, personal interviews might be conducted with a random sample of 400 Dubuque residents to identify their present pattern of soft drink consumption. These per capita consumption figures for the sample are then used to project the market potential for soft drinks for the entire population of Dubuque. Assume the resulting figure for Dubuque is 19.3 million cans. Since Dubuque has 3.2 percent of the state's population, the potential for soft drinks in the entire state would be 603 million cans (19.3 million ÷ .032).

Limitations of Index Method

Although this method is fairly simple to apply, it does have two major draw-backs. (1) It doesn't provide unit values for market potential. Thus, it must be used in conjunction with another method (that is, the survey of Dubuque residents) to identify those unit values. (2) Its second drawback is that it assumes a single factor is equally appropriate for all areas. Population was the key factor used in the soft drink example. However, soft drink sales are also closely related to age since per capita consumption is much higher among children, teens, and young adults. Census figures show that the median age for residents of Dubuque, Iowa was 27.4 years, whereas the median age for the entire state of Iowa was 30.6 years. This suggests Dubuque, Iowa has a higher proportion of younger people than the state in general. Thus, the per capita sales of soft drinks for Dubuque residents would seemingly not be equally appropriate for those Iowa cities with a different age composition.

In spite of this second drawback, there are many situations where a single factor can be used effectively. For example, the market potential of diapers (cloth or throwaway) is directly tied to the number of births in a given area and the potential for false teeth cleaners is directly related to the number of people over 55 years of age.

Multiple Factor Index Method

This method recognizes that more than one factor usually affects the potential demand for a product and each factor does not have an equal impact on sales. The most famous multiple factor index is the "Buying Power Index" developed by *Sales and Marketing Management Magazine*. This index uses three factors—disposable personal income, retail sales, and population—to determine the relative consumer buying power of different geographic areas.

These three factors represent the three components of a market described earlier, people (population), ability to buy (disposable personal income), and willingness to buy (retail sales). The following formula illustrates that model and its weights.

$B_i = .5I_i + .3R_i + .2P_i$
B_i = Percentage of national buying power in area i
I_i = Percentage of national personal disposable income in area i
R_i = Percentage of national retail sales in area i
P_i = Percentage of national population located in area i

The model assigns the most weight (.5) to personal disposable income, with lesser weights to retail sales (.3) and population (.2). Statistics from *Sales and Marketing Management* indicate that Dubuque, Iowa had .0341 percent of total U.S. personal disposable income, .033 percent of U.S. retail sales, and .0273 percent of the U.S. population. This means the BPI (buying power index) for Dubuque would be determined as follows:

$$B_D = .5(.0341) + .3(.0330) + .2(.0273)$$
$$B_D = 0.0325$$

If this index were used to assign potential shoe sales, Dubuque should provide 0.032 percent of the nationwide potential for that type of product.

The strength of this method is its flexibility since both the factors and the weights can be changed to fit a particular product. The above weights apply mainly to consumer goods that are viewed as staples. The same weights and factors would not be appropriate for a high-priced food item such as caviar. For caviar, percent of population with incomes in excess of $30,000 would be substituted for disposable personal income. Also, food sales might be substituted for retail sales. Finally, a greater weight (.6) would likely be assigned to the income factor. Thus, the buying index for caviar might be:

$$B_i = .6(I_i) + .3(F_i) + .1(p_i)$$
where I = percent of national population having incomes greater than $30,000 in area i
F = percent of national food sales in area i
P = percent of national population located in area i

When to Use Multiple Factor Index

The key questions to ask in determining whether to use a multiple factor index are: (1) Can the key factors affecting demand for the product be identified? (2) Can weights be realistically assigned to these factors? (3) Does quantitative information exist about each of these factors? This last question—availability of data—is critical, since the whole technique is useless unless accurate data can be plugged into the formula. This method also suffers from the same drawback as the single factor method: it doesn't create a potential figure in units; rather, it provides a technique for apportioning units among different segments.

Survey Method

All of the previous methods required some type of quantitative data to determine the market potential of a product. Much of this data, such as population, income, number of rooms, types of major appliances owned, can be found in Census Reports. But the firm might also be interested in that elusive factor— desire to buy—and that is difficult to quantify. A product's recent retail sales are often used as a surrogate for "willingness," but for relatively new products such as video cassette recorders or personal computers it is difficult to find appropriate substitutes. In those situations where past sales data are non-existent or the product being studied is quite unique, surveys are used to identify buying intentions.

Key Aspects of the Survey

The procedures for obtaining survey data can be quite complicated and should be performed by a qualified researcher. Although you, as a research user, will probably not participate in the actual gathering of this data, you should be involved with the following survey activities: (1) make sure the sample being surveyed really represents the likely market for the product; (2) if the product is very unique, make sure the sample members (interviewees) fully understand how the product works, its costs, and its benefits; (3) be sure the survey provides a realistic buying environment. A question such as: "Would you buy this product?" doesn't require a person to make an actual commitment and thus its results can be misleading. People are very interested in new products until it requires their financial commitment. Most marketing research books describe techniques that can be used to identify people's willingness to buy.

Two Additional Examples

Example: Automobile Replacement Batteries

Objectives: A manufacturer of automobile batteries wants to identify the 1982 market potential for replacement batteries for the five-state area of Iowa, Illinois, Missouri, Minnesota, and Wisconsin.[2]

Assumptions: (a) Normal life of an automobile battery is three years. Thus, approximately one of three registered automobiles will need a new battery each year. Since the number of new cars exceeds the number scrapped, the real replacement ratio will be closer to 31 percent. (b) Total automobile registrations will continue to increase annually at about 2.3 percent (Column 3).

States (1)	1981 Auto Registrations[3] (millions) (2)	1982 Estimated Registrations (2) × 1.023 (3)	Estimated Replacement Batteries (3) × .31 (4)
Illinois	7.59	7,765	2,407,000
Iowa	2.36	2,414	748,000
Indiana	3.89	3,979	1,234,000
Minnesota	3.15	3,222	999,000
Missouri	3.33	3,407	1,056,000
			6,444,000

Thus, the market potential in 1982 for replacement batteries in the five state area is 6.4 million batteries.

Example: Mouthwash for Young People (Ages 5–17)

Objective: A manufacturer of mouthwash wishes to identify the 1983 market potential (in ounces) for a mouthwash aimed at the youth market.

Assumptions: (a) Potential users are all people between the ages of 5 and 17. (b) Each potential user would use one ounce of mouthwash per day (one-half ounce, twice a day). (c) Approximately 20 percent (19.8) of the population is between the ages of 5 and 17.

Procedures:

Market potential = U.S. population × percent in 5–17 age bracket × annual usage of product
= 231.5 million × 19.8% × 1 oz. × 365 days
= 16.7 billion ounces

Therefore, the market potential for mouthwash in the youth market for 1983 is approximately 16.7 billion ounces.

TECHNIQUES FOR INDUSTRIAL GOODS

The basic techniques used to identify potential for consumer goods also apply for industrial products, however, the factors used in the models will differ. For example, in models used for consumer products, population is often a key factor; whereas for industrial goods, number of employees or number of plants are used.

There are also some additional techniques specifically designed to determine market potential for industrial products. These techniques frequently rely on Standard Industrial Classification data. (Readers not familiar with the SIC system should turn to Chapter 11 where a description of that system is provided.)

Tying Industry Data to SICs

The following example is a little dated but it does provide a good illustration of how industry data can be tied to SIC statistics to derive the market potential. Ready-Made Containers wishes to estimate the market potential for corrugated and solid fiber boxes in the Phoenix, Arizona area. Data from two publications are used to derive that figure: *Country Business Patterns* and the *Fiber Box Industry Annual Report.* (See Table A-1.)

The underlying assumption in this model is that a useful ratio can be established between the dollar value of fiber boxes shipped to a specific SIC industry and the number of employees in that industry. Column 3, Table A-1 identifies the consumption of fiber boxes per employee in dollars. A preferable value would have been "pounds of fiber box," to eliminate the problems associated with price changes but that type of data could not be obtained.

Table A-1

Estimated Market for Corrugated and Solid Fibre Box by Industry Group

SIC major group code	Consuming industries	Value of box shipments by end use[1] ($1,000)
		1
20	Food and kindred products	1,171,800
21	Tobacco manufactures	29,400
22	Textile mill products	121,800
23	Apparel and other textile products	54,600
24	Lumber and wood products	42,000
25	Furniture and fixtures	147,000
26	Paper and allied products	567,000
27	Printing and publishing	58,800
28	Chemicals and allied products	260,400
29	Petroleum and coal products	33,600
30	Rubber and miscellaenous plastics products	163,800
31	Leather and leather products	21,000
32	Stone, clay and glass products	365,400
33	Primary metal industries	42,000
34	Fabricated metal products	184,800
35	Machinery, except electrical	105,000
36	Electrical equipment and supplies	256,200
37	Transportation equipment	109,200
38	Instruments and related products	29,400
39	Miscellaneous manufacturing industries	403,200
90	Government	33,600
	Total	3 4,200,000

D   Data withheld to avoid disclosure of individual reporting units.
[1]   Based on data reported in *Fibre Box Industry Annual Report 1972,* Fibre Box Associatio
[2]   *County Business Patterns. 1972.* U.S. Department of Commerce, Bureau of the Census.
[3]   *U.S. Industrial Outlook 1973–With Projections to 1980.* Bureau of Dmosetic Commerce,
       U.S. Department of Commerce.

The nationwide sales of fiber boxes to SIC industry 20 (food and kindred products) was close to $1.2 billion (Column 1, Table A-1). Since that industry employed approximately 1.5 million workers, the average use of fiber box per employee was $763. ($1,171 million divided by 1.5 million) (Column 3, Table A-1) This "sales per employee" figure is then applied to Phoenix, Arizona where there are 4,971 employees in the food and kindred products industry (Column 4). When $763 is multiplied times the number of employees (4,971), the resulting potential for SIC 20 becomes $3.8 million (Column 5). When similar computations are made for the other SIC industries using fiber boxes, a total potential figure of $14.1 million emerges for Phoenix.

This procedure could also be used to identify the potential in a combination of

hoenix, Arizona, Standard Metropolitan Statistical Area, 1972

| Employment by industry group[2] | Consumption per employee by industry group (1 ÷ 2) (dollars) | Maricopa County | |
		Employment by industry group[2]	Estimated share of the market (3 x 4) ($1,000)
2	3	4	5
1,536,307	763	4,971	3,793
63,919	460	–	–
935,925	130	–	–
1,349,000	40	3,158	126
579,037	725	1,736	1,259
468,311	314	1,383	434
631,588	898	284	255
1,056,336	56	4,346	243
849,969	306	1,133	347
139,228	241	–	–
555,539	295	779	230
277,371	76	–	–
588,897	620	2,270	1,407
1,144,327	37	2,036	75
1,312,595	141	3,271	461
1,769,738	59	14,691	867
1,698,725	151	23,788	3,592
1,700,723	64	2,484	159
383,585	77	D	–
411,967	979	868	850
–	–	–	–
–	–	–	14,098

ource: Measuring Markets--A Guide to the Use of
Federal and State Statistical Data, U.S.
Department of Commerce, August 1974, p. 46.

counties or states. In reality, it is just a special form of the build-up method described earlier in the section on consumer goods.

Statistical Series Method

This method is really a specialized version of the single and multiple factor index techniques described in the consumer section. It determines the potential sales for a product by using industry data that reflects the relative buying power of different industries. The name—statistical series—was first used by Francis Hummel in his classic text on market measurement published in 1961, *Market and Sales Potential*. The following material is drawn from Chapter 6 of that book.[4]

Steps Involved in Calculating Index

There are four steps involved in developing a potential when using the statistical series method:

(a) Identify the SIC industries using the product.

(b) Establish weights for each industry.

(c) Determine the factors affecting potential of industries.

(d) Tie the weights and factors together to derive a potential for a geographic area.

If a firm produces more than one class of product, a separate index is developed for each product.

Identify those industries (via SIC numbers) that either presently use the product or, if it is a new product, are likely to use it in the future. To illustrate this method, it is assumed the product being evaluated is a specialized cutting tool. Table A-2 indicates that six industries use this tool (Columns 1, 2).

Identify the present and future usage of the product among the industries. Ideally, these initial weights (Column 3) could be derived from information in industry publications or other secondary sources. If such data does not exist, then a firm could assign weights to each industry based on the proportion of its own product's sales to that industry. This latter approach creates problems if the sales pattern of the firm's cutting tool differs markedly from its competitors. Therefore, a safer approach would be to survey a representative sample of firms from each industry to determine their ownership of this category of cutting tool, the brand used, the age of the equipment and their future purchase plans. The firm's own sales force can also provide solid information for determining the use of cutting tools by each industry.

This information is then adjusted, based on the expected changes in each

Table A-2
Present and Future Use of Cutting Tools by Six Industries

SIC (1)	Industries (2)	Initial Weight (3)	Adjustment for Coming Period (4)	New Weight (5)
3490	Misc. Fabricated Metals	12	No Change	12
3540	Metal Working Machinery	14	+20%	17
3550	Special Industry Machinery	5	No Change	5
3710	Motor Vehicles	23	Decline 10%	20
3720	Aircraft and Parts	34	Decline 15%	29
3730	Shipbuilding	7	+30%	10
		95		93
	Sold to other industries	5		
		100		

industry's purchases for the coming period (Column 4). Data from surveys, sales force estimates, and input from experts are all used to assign the new weights (Column 5).

Note that, in the coming period, the proportion of sales of the product to these six industries is expected to decline from 95 percent to 93 percent. This suggests that the overall potential for cutting tools is decreasing. These new weights (Column 5) are now incorporated with other data to assign potentials to specific geographic regions.

The third step in the statistical series method is to identify the key factors affecting an industry's purchasing potential. These factors are usually drawn from the following list:

Number of plants

Number of production workers

Value added by manufacturers

Expenditures for new plant and equipment

Value of products shipped

Value of materials consumed

In the cutting tool example, it was decided that "number of production workers" and "value added" were the two key factors affecting a product's potential. The importance of these two factors was disclosed through multiple regression analysis using cutting tool sales as the dependent variable. These two factors are then combined into a single index figure by assigning each a weight. For cutting tools, discussions with the firm's sales staff and the results from regression analysis indicate that the "number of production workers" should be assigned twice the weight of "value added" when determining an area's potential. (The regression analysis could also be used to assign these weights.)

The fourth step is to tie these weights and factors together to determine a market potential for an area. This technique is used to determine the market potential of Cleveland, Ohio. Table A-3 contains information on the two factors, combines that data with the assigned weights for each SIC, and sums this data to derive the market potential for Cleveland.

Cleveland had over 15,000 employees in the metalworking machinery industry (SIC 3540) or approximately 6.5 percent of all U.S. workers in that SIC category (Columns 3 and 4 of Table A-3). Similarly, SIC 3540 in Cleveland contributed approximately $149 million of the "value added" dollars for that industry or about 6.4 percent of that industry's value added in the United States (Columns 5 and 6).

Column 7 of Table A-3 takes the data from Columns 4 and 6 and combines them with their respective weights. Remember, "workers" were assigned twice the weight of value added. For SIC 3540, the weight is derived as follows:

Table A-3
Development of Market Potential for Cutting Tools in Cleveland, Ohio

SIC (1)	Industries (2)	Production Workers # (3)	% of SIC (4)	Value Added $(Millions) (5)	% of SIC (6)	Multiple Index % (7)	New Weight (8)	Weighted Index (7)X(8) (9)
3490	Misc Fabricated Metals	3,231	.032	79.6	.077	.047	12	.564
3540	Metal Working Machinery	15,468	.065	149.3	.064	.065	17	1.105
3550	Special Industry Machinery	1,969	.014	36.7	.030	.014	5	.095
3710	Motor Vehicles	37,164	.053	280.1	.044	.050	20	1.0
3720	Aircraft and Parts	12,558	.021	194.9	.031	.024	29	.696
3730	Shipbuilding	1,417	.008	3.2	.004	.007	10	.07
							93	3.53

$$\frac{3.53}{93} = 3.79$$

Thus Cleveland's market potential for cutting tools is 3.8% of the entire U. S. market potential.

$$\frac{\text{Multiple}}{\text{Index}} = \frac{\text{Percent of production workers} \times 2 + \text{percent of value added} \times 1}{\text{Sum of weights (3)}}$$

$$= \frac{(.065) \times 2 + (.064) \times 1}{3}$$

$$= .0647$$

The values in Column 8 are the new weights assigned to each SIC category on the basis of projected changes in their potential (see Table A-2, Column 5).

All of these calculations result in a weighted index (Table A-3, Column 9) for each SIC industry. These individual values are then summed and divided by the sum of the weights (93) to provide the market potential for Cleveland. Table A-3 indicates that Cleveland possesses 3.8 percent of the U.S. potential for cutting tools.

While the statistical series method appears to be a more sophisticated technique than some of the methods previously discussed, it still only provides a ratio rather than unit sales. Thus, to be most effective, this method should be used in conjunction with some other model that can supply the overall potential sales in units.

Market Survey Method

A shortcoming of some of the previous methods was that they can only identify a particular area's potential as a ratio (for example, 17 percent of United States). This doesn't determine a product's potential in terms of actual units or dollars. Therefore, as was the case with consumer products, it may be necessary to survey markets.

The starting point is to identify those categories of firms (or industries) using, or likely to use, the product. Then a representative sample of these firms will be contacted by mail, telephone, or personal visits to obtain data on their use, ownership, and expected future purchases of the product.

These survey results are generally used to tie possible sales to some key factor of each industry. Table A-4 shows how such results can be used to derive a market potential for a specialized machine tool. Five industries were identified as users of this tool and a sample of firms from each industry were surveyed by telephone to determine their intentions to purchase this type of tool. This data was then related to the number of workers in the firm and an "average intended purchases per worker" was derived for each of the five industries. These survey findings were then projected to the national market for each industry, and combined into a national market potential figure.

The firms in SIC 3631 expected to purchase a total of $2.6 million of this tool in the coming period. These surveyed firms had a total of 2,104 workers, which meant the average dollar purchase of the machine on a "per worker" basis in

SIC 3631 would be $1,235 (Column 4). Projecting this nationwide to that indus-
try's 23,000 workers, a potential of over $29 million for SIC 3631 emerged
(Column 6). This same process is applied to the other four industries using
"intentions to purchase" data from the surveys. Combining data from the five
industries indicates that the total potential for this category of machine tool is
approximately $415 million.

A note of caution: not all "intentions to buy" become actual purchases.
Therefore, a fudge factor should be introduced to allow for this discrepancy.

The reader should also be aware of certain drawbacks of surveys. Since it is
difficult to get a high participation rate in surveys, questions are frequently raised
about the representativeness of the responding firms. Who in the firm should be
contacted? Who can provide accurate data about the firm's purchase intentions?
Is "sales per worker" a reasonable ratio to use? Finally, as stated in an earlier
section, the survey process can be quite complicated and a knowledgeable researcher should be involved when it is used.

DETERMINING SALES POTENTIAL

Sales potential was defined as that portion of the market potential a firm
believes it could obtain under maximum marketing efforts. How does a firm
determine the sales potential for one of its products?

Input from Experts

The method most frequently used is to obtain input from people who are well
acquainted with both the product and the market. These people usually are not
asked to give precise dollar amounts but rather to identify that portion of the
market potential they feel product X could obtain.

For example, earlier the market potential for a special machine tool was
determined to be $415 million (Table A-4). Acme Tool manufactures that ma-
chine tool and is a strong competitor in many geographic markets. Based on
estimates from its salespeople, Acme's machine tool has a 30 to 35 percent
market share in those areas in which it competes. Thus, it would be realistic to
assign Acme's machine tool a sales potential of 35 percent of the $415 million,
or $145 million. This figure might even be raised to 40 percent if the firm intends
to introduce an improved version of the product along with a major promotional
effort.

Who are the experts that can provide such input? One group has already been
identified: the firm's own sales force. These people certainly know the product,
the competition, and the overall market environment and should be well qualified
to estimate the possible sales level for the product. However, a warning is
necessary when using salespeople for this task. Make clear to them that these
sales potentials will not be used to establish quotas for their territories. If this
point isn't made, they may understate the sales potential to protect themselves.

Table A-4
Using Survey Results to Determine Market Potential for a Specialized Machine Tool

SIC		Intentions to Purchase (000's of $)	# of Workers	$ Purchases per Worker	Number of Workers (Nationwide)	National Market Potential (000's)
(1)		(2)	(3)	(4) (2) ÷ (3)	(5)	(4) x (5) (6)
3631	Household Cooking Equipment	2,600	2,104	1,235	23,502	29,024
3633	Washing Machines	35,200	3,497	10,066	35,593	358,279
3635	Vacuum Cleaners	1,875	402	4,664	4,572	21,323
3636	Sewing Machines	600	912	658	8,182	5,383
3639	Other Appliances	225	1,100	205	9,029	1,850
						$415,859

National market potential for this
machine tool is approximately
$415 million.

Another group of experts would be the firm's own executives, especially those in marketing and production. A third group of "experts" could be the potential customers themselves. Through surveys, their opinions about future sales of each product could be obtained. This assumes a market where only a limited number of firms compete so that customers are familiar with most brands.

Finally, consultants could be used to identify sales potentials. In most industries there are people or firms who specialize in gathering information about the industry's past and present sales, as well as its likely future growth. For a fee this group could be tapped. (Although not mentioned earlier, consultants could also be used to develop market potentials.)

Market Opportunity Index

This method can be used to determine sales potentials in those areas in which the product is presently competing.[5] It assesses past sales performance to identify areas of greatest opportunity. Thus, in determining a solar firm's sales potential it would first evaluate its past sales performance and use those figures to compile a sales potential figure.

Table A-5 shows the number of households in Colorado's five metropolitan areas (Columns 2 and 3). It also identifies the percent of the state's solar sales made in each area (Column 4). The Fort Collins metropolitan area had 5.1 percent of Colorado households and 7.8 percent of the state's solar sales. Thus, Fort Collins has a fairly high ratio of solar usage, or a category development index of 153 (7.8 percent $\div$ 5.1 percent). A ratio of 100 would indicate that the percent of population equals the percent of product sales (Columns 3 and 4).

Column 6 contains the percent of Firm X's solar panel sales in each of the five areas. Thus, Firm X has 22.8 percent of its total Colorado sales in Fort Collins, an area that has only 5.1 percent of the state's households. This indicates Firm X's sales are over four times (447 percent) the amount expected (Column 7). This suggests that Fort Collins holds less future potential for Firm X than other areas in which it has less brand development. Therefore, when determining Firm X's sales potential for each of the five areas, their market opportunity index should be taken into consideration (Column 8).

The market opportunity index compares an area's present use of a product category (category development index, Column 5) with that area's present use of a particular brand (brand development index, Column 7). The higher this ratio (Column 5 $\div$ Column 7), the greater the brand's sales potential. Conversely, when the market opportunity index is low (.34 for Fort Collins, Column 8), this indicates that the area holds only small sales potential since it is already saturated with the brand.

Thus, if the 1987 market potential for solar sales in Fort Collins was $5.5 million, and Firm X normally gets 15 percent of a market, it would scale that figure down based on its low opportunity index for that area.

Table A-5
Market Opportunity Index for Solar Sales in Five Colorado Standard Metropolitan Statistical Areas

Metropolitan Area (1)	# of Households (2)	% of State Total (3)	% of State's Solar Sales (4)	Category Development Index (4÷5) (5)	Percent of Firm X's Sales (6)	Brand Development Index (6÷3) (7)	Market Opportunity Index (5÷7) (8)
Colorado Springs	114.3	10.5	12.5	119	10.3	98	1.21
Denver-Boulder	628.2	57.5	52.5	91.3	37.5	65	1.40
Fort Collins	56.4	5.1	7.8	153	22.8	447	.34
Greeley	44.1	4.0	2.0	50	4.5	112	.45
Pueblo	45.8	4.2	2.9	52.3	6.5	154	.34

Weakness of Technique

This technique is more appropriate for products regularly consumed (food, clothes) than for products such as solar panels that are purchased infrequently. Also, it does not really acknowledge any unique advantages a firm might have in a geographic area. For example, Firm X could be located in Fort Collins and that is why it is so successful there. Their locational advantage is lost in other cities such as Denver or Colorado Springs.

OVERVIEW

This chapter identifies methods for measuring the potential of markets for both consumer and industrial products. The resulting "potentials" provide valuable information to production and marketing managers since they can be used to estimate sales in a territory, establish sales quotas for salespeople, apportion promotional budgets, and so on. But market and sales potential data are also very useful to forecasters since they provide a profile of the industry in which the product is competing or expects to compete. It identifies the maximum sales volume possible for a firm in an industry and thus puts a forecast in a better perspective for its developers and users. Figure A-1 shows the relationship

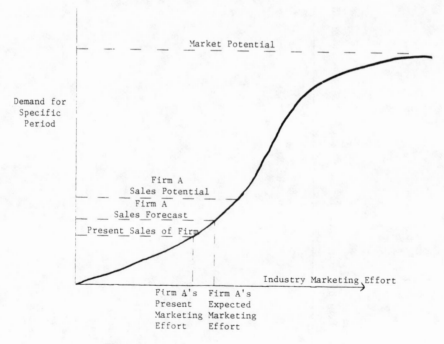

Figure A-1
Relationship between Potentials and Forecast

between potentials, forecasts, and actual sales. It also depicts their ties to the firm's and industry's marketing efforts.

NOTES

1. *Statistical Abstract of the United States,* 1984, p. 748.
2. The idea for this example came from *Measuring Markets,* a publication of the U.S. Department of Commerce, August, 1974.
3. *Statistical Abstract of the United States,* 1984, p. 614.
4. Francis E. Hummel, *Market and Sales Potentials* (New York: Roland Press, 1961).
5. The general procedures for this index are from Philip Kotler's *Marketing Management,* Fifth Edition (New York: Prentice Hall, 1984) p. 238.

Index

About the Author

GEORGE KRESS, Professor of Marketing at Colorado State University, has done consulting, research, and forecasting in both the public and private sectors. A frequent contributor to trade and academic journals, he is the author of *The Business Research Process* and *Marketing Research*.